THE BUSINESS OF BUSINESS

Also by Robert Heller

Superself: The Art and Science of Life Management
The Great Executive Dream
Can You Trust Your Bank? (*with Norris Willatt*)
The Common Millionaire
The European Revenge: How the American Challenge Was Rebuffed (*with Norris Willatt*)
The Naked Investor
The Once and Future Manager

The Business of Business
MANAGING WITH STYLE

by Robert Heller

Harcourt Brace Jovanovich, Publishers
New York and London

*To
My Mother*

Introduction and new matter
copyright © 1981 by Robert Heller
Copyright © 1980, 1981 by Heller Arts

All rights reserved. No part of this publication may be reproduced or transmitted in any form or by any means, electronic or mechanical, including photocopy, recording, or any information storage and retrieval system, without permission in writing from the publisher.

Requests for permission to make copies of any part of the work should be mailed to: Permissions, Harcourt Brace Jovanovich, Inc., 757 Third Avenue, New York, N.Y. 10017.

Library of Congress Cataloging in Publication Data

Heller, Robert, 1932–
  The business of business.
  Includes index.
  1. Management. 2. Business. I. Title.
HD31.H442   658   81–47305
ISBN 0–15–114982–8   AACR2

Printed in the United States of America

First edition

B C D E

CONTENTS

Acknowledgements	xii
Introduction: Back to Basics	3

Part 1: MANAGERIAL BASICS

1 The Objects of the Exercise 9

Competitive management requires two types of good idea: the insight and the outsight. 11

The winning manager needs the immigrant's ability to see with new eyes—and his determination to succeed against odds. 14

What matters is not how large you are, but how effectively you mobilize your strengths at the point of impact. 18

2 Mirror, Mirror on the Wall 22

All measures must be looked at in combination; and you must understand the physical reality that underlies the abstract financial figures. 24

Unless a company earns more than its cost of capital, it can't hope to finance its growth. 27

The winning feature of Added Value is that it cencentrates the manager's mind on essentials—on adding value. 33

3 The Five-Star Company 38

"Mommy, let's go back into the business we know something about." 39

Without self-criticism, the desire to be best loses virtue. 42

The five-star company builds the questioning attitude into its concentrated, perfectionist, self-critical, plural, and economical way of life. 46

4 The Seven Pillars of Management 51

It's unlikely that a manager who isn't interested in maximizing his own resources will be interested enough in maximizing his employer's. 52

If you ever reach a point of no return, with a project that offers no return, you shouldn't be in business. 56

The manager intent on winning searches for the Vital Fifth: the 20 percent on which four-fifths of the outcome depends. 59

Part 2: ORGANIZATIONAL BASICS

5 Love That Company 67

Only one question counts: does the organization itself, and the style which managers adopt within it, stop people from achieving their potential? 68

In real-life business, as opposed to the vertical world of the organization chart, anything worth doing is usually a lateral achievement. 72

"We're trying desperately to hang on to that early successful formula of a very small company." 75

6 Command, Consent and Control 80

The winning combination, the old one-two of Theories Y and X, is as follows: first, get their consent, then tell them what to do. 81

Within the organizational framework, people need the controlled freedom that "advise and consent" suggests. 85

The true authority of expertise automatically carries with it both obedience and consent. 88

7 To Market, to Market 92

What matters in marketing is whether a line drawn around customers and business envelops a coherent whole. 93

"Prepare an order of battle beforehand. By this means, a methodicism is instituted which takes the place of art, where the latter is wanting." 97

In marketing, whatever the truth about war, it's all too common to underestimate the enemy. 101

8 The High-Octane Outfit 105

If you decide that—come what may—you will always provide the market with its top quality, many beneficial results must flow. 107

"If you start confusing quality with elegance, brightness, dignity, love or something else, you will find that everyone has different ideas." 111

All the boss wants to know is "whether you made what you said you would. If not, why, and what have you done about it?" 115

9 Group Therapy — 120

Successful groups need members to play several different roles, and successful top managers must play all of them themselves. — 122

Given that every person is imperfect, who's the partner to supply his deficiencies? — 126

The idea of subordinates voting down their superior—even one whose name is on the label—shouldn't be strange. — 130

Part 3: WHAT MANAGERS DO—AND DON'T

10 The Managerial Potential — 137

A healthy executive mind in a healthy executive body requires a healthy company. — 139

All managers, like it or not, are in the business of words. — 142

How managers organize their own time and the work done within it is the biggest single determinant of their success. — 147

11 Questions, Answers and Problems — 151

The definition of the perfectly right question is one that answers itself. — 153

A problem is far more likely to find a solution than a solution is to find a problem. — 156

It always pays when confronted with an apparent problem to ask: "Is this a problem or a question?" — 159

12 The Days of Decision — 164

Any worthwhile routine will include the PROBE elements—Plan strategy, Review, Operating plans, and Budgets Evolved from the latter. — 166

Even if the idea passes all the tests, the decision phase involves answering a more difficult question. Can *we* do it?   170

Making the decision guilty until proved innocent is an excellent way of avoiding voluntary defeats.   175

Part 4: THE HUMAN FACTOR

13 Making People Pay   183

"He's the worst sort of boss, because he makes you forget the basic injustice of capitalism."   185

"It isn't necessary to give them a veto or even a vote, but it is wise, indeed, to hear them out and to try to accommodate their wishes."   189

If managers can't "take the initiative," aren't stimulated to "pride in performance," don't have their "self-confidence" built up, and aren't allowed to be "open-minded," everybody loses.   194

14 The Communication Trap   201

If you don't know what you're saying, nobody will ever understand you.   203

Tell the truth and act accordingly, and you can't go wrong.   207

When the pervasive good image matches a pervasive truth, it's the ultimate in excellent communication.   211

15 The Participative Panacea   216

The good manager doesn't run a social laboratory, but a place where people work effectively and willingly.   218

In any workplace, there's an implicit social contract between workers and management.   222

x   *Contents*

"People must feel they are part of an organization where their contribution is properly measured." 226

Part 5: **CHALLENGES FOR THE MANAGER OF TODAY AND TOMORROW**

16   Swings of the Seventies   233

Managers, under duress, have been quick to learn the lessons of their failure in the seventies. 235

Compound annual growth plans are creeping back, and the crawly accountants will come back with them. 239

The iron laws of economics, not the discoveries of technology, are the ultimate deciding force. 243

17   Plus Ça Change   248

Use of managers should conform to the value analysis ideal of Least Input for Most Output. 250

No matter what relation the price paid by the immediate user bears to the full cost of the product, somebody, somewhere, somehow, is bearing that full cost. 254

"Make quality products, constantly strive to improve, take care of regular customers and maintain good relations with suppliers." 258

18   Five Who Won Big   263

"If that simple system had not been there from the beginning, I would have stayed in two shops." 265

"I am working here for myself, not because I am the company president, and I hope you're working for yourselves, too, and not for me." 272

"I'd noticed that a few companies like Du Pont

	and G.M. made 20 percent on equity, so I said, 'Why not shoot for that?'"	276
19	The Winning Combination	282
Appendix:	**Big Names in Business**	287
Index		301

ACKNOWLEDGEMENTS

The author and publishers would like to thank the following for permission to publish extracts from copyright material in their possession: *Business Week*; *The Financial Times*; *The Harvard Business Review*; *Management Today*, for extracts from articles by John Child, Saul Gellerman, Bill Reddin, John Saunders, and John Thackray; Management Resources Inc., for extracts from *The Gellerman Memos* by Saul Gellerman; McGraw Hill, for extracts from *Quality Is Free* by Philip Crosby, and *The Human Side of Enterprise* by Douglas McGregor; *The McKinsey Quarterly*, for extracts from Konichi Ohmae's article "The Corporate Strategists"; and *PHP* for extracts from Konosuke Matsushita's article "The Public Is Always Right."

THE BUSINESS OF BUSINESS

INTRODUCTION

BACK TO BASICS

Once upon a time there was a company. For years, like the Sleeping Beauty, but not half so beautifully, it had lain asleep. Its old product lines were slowly dying, its new ones, all purchased along with other firms, were little better. Some were much worse—they lost large amounts of money which the company could ill afford. That was because the flow of profits generally was drying up. Most years, the group made an inadequate profit. Two years out of ten, it made thumping losses.

No Prince Charming came to kiss this Sleeping Ugly into life. But one day its senior executives realized that, unless they did wake their sluggish employer, the group would slumber itself into liquidation: and with the company would go their jobs. Like their products, they were not very glamorous, these men, nor were they especially clever. But they sold or closed businesses that were making poor returns on capital. They reinforced the good operations by buying others that fitted, not the group, but the particular business.

On organization, they followed the simple rule of grouping like activities. They put each business thus formed into the hands of a single boss. The bosses chosen were no brighter than the senior group. But it was made clear that they were in charge; and they knew full well what they had to do—raise profits and go on doing so, in whatever ways suited them, their people and the business.

The top men could not even try to run the individual businesses any more: they lacked the means. They had cut the headquarters staff to a sixth of its former size, leaving finance as the only central function—and in that area no stone was ever left unturned. All the centrists concentrated, not on detail, but on helping the individual business heads to do their job of raising profits. The men at the center, though, worked very hard—and so, encouraged by their example, did everybody else.

An amazing thing happened to the slow, Sleeping Ugly. In less than a decade, profits multiplied nearly thirty times on turnover that rose almost fivefold to half a billion dollars, yielding a pre-tax return on capital of a third. The name of the company (for this is a true story) does not matter. What matters is that anybody else—who wants to—can follow the same prescription.

Like those not exceptionally clever men, you must go
BACK TO BASICS

1. Behave toward others as you would wish them to behave toward you.
2. Assess each business and business opportunity with all the objective facts and logic you can muster.
3. Concentrate on what you do well.
4. Keep the company flat—so that authority is spread over many people instead of being piled up at the apex of some unnecessary pyramid.
5. Think as simply and directly as possible about what you're doing and why.
6. Own up to your failings and shortcomings—because only then will you be able to improve on them.

7. **B**udget your time, and tighten up the organization wherever you can—because even success tends to breed slackness.
8. Ask questions ceaselessly about your performance, your markets, your objectives.
9. Save costs—not just because economizing is an easy way to make money, but because doing the most with the least is the name of the game.
10. Improve basic efficiency—all the time.
11. Cash in—because unless you do make money, you can't do anything else.
12. Share the benefits of success widely among all those who helped to achieve it.

There are other key concepts in the new-old vocabulary of managing to win, and each of the sections concentrates on one. Each section is self-contained, but each links with the others to form a complete description of the winning style: not *theory*, but style. Part of the successful style is the knowledge that, in business management, a theory is only as good as its practical results, and the practical results are only as good as they last.

It will be a long time (if ever) before the twelve rules to live by in **BACK TO BASICS** become obsolete. They do, after all, embrace some truths that have already lasted as long as business itself—which is longer by many centuries than the concepts of management and the manager.

The twelve rules apply to the manager as an individual just as strongly as to his organization. Remember, though, that nobody ever manages well in a Sleeping Ugly—while everybody looks good in a red-hot firm. That's what the Prince Un-Charmings in the true fairy story found and demonstrated. It became beautiful, and they became successful. That's what the business of business is all about.

PART 1

MANAGERIAL BASICS

1

THE OBJECTS OF THE EXERCISE

A few years ago I wrote a book called *The Naked Manager*. It was meant to be an exposé. I wanted to prove that the hero manager of those days, who preached and pretended to practice a new, supposedly scientific brand of management, had no clothes. Today, that idea is generally accepted, not because of what I wrote, but because events have proved just how naked those heroes of the sixties actually were.

But managers today owe the nudists a great debt. Their failure has pointed the way to success, while stripping away the veils that blurred the vision of many intelligent and excellent people. Today, managers are within closer reach of the promises that their predecessors held out so falsely. The modern manager does have all the equipment and opportunity he needs to make the modern company work—even the company whose huge size and stretch seem to make the job impossible.

The way forward turns out to lie in going back. It's necessary to rediscover the truths of the old-fashioned way of running a business before the new methods and technologies—which do have a part to play—can prove their worth. The merits of old business virtues were discovered under the duress of cash crises, collapsing markets and inflationary squeezes. But one of the best old truths of business is that the lessons of adversity last longest and teach most.

This book is about that effective one-two combination of the old and the new, used for the only purpose which ultimately makes the work of a manager worthwhile—to win. Winning doesn't mean trampling over some adversary. It means doing *better*: better than the competition, better than your own past performance, better than the challenge of people, economics and events might have led you to expect. Like it or not, the manager is always in competition; but the competition which matters most is with himself, with his own stubborn inability to perform as well as his talents, energy and chances make possible.

The problem for many managers is that they work for large companies which have lost the habit of winning, and where winners haven't been encouraged. Both the organization and its executives are like flies in amber: trapped by the past and the present in attitudes they can't change. These outfits come dangerously close to existing only to be. The idea of a real objective, call it winning or anything else, has been lost.

In managing to win, the first object of the exercise is to *have* an object. It has been well said that, if you don't know where you're going, and don't know how to get there, any arrival will be strictly by chance.

Take car companies which thought they existed solely to make big cars, or steel makers who believed only in manufacturing steel. The first lot had no right to complain when small foreign cars captured a vast and valuable chunk of their market. As for the steel men, the evolution of the world economy away from their beloved metal has left most of them stranded like overturned giant turtles.

The fate of any individual executive who opposes such conditioned corporate reflexes is rarely happy. When one great manufacturing firm, chasing multinational dreams down the road of a giant merger, plunged into financial disaster, the sole member of the executive élite to leave was the plan's only opponent. Ghosts are no more welcome at funerals than at weddings. But the funeral for companies like this is their own. In today's world, when avoiding failure may produce it, the search for success is the only real option.

> **Competitive management requires two types of good idea: the insight and the outsight.**

There's still plenty of room for managerial time-servers. The corporation man who imitates the Vicar of Bray, changing his position with each change of regime, is hard to stop. If he is serving his time in a time-serving company, the two have a great chance of being deadbeats together. It's not just that challenge and opportunity are more exciting than staying put. Seeking to win is an insurance policy against corporate and personal obsolescence: and that's more of a threat today than ever.

This isn't because of supposed acceleration in the pace of technological change, although technology surely has something to do with the lessened security of the executive. But it's not clear that today's changes will do as much to create or revolutionize whole industries as did the inventions of the postwar era which spawned the jetliner, antibiotics, the computer, the supertanker, the semiconductor and other fantastic, far-reaching innovations.

These leaps forward were often translated more rapidly into marketable products than has happened, say, with large-scale integrated circuits—the now infamous silicon chip. The manager has less need to worry about the threat of new technologies than over the breakup of the old, safe, corporate lifestyle. Many of the ideas in this book are being applied with remarkable success by corporate managements all over the world—that's how I came to notice and establish the validity of these ideas. These managements have chosen to win—and anybody who hasn't made that choice will face a harder and harder challenge from those who have.

Choosing a vigorous and competitive policy gets neither you nor the company anywhere if the commitment is mostly in words. To win doesn't just mean staking the corporation's money, and perhaps its future, on the lure of brave, bright, new horizons. Illusions about dynamism lay behind many of the awful corporate disasters of our times—illusions which trapped companies as far apart as the red-hot, highly professional Xerox, which dropped a $300 million bundle in computers, and a corporate cold turkey like Britain's Burmah Oil, which destroyed itself by gadding about in diversions from car parts to supertankers.

In these two cases (and in all such cases) there was a basic failure of thought. Competitive management requires two types of good ideas: the "insight" and the "outsight." The *insight* is much more difficult than it sounds—it's the idea about oneself, about what a company and its managers really do well, about how what they are doing can be improved. The *outsight*, which sounds difficult, but can be surprisingly easy to obtain, is the vision and understanding of the world beyond the company's own or present frontiers—the feeling for the present and future events which must shape the company's destiny.

The Xerox failure was predominantly one of outsight. The company simply did not gauge accurately how the computer market was likely to develop, or what role, if any, computers needed to play in its own affairs. Had Xerox been right on these points, had it really required a computer capability of the kind it bought so expensively, then the associated failure of insight (the inability of Xerox's managers to see that they weren't equipped to handle expensive acquisitions in strange businesses) would eventually have been overcome.

In Burmah Oil, the essential failure was of insight. Its

managers couldn't see that they weren't the kind of businessmen they had set their hearts (and the company's millions) on becoming. Had they been, then the blunders made in buying and managing their enormous volume of corporate purchases would have been less grave. Apart from anything else, they wouldn't have bought so much so expensively. It was that enormity, not just failure of outsight about the tanker market, that laid Burmah low.

Customarily, the modern business devotes a great many costly man-hours to seeking more and better outsights. It spends little or no time searching for insights. Yet very often the need for outsights can be kept within limits at the very beginning. For example, if a company decides that it can win without any need for major diversification outside its existing activities, then it may not require to form any vision, accurate or otherwise, about the future development of, say, micro-electronics. The winning manager never forgets that the further an outsight moves from the present, the more inaccurate it is likely to be: he thus avoids the trap into which the Harvard futurologist, Daniel Bell, fell headfirst—predicting a "surprise-free economy" for the rest of the century, six years before the start of the Yom Kippur war.

Generating good insights and outsights can never be the object of the management exercise. No idea in business is of any use until it is translated into action: effective action—the kind that wins satisfactory results. "Satisfactory" is usually an unsatisfactorily vague word, but not in this instance. Very precisely, no result is ultimately worth having unless the outcome includes a mint of money, a deeply satisfying pot of gold.

Under any name, money has to be the goal. Managers have always, of course, known this. They are now more immediately aware of the truth than they were. Time was, not so long ago, when profits (another, not very precise, name for the game) were so unfashionable that some managers almost apologized for making any. More recently, when adequate earnings in large companies have been few and far between, there's been real reason for apologies. That's because money is the only possible general measure of success in creating new resources out of old ones: and that phrase in turn sums up the whole process and urgency of economic growth.

A company which loses money, or fails to generate enough to replace its aging plant properly, is consuming capital, eating up resources. A company which makes money in abundance is creating the new resources whose use, either within the business or outside, will develop other resources still. The making of money and managerial success go hand in hand with each other—and with managing to win.

> *The winning manager needs the immigrant's ability to see with new eyes— and his determination to succeed against odds.*

Even people of supposedly stern anti-capitalist principles (like Labour politicians in Britain) have a sneaking fondness for the men for whom success and money go hand in hand, the entrepreneurs. Though the personal judgment of the fanciers is often bad, the general principle behind the politicians' fancies is right. The economic rewards of the winning entrepreneur stem from the initial quality of the insight/outsight perception. When it's said that such businessmen spotted a gap in the market, the cliché really means that people at large wanted important products or services: and that these entrepreneurs were able to supply what was wanted at a cost lower than the price the market was happy to pay.

Very often, the man who spots such a gap is an outsider: sometimes the rankest of all outsiders—an immigrant.

The generation of powerful insights about yourself, and outsights concerning the world beyond, is easier if your mind is not cluttered with preconceptions, built up over years of experience in a particular industry or country. That's why a manager seeking to improve his insights is well advised to pretend as follows:

1. I know nothing about the company;
2. I need to have everything explained to me;
3. I take nothing for granted.

Occasionally, towering fortunes have been built on a single perception. Such a phenomenon was the realization of individual entrepreneurs that, in a postwar world hungry for bulk cargoes, notably oil, a ship was a license to print money. Not only would shipyards, often backed by governments, fall over themselves to win orders by offering cutthroat prices and generous credit—but, when it comes to approaching banks, a leased ship is among the easiest assets to finance. Not only is a ship security in itself, but a long-term charter—to an oil company, say—both guarantees the cash to pay the interest and doubles the security. Any of the established shipping companies could have spotted such possibilities. None did—not because they were stupid (though some were) but simply because they had far too much of one non-winning quality, Establishment, and far too little of a winning one, Motivation.

The immigrant has none of the first and a lot of the second. To succeed in a strange society isn't so much a challenge as a necessity if you've arrived with no position in the society, and often with no money. The winning manager needs the immigrant's ability to see with new eyes and also his determination to succeed against odds. You don't have to be an immigrant—but it helps.

Take the case, recounted not long ago in *Fortune* magazine, of Samuel Regensbrief. Almost nobody in America would recognize the name of the country's largest maker of dishwashers. Regensbrief, a baker's son, had come to the United States from Vienna aged four. He first made his living as an efficiency expert—what is now known as a management consultant. Regensbrief got into appliances by saving the hide of a refrigerator firm; when that merged with Philco, he became a company man, but moved out, richer by millions of Philco stock, when his employer merged with Ford.

A stone's throw from Philco's Connersville site, where Regensbrief was looking after the construction of a new plant, was a deatbeat dishwasher operation, with 6 percent of the market and only one real asset: its largest customer, Sears, Roebuck. But that contract was in danger, which explained the low price—$2.6 million—that the owner, Avco, accepted from Ragensbrief over twenty years ago. The buyer was totally innocent in dishwashers. But his outsight was correct: that with penetration of only 10 percent of households, these appliances had wonderful market potential—if their price could be brought down.

For an old efficiency expert, that didn't look like much of a problem. But Regensbrief's major insight, when he looked into his acquisition, was that its dishwashers—like everybody else's—were loaded from the *top*. The obvious inconvenience could be avoided, provided the design was watertight, by loading from the *front*: and that was the proposition with which Regensbrief hung on to the Sears account. According to *Fortune*, "Other manufacturers scoffed when they heard of Regensbrief's brainstorm." "Everybody thought we'd be a dead duck," he recalled, "but you just can't be a me-too and succeed in business." In 1979 his company, Design and Manufacturing, had 40 percent of the U.S. market and claimed to undercut General Electric (the also-ran, at 25 percent) by a fifth in price—thus demonstrating that victory doesn't always go to the big battalions.

Such achievements make fine reading for outsiders seeking to muscle in. But what about the corporate insider? Is he condemned to lose? To be defeated by the forces of inertia in the company? Not if the company can see itself as a dialectical process, in which the truth, or the true way, is established by stating a thesis; countering with an antithesis; and arriving at a synthesis.

What the company is right now, what it does and how it does it—these constitute the thesis. The alternative activities and methods which it might adopt are the antithesis. Their combination, the corporate synthesis, should provide the essential blend of stability and progress. It's obvious that the element which may well not be present, and which must be injected if it isn't, is the antithesis, the voice of questioning, criticism, argument and dissent.

Where the emphasis should go varies from time to time as circumstances change. But the company will always gravitate towards stability, or stasis, given the chance. The tendency isn't unhealthy in itself. The economic world needs continuity no less than the political one. So it's in a way comforting that, of the ten non-oil companies which *Fortune* magazine ranked top in sales in 1969 (General Motors, Ford, G.E.—the very same company which was out-dishwashed by Regensbrief—I.B.M., Chrysler, I.T.T., Western Electric, U.S. Steel, Westinghouse and L.T.V.), only the last two had left the list in 1977. Their replacements were Tenneco and Du Pont, which are not exactly bright young newcomers.

Stability and survival are the *sine qua non* of management. But if they become the objects of the exercise, the game is lost. To survive is no great trick. To use the stable strengths of the corporation to make new competitive advances is far harder and far less often achieved. That's why, to make full use of the potential of the new—the really new—management, the large corporation, like management itself, may have to turn backwards towards its own past (possibly one formed by an outsider, even an immigrant). It may have to seek ways of returning to the smaller, more compact organizational forms that firms which are managing to win have found increasingly applicable in today's conditions. If you can't beat the Regensbriefs, it makes sense to join them.

> *What matters is not how large you are, but how effectively you mobilize your strengths at the point of impact.*

It may help to be an outsider; but the corporation man can also outdo other corporation men by following the correct outsider techniques. Even a big firm can find both opportunities and times when it has to buck the odds. A Japanese company called Sakura proved this in the market for color film. Local sales were dominated by Fuji, which, since it was named after the mountain which the Japanese worship and photograph incessantly, had the humdrum Sakura in an apparently hopeless position. The Sakura people (insight) came to the conclusion that they had no hope of beating Fuji by any method of marketing known to man. But from this depressing insight came a deeply constructive thought, or question. Was there any other way in which Sakura could compete more effectively?

The company spotted (outsight) that people buying twenty-exposure film always tried to squeeze in extra frames. In contrast, buyers of thirty-six exposures commonly wasted a few. So Sakura launched a twenty-four-frame film. It proved so successful that the company's market share doubled—and it began to compensate for its lack of holy mountains by a reputation for technological innovation, even though the twenty-four-frame film had involved no technical effort at all (and, for that matter, very little cost).

The Sakura story has deeper implications still, which will appear a little later in the context of why odds only appear to be overwhelming. The choice of a Japanese example is significant, because that whole nation appears to have behaved in the world economy like an outsider, an immigrant at large. Having nothing after the war, never having loomed large in any of the markets they proceeded to tackle, from civil shipbuilding to pocket radios, the Japanese have consistently shown original thought. They have been forced to do so because their original technology has been borrowed, with very few exceptions.

Outdoing your competition while using its own inventions demands assets far greater and rarer than cheap labor. The Japanese manager has consistently spotted opportunities in products and markets that were under the noses of big, rich, fully established Western competitors. Sometimes the chances were in technology—like the extreme improvements Honda made in motorcycle engines. Sometimes the opportunity lay in market exploitation—like the widening of 35mm photography from an expensive specialist hobby into a mass market. Sometimes the brilliance lay in creating a wholly new market—like the adaptation of the transistor to create mass sound. Sometimes the chance was taken by painstaking imitation of a competitor's success in circumstances which were geographically more favorable to the Japanese firm—like Toyota's invasion of California in the best Volkswagen style.

The firms consistently taken on and defeated by the Japanese had enormous technological and financial power, coupled with apparent strangleholds on their markets. One by one, these giants have toppled—Leitz and Zeiss in cameras, Norton and Vespa in bikes, every single United States radio manufacturer. Very few firms have felt safe in the face of this ferocious competition from the East.

The precise opportunities taken are significant; but less so than this consistent theme of searching for openings and then pushing through the breach in the Siegfried Line in steadily increasing force—until the small aggressor becomes the dominant power.

The success of Japanese companies in several of the best markets flies in the face of much conventional wisdom. The fashionable school of corporate strategy holds that the firm with the largest market share has the highest profitability; that the race goes, not to the swift, but to the rich; that the rich get richer, because of the economies of scale which only they can obtain; and that market after market will consequently end by being dominated by a tiny number of gigantic firms.

Up to a point, every one of these notions is correct. But the point at which they cease to be correct is crucial. The larger firm presents a larger target at which to aim. Not only that, but the cost of defense against a new competitor may be so much greater than the latter's cost of attacking that the defense may not seem worth the price.

Sakura's successful attack on Fuji is an overwhelming proof. By selling its twenty-four-frame film at the same prices as Fuji's orthodox twenty-frame product, Sakura posed a painful problem for the stronger firm. Fuji could have retaliated by cutting prices, but that would have been twice as costly as Sakura's certain response—which would have been to match the cuts, yen for yen. Fuji, moreover, would have gained nothing from the exercise; it would have ended, at best, with the same share and much lower profits.

Or Fuji could market a twenty-four-frame film itself. But this response would take time, during which Sakura would be able to establish its "new" product in the marketplace. Again, any extra sales Sakura made would be additional business, while any sales Fuji made would merely replace its twenty-frame products. Thus Fuji was faced, either way, with unwanted and, from its point of view, unnecessary expense, magnified by the sheer size of its market share; an expense forced on it by an apparently much weaker opponent. In the end, Fuji was compelled to meet Sakura's competition anyway by introducing a twenty-four framer, but the damage had been done—and it was Sakura which came out on top.

Effective competition is not prevented by the opponent's size—it's facilitated, if you can hit him where it hurts. One of those places is certainly the very tender spot where he must incur considerable loss of profit for no compensating gain.

He who starts small in a giant's market, moreover, can win

highly satisfactory growth in the early years, even though the total market share remains small. A barely noticeable loss of share for the giant (and it probably won't be noticed if the whole market is growing) can add up to highly profitable volume for the newcomer. In addition to these economic advantages of being small, the invader has the priceless psychological asset of his large opponent's built-in inertia. In part, this inertia is economic, too: the cost and difficulty of modifying a product line selling millions of units are a powerful obstacle to the kind of change which, anyway, large established organizations are always reluctant to make—despite their protestations.

Size, of course, is relative. The ABC television network is no small fry, with a turnover of $2.26 billion. But the sales of CBS are $1.75 billion larger still, and those of R.C.A., the parent of the NBC network, are four billion higher than those of CBS. Yet a year or two back the two larger networks were comprehensively and humiliatingly pushed into second and third place in the ratings competition by the smaller battalion —whose chances of winning at the start would have been dismissed as negligible by anybody in or out of the know.

What really matters is not how large you are across the board, but how effectively you mobilize your strengths at the point of impact. For those who master these lessons, managing to win is possible in even worse circumstances than ABC's. The object of this book is to show how it is done.

2

MIRROR, MIRROR ON THE WALL

Managing, then, is about getting results, and those results must be translated into money, the mirror of business reality. Saying that is the easy part—not because obtaining good results is hard (it's usually the manager's fault if it *is* hard), but because measuring results is tricky. Measurement means applying the right rule or yardstick to what is being measured. In business management, however, choosing the right yardstick—let alone deciding what it should measure—is as contentious as the meaning of the Book of Revelation.

This uncertainty opened the door to some assorted rogues of the sixties, the conglomerateurs and whiz-kids who briefly convinced the world that new methods of scientific management had been mastered and promulgated at the Harvard Business School and like institutions. The name of their particular game, however, wasn't great management, but its illusion: an illusion created by the sight of ever-rising "profits" and "earnings per share."

Since earnings per share are merely profits at one remove (the remove being the fact that, to find the e.p.s. figure, you divide a company's profits by the number of shares it has issued), the e.p.s. figure offers no escape from a central difficulty: that the profits element is an uncertain quantity, even in conservative companies which would no more cook a balance sheet than serve horseflesh in the executive dining room. Profits and e.p.s. figures alike should be approached with caution and handled with care. Yet many informed, alert people completely swallowed figures cooked to a turn by the rogues.

Letters of intent were treated as actual sales; companies were bought hastily towards the end of the financial year so that their profits could be thrown into a whole year's "growth" kitty; expenses were shifted forward, as if by magic, into the year after they were incurred; and to all these, and many other tricks, honored members of the accountancy profession gave expensive blessing. You could argue that the rogue managers, of whom many are still not down to their last yachts, won. But some are in jail; many of their firms sank; and such victories, anyway, are not management, but manipulation.

The true manager builds for the future of the business, for that is also his own. Even if his game plan includes company-hopping, it's foolish to foreclose the possibility that a better personal future may well be available on the spot. The grass *can* be greener in your own backyard, and there's no inherent contradiction between developing the business (or ensuring that it has a better future than its present) and developing a personal career.

The relationship between the two is that between the three time zones of business, the "terms": short, medium and long. The super-economist Keynes was wrong: it's in the short term (not the long) that we're all (or may be) dead. The wise manager ensures, first of all, that the short-term needs of the business can be met. At the same time, he makes equally sure that no short-term moves jeopardize the business in the long term (that being as far as the eye can see). The medium-term ties the other time zones together: it's tomorrow's short term, which will need all the resources for day-to-day prosperity and long-term survival that today's short term should already be enjoying

The winning manager seeks to strike the balance between short- and long-term needs that will maximize medium-term results. That way, he's highly unlikely to come to short-term personal disaster. The measure is what should guide him to the right choices: to strike a balance, you must have weights on the scales.

> *All measures must be looked at in combination; and you must understand the physical reality that underlies the abstract financial figures.*

The choice of the right measure is a creative management task—or would be so called if the conglomerate gunslingers hadn't debased the word "creative." In the sense of creating profits out of thin air by fancy paperwork, creative accountancy is to be shunned. So long as business continues to be taxed on profits, any corporation that shows more profits than it positively has to will, in most circumstances, be run by criminals, incompetents or both. The right measure of business is creative in a quite different sense.

A measure is creative if it reveals that labor costs are too high for the good of the business (a condition from which many companies, great and small, were suffering, often in ignorance, in the middle seventies). But ailments like that, or the onset of a significant weakening in competitive standing, aren't revealed directly by a conventional profit and loss account, nor by the cold statistics in a balance sheet.

The creative act is to find the measure that will unveil the truly warm, vital statistics, and it's doubly or trebly creative to follow up the discovery by taking action. The acid test of an accounting system or any other statistical tool is whether it's of practical use. Information in itself is at best merely interesting.

As a means of discovering the right action to take, and monitoring its results, information is the bloodstream of the well-run business.

The tried and trusty old retainers of management accounting have not been retired, however. Growth in sales will always start the adrenalin flowing as long as business exists. But expansion in sales is usually less important than growth in market share; and the latter in turn is less important than growth in profits; and the latter in turn . . . But that's to anticipate. The first point here is that none of the measures mentioned is good enough without the others.

It's elementary that you haven't won if sales have boomed by 38 percent while the market has advanced by 70 percent. Equally, even if sales growth has been double the overall market rise, that victory will not have been well won if there has been a catastrophic decline in profits. There are exceptions, true. Loss in market share could be desirable if prices are being slashed, and you're deliberately opting for a corner of the market where profits can be maintained. Similarly, a deliberate decision to seek a large increase in market share at the expense of margins can sometimes be justified.

The key word is *deliberate*. The performance according to the measures, if the manager has calculated correctly, will be relatively poor, but it will be according to plan. The exceptions only prove the rule: that all measures must be looked at in combination, and that you must understand the physical reality which underlies the abstract financial figures.

In that hierarchy of growth in sales, growth in market share and growth in profits, the last is really first, because higher profits, other things (like accurate and honest financial reporting) being equal, mean the creation of additional resources. That can't be said about higher sales or deeper market penetration in themselves. But profits, even honestly reported ones, have several disadvantages if used in isolation.

One of the oldest adages in business states that nobody ever went bust through making too little *profit*. It's too little *cash* that proves fatal. Many companies have failed, while reporting high, wide and handsome profits that may even, at least in part, have been genuine. The classic form of bankruptcy is an example: over-trading. The over-trader may have a bulging order book taken at prices which guarantee a huge margin of profit; every product leaving the plant embodies that margin; he still goes bust, because he can't find the cash to finance the production which, if he could only pay for it, would prove so profitable.

The modern professional manager knows as a matter of routine that cash-flow management is basic to business. Unless his finance people are half-witted, cash coming in will be efficiently budgeted, controlled and monitored, so that enough will always be available when needed. (Money won't always be available at exactly the right times and places—that's what banks are for, to bridge the gaps; when banks won't, the death rattle is usually heard.) Rather, today's pro manager faces another danger, spiritually akin to over-trading, but bearing no technical similarity: under-financing.

Its existence was barely noticed until record inflation exposed many companies to its dangers for the first time. The conglomerates had inadvertently pointed the way. Their exclusive concern was, as noted, with growth in earnings per share. This measure wasn't chosen because it said much more about the intrinsic health of a business than the straight, unadulterated figure for earnings. It was chosen because of the intimate connection between the e.p.s. figure and the share price.

In the days when, to win, a manager engineered the highest possible share price, and the fastest possible rise to that peak, it made apparent sense to aim for the quickest possible appreciation in e.p.s. Share prices are a multiple of earnings, and will move up, not just in proportion to earnings, but much faster, if only the speedy advance of e.p.s. persuades investors that a hot "growth stock" lies before them.

Many a staid company adopted corporate targets expressed in terms of the rise in earnings per share. This was justified on the grounds that the business ultimately belonged to the stockholders (who, by virtue of rich stock options, conveniently included the directors and senior management). Since the investors were predominantly concerned with the value of their investment, the right and proper procedure for corporate planners was to set an e.p.s. target that would rejoice the owners' hearts, and to work back to the underlying fundamentals, like sales and margins, products and diversification.

The danger isn't only that of missing e.p.s. targets altogether (as many companies did). It shouldn't, either, have taken the Second Great Crash, when Wall Street, London, Paris, Tokyo and all the other stock markets collapsed, to prove, as well, that market prices are not within any man's power to command. Investors are absolutely right to be deeply interested in the market value of their investment, and managers certainly must concentrate on protecting and enhancing that interest. But aiming at some given rate of increase in e.p.s. has nothing to do with the safety and succor of investments. Something else is required, something very old-fashioned: a high rate of return.

Unless a company earns more than its cost of capital, it can't hope to finance its growth.

The apparent dynamism of a target of 15 percent a year growth in earnings per share is illusory—so illusory that it can lead to *negative* growth. A brilliant study in the *Harvard Business Review* (March–April 1975) by Fred Searby stripped away this particular veil. It compared companies with e.p.s. targets with firms which chose the apparently static corporate objective of return on investment (probably the oldest yardstick in business); and concluded that those which used the

Neanderthal measure of R.O.I. were actually much better placed to grow.

Why so? Put yourself in the shoes of a manager whose business returns 30 percent net of tax. We know one thing about his company for a start: it either has fine management, or an excellent line of business, or both. We also know that, with so high (but by no means improbable) a return, the firm is unlikely to be short of funds, for expansion or anything else; what it can't generate internally, it can (because of its extreme profitability) borrow with ease. One thing more: it has a yardstick and target rolled into one.

The obvious target for such a company is to maintain its high return. It follows that the manager in these shoes won't buy a business that can't (either before or after improvement) match the return on funds already employed in the firm. The obvious yardstick for existing operations is that same return: operations performing below the 30 percent need either revival or disposal. More important still, all modernization and expansion plans will be expected to maintain or protect that same 30 percent. In other words, they will be high-value projects, rigorously selected and strictly monitored. As their benefits flow, too, the company's rich ability to finance itself will be enhanced.

It's the opposite of a vicious circle: a beneficent round. Now, swap shoes for those of an e.p.s. enthusiast. We know only one thing from his fast percentage growth rate: that earnings are increasing rapidly in a way that doesn't dilute the stockholders' equity (the object of the exercise is defeated if he issues stock as fast as he boosts profits). The snag with all percentage growth targets, however, is that the *absolute* figures keep on getting larger.

At $100,000 of profits, an increase of $50,000 (perfectly feasible) raises earnings by 50 percent. The next year, the same $50,000 rise will only boost earnings by a third. In the third year, $50,000 is a rise of only a quarter . . . and so on. A company aiming at a 24 percent rise in earnings per share, and starting at $1 million of net profit, will in three years need, not $240,000 more to keep up the pace, but $480,000. In six years, profits equal to those which the whole business was earning at the start are required to keep the 24 percent ball rolling.

To be fair, even the wildest corporate gunslinger might jib at an e.p.s. target of 24 percent. But even a lower, more accessible figure puts the emphasis on adding profits—even if the company's basic financial performance, its R.O.I., deteriorates as a result. In the example above, it makes no difference whether, after three years, the company has added $480,000 of earnings at sales margins of 1 percent or 10 percent. In fact, from one angle, the first and worse case might even seem to be *better*. Adding $48 million of sales looks a great deal more impressive than a mere smidgen of $4.8 million. Anyway, it's easy to raise a feeble 1 percent on sales to 2, 3 or even 4, isn't it? Especially for boy geniuses like us . . .

In harsh fact, a big business with a small return—on either sales or capital—is often afflicted with deep-running ailments that the kind of boy genius who buys such properties is ill equipped to cure. Many e.p.s. enthusiasts made bad and costly buys simply because, in the short term, the purchases appeared to offer an easy boost to the precious e.p.s. growth rate. Any target that puts the emphasis on growth, but not on its quality, is putting the cart before the horse; and, as the *Harvard Business Review* study showed, in the result the horse may simply not move at all.

The explanation lies partly in the different psychologies that produce the different choices of method. But the major factor is entirely economic. Fast e.p.s. growth can be achieved on an inadequate operating base. Thus, in 1966, when Litton Industries was still riding high as the Big Daddy of the conglomerates, it could point to a ten-year growth rate in e.p.s. of $36\frac{1}{2}$ percent. But its return on sales was only 4.7 percent at the time; this anaemic figure was only elevated into an 18 percent return on stockholders' equity by some heavy gearing: in other words, by debt financing.

The relative merits of businesses that earn the same profits on the same capital are not changed in essence by the fact that one borrows half its capital (Litton's long-term debt in 1966 equaled half its stockholders' equity), while the other doesn't. But in olden days, the unborrowed firm would have been considered intrinsically stronger. And the olden view was right.

Move on to 1977, and Litton's e.p.s. growth over ten years has turned negative: from 1967 to 1977, e.p.s. *fell* by an average 4.11 percent a year. Litton's net return on sales (1.6 percent) was still pitiful by the standards of the 433 other companies in *Fortune*'s list of the 500 largest American companies which outranked it in this respect. Its former, seemingly excellent, 18 percent return on stockholders' equity of 1966 had become only 6.5 percent—not that stockholders' equity, the stake of the investors in the business after all other claims on the assets have been met, is as logical a base as it may seem. It relates clearly enough to the earnings per share measure. But like e.p.s., and for similar reasons, it does not give a reliable guide to the health of the company.

The confusion is between two different matters: the performance of a business, and the way in which that business is financed. In the end, there's only one source of finance: the extra resources generated by the business, which (roughly speaking) equal the net cash flow, which (roughly speaking) equals the available profit plus depreciation. Borrowed money, or fresh cash raised from the shareholders, will do just as well: but bankers or other lenders don't like lending money that won't be repaid, and shareholders won't throw good money after bad (unless they are being well and truly deceived).

That happened to the shareholders in the aero-engine firm of Rolls-Royce, who once coughed up the money from which their own dividends were paid. But classic corporate failures offer no recipes for would-be winners. The winning idea is an apparent statement of the obvious: *expansion follows from the means of expansion.* Unless a company earns more than its cost of capital (as Fred Searby argued in the *Harvard Business*

Review article mentioned), it can't hope to finance its growth. Searby has charted a Rake's Progress, to prove his point. It starts by analyzing what happens if the company consistently earns *less* than its cost of capital.

   a. The company's growth of reinvestment is slowed.
   b. Dividends are reduced.
   c. External financing must provide an increasing proportion of capital needs.

The consequence of (a) plus (b) is that shareholders' returns and expectations are reduced: as for (c), as the company's borrowing rises, so must its risks and its financing costs also increase. In consequence, capital costs rise overall; market value and stock price decline; and the risks being run by the shareholders, and the returns on their money, simply become less competitive compared with other available investments.

Searby, a McKinsey consultant, points out in sorrow that "most executives are exceedingly reluctant to accept any e.p.s. penalty, even within a balanced program for improving R.O.I." He cites "a primary metals producer" that could have bought a company which "if acquired through common stock, would have increased the overall company's R.O.I. by 30 percent. A debt acquisition was not feasible because of a self-imposed debt/equity ratio. Management balked at and eventually declined a stock merger because of a 20 percent e.p.s. dilution, although the dilution would have been fully recovered in five years."

This sad short story is matched by another: that of a "growth-oriented company," which from 1969 to 1974 increased sales by 15 percent compound annually; raised invested capital by 18 percent (with debt multiplying fivefold); and elevated e.p.s. by 10 percent. At the same time, though, return on investment declined by a fifth, from 10 percent to 8 percent. "Growth-oriented" managers like that don't know the answer to a basic question: Just what are you in business for?

The answer is outlined in another Searby case:

A $20 million division of a diversified industrial-goods supplier, once a major profit support, had gradually slipped into a cash-loss position . . . the overall corporation . . . had not earned its cost of capital in eight years. Ultimately, the corporation cut the division back from over 100 product/market sectors serving 11,000 customers at 70,000 shipping points to two product/market sectors serving twenty-five major customers from seventy shipping points. Three of its five plants were sold (for nearly book value) and two-thirds of an expensive division overhead was eliminated. Now, two years later, the division is producing $15 million in sales and an after-tax R.O.I. of 18 percent.

The name of the game is the constructive employment of the assets in the business. As Searby points out, you can improve R.O.I. by divestment of businesses or major operations. (Potential leverage in this case, he says, is "very high: can be the fastest and surest way to improve return on investment.")

Then there's acquisition, but that won't raise R.O.I. in the short term.

Pruning the product line, however, is "good": relatively little risk, "but payoff may not be immediate."

Cost reduction/profit improvement is another "good" approach to R.O.I., but it's unlikely to solve the fundamental problem if the company is persistently failing to cover the cost of its capital. As Searby says, "the primary value is in buying time"; you can seek a fundamental, long-term solution while the short-term economy-cum-improvement measures are paying off.

Improving asset utilization is "good: can be very quick and sure in cash-management area, less quick in areas of inventory management and plant consolidation."

Finally, changing the financial structure: "Very good: can be quick, especially through stock repurchase [a maneuver that used to be illegal in the United Kingdom] or exchange of debt issues."

The key to all these approaches is the same: raising the return without increasing the capital: more bang, in other words, per buck.

The rules are:

1. Maintain the target of a *"satisfactory"* return on total capital employed at all times.
2. "Satisfactory" means achieving a *substantial* margin over the cost of borrowing money—even if you're *not* in debt.
3. "Substantial" means enough to allow for:
   a. the risks of equity capital,
   b. inflation,
   c. maintaining adequate investment.
4. Don't confuse the R.O.I target with *growth*: profitability can be greatly improved by constructive shrinkage—or selling the bad apples.

It's the last point that's often the hardest to swallow. Rather than get smaller, even as the foundation for new growth, managers would prefer to add sales, even if no extra profits result. So long as capital employed stays constant, they can even cover their shame with an unchanged R.O.I. But the whole exercise would then have very little point: the object of winning management is to add, not just business, but *value*.

The winning feature of Added Value is that it concentrates the manager's mind on essentials—on adding value.

One British conglomerate has grown mightily by applying to its subsidiaries a single yardstick of great and effective simplicity. So long as they increase profits year by year, the managers may continue to bask in the golden approval of head office. Fine and good, so far as it goes. But as the index of health and efficiency, simple profit doesn't go far enough. It only measures one dimension of the business—a narrowly defined financial dimension, based on the principles of double-entry bookkeeping and on accounting conventions evolved (with some difficulty and much obfuscation) through the years.

The classic case of corporate revival, raising a business Lazarus from the near-dead, is that of the General Electric Company in Britain. Company turnarounds exist in plenty, on both sides of the Atlantic. But no other has involved three companies which were big even by world standards: the original G.E.C., Associated Electrical Industries and English Electric. The three were welded into a mighty group—which had £476 million of pre-tax profits in 1980–81—by profit-oriented management of the highest order.

Its architect, Lord Weinstock, is down on record as opposing profit as a target, arguing that profits are the *result*, not the aim, of effective management (note the analogy with the R.O.I. and e.p.s. firms described above). But although Weinstock argues against putting the profit objective before the management task, he does use profit for three of the seven key ratios with which his businesses were judged in their famous revival. They weren't the only ways, by any means; Weinstock, an arch-pragmatist (as all good managers should be), is no man for magic formulas.

Still, the ratios are an interesting bunch; and to the extent that they helped to raise G.E.C. earnings by exactly 100 times between 1960/61 and 1977/78 (or seventeen years), they are not to be sneezed at. There are seven in all:

1. Profit divided by capital employed.
2. Profit divided by sales.
3. Sales divided by capital employed.

4. Sales divided by fixed assets.
5. Sales divided by stocks.
6. Sales per employee.
7. Profit per employee.

First, note how *many* ratios there are. As Peter Drucker has written, business is multidimensional, and needs measures for each dimension. Second, it doesn't follow that all these measures would be equally important for all businesses. Each business has its own unique, indispensable ratios of operating efficiency. For instance, in fast-food catering, the ratio of material costs to turnover is bound to hold one key to success.

A third point is that the Weinstock ratios are readily translated into the terms of a *conventional* profit and loss account. Accountants have built up a complex set of conventions which not only deliberately depart from reality but are highly variable as between accounts and accountants. One man's profit, you might say, is another man's loss. However, there is another, less variable way of looking at the money flows of a business: *added value*.

The measure is less useful in a service business, which is often really selling the time of people, than in manufacturing or retailing. But even the people employed in an advertising agency can only gain any loot if there is enough margin between the prices paid to suppliers *outside* the business and the prices paid by customers *outside* the business.

That's the philosophical starting point: the idea that a firm, any firm, is nothing but a device for taking in supplies at one end and pushing out those external supplies, in one form or another, at the other end. The difference between the price received at the far, customer end and the price paid at the incoming, supplier end is the *value added*. It has no exact correlation with any single conventional accounting figure, not even the American gross profit or the British trading profit. But it is exactly the same as the following combination of conventional numbers: external sales, less all external costs of sales, but including wages, tax, interest, depreciation, dividends and profit.

The notion stands Karl Marx on his head. Marx took all the prices incurred in the business, from materials to rents, added the wages paid to labor, subtracted the total from the income received from sales, and called the difference "surplus value"—the wealth extracted or exploited from the workers by greedy capitalists. Added value, in contrast, stands for a pool of wealth from which everybody involved in the operation has to be recompensed: labor, providers of capital, owners, government.

The winning feature of A.V. is that it concentrates the manager's mind on essentials. For instance, an excellent stockturn (that being the ratio of sales to inventory) is not excellent if the stock turned over so rapidly is adding no value. The Weinstock ratios, in fact, can be revised as follows—remembering that added value is simply established by counting in all cash proceeds from sales in the financial period concerned, and subtracting all cash expended on bought-in supplies and services, but nothing expended on the internal labor supply.

1. Profit divided by capital employed (*the same as above*).
2. Profit divided by added value.
3. Added value divided by capital employed.
4. Added value divided by fixed assets.
5. Added value divided by stocks.
6. Added value per employee.
7. Wages and salaries divided by added value.

Of these seven, the last two are the most penetrating. If you're paying your employees an average of £10,000 a year, and A.V. per employee is only £10,000, you're in business for nothing except your salary. Equally, the really successful firm will show both high and rising wages and salaries *and* a low, even falling percentage of added value going to labor. To put it the other way around, if labor is raising its share of added value, then somebody else's percentage must be shrinking.

Since, in these times, that's unlikely to be the government, either investors, or reinvestment in the business, or both must be getting (relatively speaking) short-changed.

The lower the percentage going to labor, the more room for that proportion to be raised without causing the proprietor any pain. But there's always a point (and most long-established businesses will be near it) where increases in the wage-cost percentage must seriously affect the interests of management—including management's sovereign interest in the medium and long-term health of the operation. In many British companies in the late seventies the ratio was around or above 80 percent—far too high for anybody's comfort, including that of the workers.

But much more important than whether any ratio features profit or added value is the dynamic factor: which way the ratio is moving. The trend tells a manager the one thing about which he can be certain: whether, on that particular score, he's getting better or worse. No static figure can ever tell a business or its boss whether either is good, although it may demonstrate that both are bad. A trend-line, especially in a relationship between two variables, shows much more effectively where a business is heading. Properly interpreted, the trends can help any manager to add value to his own performance—and that's an essential personal victory, irrespective of whether he is (as he should be) or isn't (which he can hope to change) outperforming the competition.

3

THE FIVE-STAR COMPANY

There are no good companies and no good managers: only those who do the best they can. These heroes and hero organizations deserve their five stars. They have achieved the most that is allowed to management. The five stars are linked to five attributes. The five-star company and its executives need:

1. The ability to concentrate on what they do well.
2. A prevalence of self-criticism.
3. The desire to be the best.
4. Evolution into plurality.
5. Economy of effort.

These five attributes are basic, even though many managers have never given them any thought. Take the first—the answer to the question: What do we do well? There is an inherent supposition in companies that they could do equally well in any line of work. This is nonsense—although it is nonsense of a different order from that encouraged by Ted Levitt in a famous 1956 article, published in the *Harvard Business Review*, and entitled "Marketing myopia." In Levitt's view, companies should inquire, "What business are we in?"

The answers usually drew a circle around the various businesses a company happened to have: thus (among other things) denying to itself the wondrous benefits of quitting a business altogether. It's far more important to establish the real *talents* of a company: attributes that owe as much to history as anything else. Companies find it agonizingly hard to change their historic character. When the big U.S. car companies failed to compete with small imports conceptually, they were, of course, acting as prisoners of their past. They were good at making large, extravagant cars for the traditional American buyer. They were bad, terribly bad, at making cars for an economy-minded compact or sub-compact buyer in whom they didn't really believe. The business they were in was clear enough. Their myopia was failure to see they had carried concentration to the level of a fault, even though it is one of the basic business virtues and the subject of the next section.

Never do *anything* to excess is a sound maxim in management. With that sixth proviso, here's the five-star guide.

"Mommy, let's go back into the business we know something about."

One vital word for winning management is *concentrate*. With almost no exceptions, the most successful companies down the years have been the most concentrated. The super-company example is I.B.M. Throughout its history, this corporation has concentrated on data processing; the strength of the company lies in its fantastic customer base, not in its technology. The latter is vital, true, but only as a means of securing that base. The new-technology companies—I.B.M., Polaroid, Xerox—are marvelous modern examples of the old truth that a properly identified and serviced market need is the foundation of corporate growth into, to all intents and purposes, an infinite future.

Each such market need demands a particular body of skills; and each company consequently develops its own specific skills package. Much the same is true of managers. Nobody is universally good; everybody has specific strengths; the only universal strength is an ability to play to those specific talents. It is true that an executive's specific gift may be to have many talents, none overwhelming. That man will go far —just like the company whose talent lies in running several different businesses at once. But this is a very special ability— and no company that is especially excellent at one core activity is likely to have this particular knack.

Naturally, every company (though not every manager) needs to be at least passably good at several things. If financial control is lacking, or marketing ability non-existent, or personnel policies abysmal, or product design and manufacture defective, or other business basics wrong, the company may still succeed (just as a football team can sometimes win despite basic deficiencies). But sooner or later, the corporate fungus will threaten the entire business.

The mid-life crisis of the entrepreneurial firm commonly arrives when it outgrows the ability of the original proprietor, with his rudimentary management skills, to control what he has created; much the same problem confronted Dr. Frankenstein with his monster. The man's strength is the ability to conceive a business idea and follow it through by creating some kind of organization which is at least adequate for concentrating on and exploiting that idea.

So Levitt's question needs to be reworded: not, "What business are we in?" but, "What do we do *well*?" Meaning, in this first and most important instance, not, "What management and business skills do we deploy?" but, "How do we really make our money, and why?"

Is the company really good at consumer marketing (like Procter and Gamble)? Or only at marketing a specific type of product to the consumer (like the car-makers)? Is the firm (like Xerox) good only in professional markets? If so, it would make little sense to tackle consumer selling without solid evidence that the skills and assets are transferable—or obtainable.

Is the company good at making expensive specialty products? Then it should think twice, thrice and thrice again before venturing into broad-based volume sales, even in the same industry. Is the industry which it knows, backwards, forwards and sideways, food? Then it should think long and hard before moving beyond those confines—and then think again.

Enter the buggy-whip. Levitt made telling play with the whip-makers who, by failing to realize that they were in transportation accessories, died with the horse-drawn carriage. Being "good" at something which nobody wants is self-contradictory and self-defeating. But in truth, it's really being *bad*—bad at the critical initial selection of the business idea.

But was the business of those failed whip manufacturers really transportation accessories? If their special expertise truly lay in processing leather and distributing the product to the carriage trade, should they have converted their talents to making high-class luggage?

Maybe that wouldn't have been a particularly bright or winning idea. But the whip companies could have much less easily converted themselves to making starter-handles, or any other parts of automobiles (except, perhaps, leather upholstery). Some Americans did see the need for newfangled accessories, like Charles F. Kettering with his self-starter—and where would *that* have left a converted whip-maker? But inventors like Kettering usually and typically came from different, new worlds.

Part of their triumph lay in being first. Their skills included innovation, which involves, by definition, beating competitors to the punch. It's also the case that any well-timed idea (from hula hoops to combine harvesters) will carry its inventor through a horrifying number of failures in the more routine areas of planning and execution.

Whether the bungling innovator is really "good" at his business is beside the point. Good in such matters is a strictly relative term. By being first with the most, the innovator is automatically "good"—at least to the point where he attracts "better" competition. From that point, however, the victory goes to the managers who maintain and intensify their concentration on the basic business; who defend it by eradicating the sloppy faults of inattention and incompetence which always gather around that solid core; and who don't clutter up their minds and their management by running away from the threatened activity into other fields.

No manager should ever forget the words of Bill Lear, the great inventor (car radios, eight-track stereo) and executive-jet pioneer. Despite his genius, Lear dropped a $17 million bundle on steam-driven road vehicles. He then said to his wife and partner, "Mommy, let's go back into the business we know something about." That's what concentration means.

> *Without self-criticism, the desire to be best loses virtue.*

The entrepreneur often seems to know by instinct what "good" professional marketing men have to discover by painstaking, systematic search. But you can't win, systematically or intuitively, without really knowing the answers to the marketing man's professional questions as set out in an article in *Management Today*:

1. What is the product or service?
2. Who will make the buying decisions relating to the product or service?
3. What is "the market?" Where is it? What market segments are there?
4. How does the product satisfy a market need better than the competition?
5. What is it that makes this product or company or service unique?

6. How much investment is required—and when? What are the sales patterns? When is income received?
7. What managerial resources are currently available, or could become available?
8. What response do "sources of information" make to these plans? Are the plans adjusted in the light of other people's views? If not, why not?

Note that some of these questions are internal checks, demanding judgment on the quality of the organization. This is the second meaning of "What do we do well?" It is a tougher question than it sounds, because self-deception is much easier than self-criticism—which is the second necessity of the five-star company. A prevalence of self-criticism is characteristic of good companies—even companies that on first observation appear to be smug and self-satisfied rather than self-critical.

Before opening a single international store, the Marks and Spencer store chain had achieved an international reputation that was enough to turn the hardest head. The typical Marks executive is not prone to doubts about his company; not only (he believes) the best-managed retail chain in the world, but one of the best-managed businesses: a view with which the world, by and large, agrees.

Now, the desire to be best is the third attribute of the five-star company. But that driving passion is no use unless the passionate manager is realistic about merits and defects. In the case of Marks, the impervious self-confidence shown to *outside* critics is balanced by a heavy weight of *inside* scrutiny. Everything the business does, everything it sells, is subjected to endless critical analysis and questioning, but not with the object of self-flagellation, nor even of avoiding error.

Of course, Marks makes mistakes. One critic claims that Marks spent two years developing a line of household paints, only to find what it should have known from the start—that highly inflammable goods are unsuitable for a department store to carry. If true, that kind of mistake, while not particularly excusable, is part of the price of seeking profitable extensions to the range, the only way in which a broadly based retail group can hope to outgrow the economy in which it operates.

Without self-criticism, the desire to be best loses virtue. The strange story of the collapse of the Rolls-Royce aero-engine company epitomizes many business failings, but this one above all. The company's managers wanted to be the best in the world at making aero-engines and (of much less importance commercially) cars. So in the boardroom and right down through the company, the conviction was absolute: Rolls-Royce *was* the best.

In this conviction, Rolls-Royce did many dangerous things: it underestimated the abilities of its American rivals, Pratt and Whitney and later General Electric; it overestimated its own market penetration, and it believed its own wrong presentation of the figures; it underestimated its costs and incurred them too heavily; it grossly overestimated profits.

Far from being "best," it simply wasn't in the running on matters like financial control, strategic planning, organization structure; or even the project planning and execution which became dominant, especially after the massive RB-211 engine loomed into life.

This single project wasn't what laid the company low: it only brought to a climax all the faults from which Rolls-Royce had been complacently suffering for years. The RB-211 program, a technical headache, extremely late, and vastly over budget, gravely endangered the equally guilty customer, Lockheed.

The apologists for the RB-211 talk about the perils of all high technology. But managers are paid to cope with risk and control its consequences: not to forge blindly ahead, compounding the risks with bad decisions (like the initial choice of carbon fiber for the turbine blades) which are based on irrelevant considerations—like producing the "best" engine in the world: best in the sense of "most technologically advanced."

General Electric's less ambitious development met the customer's criteria perfectly well, and that is the only consideration which ultimately counts in most markets, whether the technology is high or low.

There couldn't be a sharper contrast than that between Rolls-Royce and McDonnell-Douglas, whose competitive plane, the DC-10, fitted the G.E. engine. This was another example of Rolls's bad luck or bad judgment: the DC-10, before its Chicago disaster, had enjoyed a far better, more successful run commercially than the Lockheed TriStar. But it was not successful enough to satisfy "Mac" McDonnell, the octogenarian founder of the St. Louis firm. The DC-10 may be "best," or, rather, "better," in market penetration, but it falls short by one indispensable McDonnell criterion: it has never made any money.

In McDonnell's main trade, the manufacture and supply of military hardware, you can afford to be "best" at any price: you can hardly afford not to be, since the armed services will probably always pay for the extra performance and capability which might win a war. In a generally cheese-paring company, McDonnell spares no expense to maintain the company's technological strength. But the management has not allowed its civilian thinking to be infected by its military business.

The consequence was a strategic decision to leave Boeing, as the top civil aircraft manufacturer, to battle it out with the Europeans in the next generation of wide-bodied transports; while Douglas concentrated, much more cheaply, on developing what it already has (the DC-9 and DC-10) in the hope of at last making money. Douglas has wobbled in its self-denial since. But to be best—market leader right across the board, say—is not enough in itself; choosing what to be best at is crucial, and must be related to the other purposes of the outfit.

Boeing, too, is an object lesson in self-dissatisfaction. Awful inefficiencies were discovered when a slump in orders for civil aircraft in the sixties threw the company into severe crisis. Boeing duly analyzed and eradicated those weaknesses (most of them elementary wastes of men and materials) and *admitted to them publicly*. The desire to be the best in the business, while essential, would need to be counterbalanced by self-criticism for the following reason alone: however good an operation is, it can always be improved, and improved substantially, at that.

> *The five-star company builds the questioning attitude into its concentrated, perfectionist, self-critical, plural and economical way of life.*

The case of McDonnell-Douglas and Mr. McDonnell, its founder, seems to contradict the fourth-star principle: evolution into plurality, an ugly phrase which means the beautiful substitution of many heads for one. Even in a one-man foundation like McDonnell-Douglas—and such businesses are by definition exceptions to rules—the plurality movement must start long before the old man retires or dies. (The increasingly plural management at McDonnell has one excellent habit to stop plurality from becoming cumbersome—at the daily management meetings throughout the enterprise, nobody is allowed to sit down, which is one way of guaranteeing that meetings stay short.)

Plurality—or at least its appearance—is powerfully evident in Japanese management, where meetings are enormous in numbers and often in length. That this is a national tradition, not a mere management theory, can be seen from the brilliant film about the raid on Pearl Harbor, *Tora! Tora! Tora!* The reconstruction of the Japanese side, filmed by a Japanese director, showed vast meetings chaired by Admiral Yamamoto, at which the general policy was decided; the details were then entrusted to relatively junior officers who happened to be the best in the fleet at their specialties.

In contrast (in reality, as in the film), the disastrous American decisions were taken—either singly or in small meetings of top brass alone—by the responsible commander. He often acted directly and wrongly against the specialist advice of junior officers, such as intelligence and air-power experts. Many reports have testified that in modern Japanese industry, which has inflicted so many Pearl Harbors on American and European business, the collective decision-making is associated with explicit reliance on the proven expertise of the specialist.

Such Japanese meetings do not so much take decisions as *evolve* them. By the time an issue has been thoroughly, exhaustively, competently discussed, the decision is not only clear to all participants, but all are committed to that decision by virtue of their active participation in the discussion. Western managers who sincerely want to win must achieve a similarly successful approach to plurality. In modern conditions, companies can't afford the loss of contribution that goes with the exclusion of talent by rank or some other artificial restraint.

One British case proves the point—a company which has had to buck not only the national traditions of aristocratic leadership (from the "Charge of the Light Brigade" downwards), but also its own vast size and powerful feelings of inadequacy. The company is Imperial Chemical Industries, Britain's biggest manufacturer, which has faced decades of formidable competition from Germany's Big Three chemical companies and from the American giants, led by Du Pont. Taking the latter as benchmark, the comparative performance over the period 1968–77 was:

Sales: Du Pont +140 percent, I.C.I. +277 percent.
Total investment: Du Pont +112 percent, I.C.I. +159 percent.

Net profit: Du Pont +43 percent, I.C.I. +197 percent.
Earnings per share: Du Pont +38 percent, I.C.I. +242 percent.

The growth figures show how Du Pont's return on investment fell over the period, while I.C.I.'s increased (since its net rose faster than its total investment). At the end of the day, the American group, once famous for its profitability, had a net return on total assets virtually identical with the British figure (around 4 percent). The Americans had cause to worry, not only about their drop in profitability, but about a sluggish sales performance—a definite loss of world market share.

The British can't congratulate themselves so long as their R.O.I. is down at this basement level: the 1980 recession took it through the floor. But their growth victory, which actually left the British firm ahead of the American giant in total sales, is still remarkable. In the course of a series of voyages around I.C.I., I tried to isolate the causes.

A more ambitious and successful program of geographical diversification was plainly one factor: but what force had inspired I.C.I. to diversify? My conclusion was that I.C.I. differed from other British companies in two critical respects. It hired graduate talent on a massive scale; and it was managed in a collegiate style (for which read "plurality")—so much so that the post of chief executive officer didn't even exist.

The two characteristics interlock. For graduate talent to be effective, it must have room in which to move. Interviews up and down the hierarchy—and later confirmation of the findings—implied that, within the framework of a strong housekeeping administration, I.C.I.'s many levels of managers were left surprisingly free to pursue interests which the corporation shared, but which the manager thought of as his own; whether it was a youngster trying psychological testing on blue-collar job applicants or a research director forging ahead with a possible half-billion pound project in synthetic protein.

What stops such people wasting the company's time and

money on worthless, unprofitable activities and ventures? Corporate culture is part of the answer. In a company with a strong, shared culture, managers tend to share assumptions about what is and isn't done. But it's also true that *plurality is its own safeguard.*

Because the company is genuinely collective, the manager doing his own thing can only pursue that thing with the knowledge and support of his peers, subordinates and superiors. Culture helps stop him from attempting the absurd. Collectivism keeps him from converting the absurd into reality. Neither should prevent him from having ideas and taking initiatives—the vital ingredients of winning. And if the goal of plurality, harnessing individual drives and expertise to the collective cause, has been achieved in a group as vast as I.C.I., it can surely be achieved anywhere.

Does plurality offend against the fifth five-star principle, in that it doesn't, apparently, economize on effort? The appearance is deceptive. Economy in this context means concentrating on what really matters—like the market from which the main proceeds of the company derive—and not dissipating effort on what is either irrelevant or impossible.

Ideally, of course, you can't be too thorough. A company like Mars, whose record in confectionery and other foods is studded with victories, is so imbued with the habit of thoroughness that it knows no other method of proceeding. But take one example of good Mars management: paying a 10 percent attendance bonus to encourage good timekeeping and discourage absenteeism. The object and the excellent results are worth a great deal of managerial effort; but the *actual* effort expended is small. The winning manager constantly seeks ways of achieving his ends by the simplest, least intensive route; or by abandoning activities altogether, that being one of the easiest means of economy.

By the same token, the inferior management spends time and money on the inessential. Thus Rolls-Royce, before its crash, would insist that unimportant parts received the same machining, to tiny tolerances, as the significant parts; while simultaneously doing nothing to stop the ruinously expensive waste of material machined off precious titanium metal. The principle of economy of effort obviously relates to the first five-star quality—the ability to concentrate on what a company does well. But it also, less obviously, marries with the principles which should govern a winning manager's use of his own personal time (see p. 147). The key questions are:

1. What am I doing that could be done by somebody else?
2. What am I doing that needn't be done by anybody?
3. What am I doing that could be done in less time ("time" being the synonym for all the manager's personal resources)?

The answers are never absolute. They change with changing situations. But the five-star company builds the questions, and the questioning attitude, into its concentrated, perfectionist, self-critical, plural and economical way of life; and it changes itself as the answers change. Nor does it ever confuse effort with virtue. In *The Naked Manager*, I approvingly quoted the Weinstock maxim that if you need complicated calculations to justify doing something, you probably shouldn't. If a manager or a company is doing something the hard way, they probably should be doing it differently—or not doing it at all.

4

THE SEVEN PILLARS OF MANAGEMENT

Managers have one especially endearing quality. They are always tempted by Holy Grails: by the search for a perfect solution to any or all of the problems they meet in an imperfect existence. There's one otherwise completely sane executive, a manager I admire, who has a passion for psychological tests. Anybody who wants a promotion or a job in his company has to be assessed by a psychologist—even a man who had come thousands of miles to offer a spot of informed advice found himself whisked straight from the airport to confront the company shrink in a hotel room. But, as an insider pointed out, the game wasn't worth even a small candle. The assessments were used mainly to reinforce personnel decisions that had already been made and *were almost never changed*.

As a British expert, John D. Handyside, has pointed out, psychologists are not yet in a position to tell us what identifiable attribute will produce what desirable results. For instance, you may decide that a certain job requires somebody especially good at lightning decisions, while another post needs a ruminative fellow who is expert in taking his time over the more difficult questions. But it is clear from experimental studies, says Handyside, that people who are good at the "rat-a-tat" handling of relatively simple problems are also, broadly speaking, the same people who are good at solving more complex problems, when the time pressures are not so marked.

In other words, don't waste time searching for the perfect psychological fit. It may exist, but you won't find it for looking. What can—and should—be sought are positive symptoms of essential qualities. Ideas will differ on which qualities really are indispensable. But my own list, culled from observation of winning managers through the years, contains seven pillars of managerial wisdom:

1. Put results ahead of personal prestige.
2. Maintain high personal ambition.
3. Aim to achieve success through others.
4. Never over-commit yourself emotionally.
5. Persist, but never with error.
6. Sort the essential from the inessential.
7. Constantly direct effort into rewarding channels.

The seven pillars fall naturally into three groups. The first of these can be summed up in one word: prestige.

> *It's unlikely that a manager who isn't interested in maximizing his own resources will be interested enough in maximizing his employer's.*

Ambition, getting results, success, prestige and working through others are intimately woven into each other. Very few activities in life—and even fewer in management—allow individuals to win with absolutely no assistance from anybody else.

Very few winners are without ambition or fail to gain prestige as a result of their success.

But what about the obvious contradictions? Isn't the ambitious man hungry for prestige? Doesn't he get to that pinnacle on the backs of other men? Won't—and don't—conjuring tricks and illusions (the original definition of "prestige," in fact) work just as effectively as real achievement in the eyes of the world?

The short answer is that prestige built on deceit (a better and stronger word than illusion) dies even faster than it arises. The real, long-distance winner begins with personal ambition; without it, he isn't even in the race. But his only target is results—the measurable ones described in Chapter 2. He knows that good results can only be obtained with and through others—and *he doesn't care if they get the credit.*

That isn't as altruistic as it might sound. It's quite hard, even in an intensely political organization (from which the Good Lord preserve us), to succeed, even in the most self-effacing manner, without the world noticing. After all, there are few reputations more prestigious, and rewarding, than that of being a superb picker of men and women.

The converse of this truth is that managers whose victories are illusory are customarily surrounded by people of insufficient ability. Maybe it's because superior people would find him out. Possibly, the tendency to pick losers is merely another aspect of the general incompetence which the illusionist disguises by his conjuring tricks. But the result is to guarantee the eventual failure of the man and the business.

Few stories of the go-go era reveal the risks of allowing the image to outshine the reality more starkly than the rise and fall of Jim Slater, the investment adviser who succeeded in identifying himself with—even as—the City of London. In fact, even on the known evidence, Slater Walker (a name now as deeply lost as the company's managerial reputation) was a minor-league player by the standards of the major clearing banks, insurance companies, property developers, investment-trust operators and merchant banks whose limelight Slater stole.

Later investigation showed that the apparently big scale of the operation, even though so limited, was illusory—the banking business depended overwhelmingly on in-house clients for its deposits. In getting outside customers, for all his fantastic public relations impact, Slater proved as unsuccessful as he and his minions eventually were in most of the basic operations at which the established City firms show practiced competence every working day.

No reputation ever grew faster or fatter than Slater's. Given that flying start, if, having hired the best available managers to run his operations, he had settled down to the long, unglamorous task of building better and more solid businesses than his competitors; if he had insisted on real growth, not illusion—then, perhaps, Slater really would have been the "City of London." But would he have been Jim Slater? The man and his mistakes are generally one and the same.

Take, in total contrast, the saga of Sir Siegmund Warburg. His reputation and prestige, in the City and on Wall Street (the places where it counts), are as great as Slater's were in the press (where—never forget—it doesn't count nearly as much). Warburg, too, had to crack the City establishment to win, but he succeeded in the solid way: by employing very clever people who put in long hours to provide a much better service in the growing areas where the traditional City was vulnerable—like looking after industrial clients.

It's questionable whether Warburg has ever thought about public relations, let alone worried over his public image. He doesn't have to. Today S. G. Warburg, the bank, which didn't exist until Siegmund started operations in London after the Second World War, is as "established" as any City blueblood: and Mercury Securities, the master company, has grown in the last decade alone threefold, to declared net profits of £11.6 million (though merchant-bank profits are notoriously understated). Yet, little known though Warburg himself is to the general public, the names of his associates are even less familiar—even that of his key long-time colleague, Henry Grunfeld.

The personal ambitions of such unsung heroes will obviously vary. There's a lovely story told by a British journalist who was once invited to the south of France by Lord Beaverbrook, on the hunt, as usual, for talent. "What do you want, young man?" barked the newspaper tycoon. "Women? Power? Money?" The young man didn't know, and he didn't join Beaverbrook. But of the old boy's unholy trinity, one usually does and should outweigh the others: money. Almost by definition, it's unlikely that a manager who is uninterested in maximizing his own resources will be interested enough in maximizing those of his employer—and that, remember, is the objective. Politicians sometimes fall into the trap of the clergy, suggesting that laborers at this exalted level should labor for the sake of the job, not for their salary. This conveniently overlooks the fact that living like a president, pope, archbishop or prime minister requires a millionaire's income—and, anyway, the top practitioners in these noble professions invariably have the highest cash incomes in their hierarchies.

There's nothing wrong with such exalted pay. What is wrong is the denigration of financial ambition by people who apply hypocritical standards. Occasionally, true, an individual appears to be pouring huge endeavor into a business cause from which he is gaining no direct personal profit. But such cases may not be what they seem.

The Herculean efforts of one young manager to push a major new product uphill thus stunned me into slightly uncomprehending admiration: he turned out to own half the equity in the new venture, and his own financial future depended heavily on its success. The question "What's in it for *me*?" may sound amoral and harsh. It is greatly softened if put into the mouth of the employer: "What's in it for *him*?"

Any good managerial situation has enough for everybody: enough money, enough prestige, enough satisfaction. There won't be enough, though, if any party to the proceedings attempts to hog the lot. Worse still, the very attempt is more than likely to reduce the size of the total pie. There is precious little real prestige in that.

> *If you ever reach a point of no return, with a project that offers no return, you shouldn't be in business.*

Much the same difficulty of balance which makes the tightrope between personal ambition and real success so hazardous also besets the question of emotional drive. One group chief executive I know has a subordinate who is both his boss's pride and his despair. The man is always putting forward ambitious plans that, on head-office analysis, make no sense. With equal regularity, though, the subordinate delivers the apparently impossible goods—because (or so his superior believes) the man has the force, the sheer energy, to make things happen as planned: or, rather, as not planned.

Maybe, in this case, the boss is wrong. Possibly the man's plans are perfectly sound—this must be true, in essence, or they could never succeed. His problem, in that event, could partly be one of articulation. The fellow is a dumb genius, a type common enough in the arts, but rare in business. This probably isn't the whole story, as we shall see. But it has a foundation of great truth. Energy, the amount of emotional force committed to a project, can turn failure into success; and, the other way around, inadequate commitment can be the kiss of death.

The converse is also patently true: if people don't believe in a project with heart and soul, as well as mind, it won't succeed. That is the explanation put forward by those involved in one of the larger debacles of the American car industry in

Europe: the scrapping in the sixties of a British-designed replacement for the Ford large-car range and the substitution of a design more to the liking of Dearborn, Michigan. The British managers were simply not committed to the project (the car was fairly awful, too), and it failed catastrophically to capture more than a tenth of the range's previous sales.

Ford subsequently abandoned the approach in favor of European models conceived in collaboration across Europe. It thus obeyed the second injunction in this pair: persist, but never with error. The manager must never be so deeply committed that he is emotionally blind to his mistakes; but he must always be so fully committed that no drop of blood will go unexpended in the effort to make a project or operation succeed. How does he establish the balancing point? How does he judge when to call the whole thing off? Or what makes him, justifiably, go for one extra, final push?

The answer must lie partly in judgment, instinct, intuition: every winning manager has in his equipment the sixth sense which tells him when a plan is doomed. The sense is developed by the experience of failure or adversity. Only those who have struggled, and either won or lost, are likely to be sensitive to the point of balance. But certain objective rules help greatly. One is an old and trusted favorite, the fail-safe routine:

1. What is the worst possible outcome if I continue?
2. What is the likeliest possible outcome if I continue?
3. What is the best possible outcome if I continue?
4. Am I prepared to accept the outcome in (1)?
5. Is the outcome in (2) worth having?
6. If not, is the outcome in (3) worth having?

Obviously, if you or the company cannot stand the financial strain of an adverse (but, remember, possible) outcome, it makes no sense to proceed. If the worst scenario is tolerable, you can then proceed to questions (5) and (6). But there's a seventh question that should be asked even if (5) and (6) above get affirmative answers: "Can we afford the cost, in time, effort and money, of achieving the necessary outcome?"

Subjective answers to these questions are futile. The best possible objective numbers have to be put against the queries. But even if the answers and the numbers come up with a firm "no-go," the negative need not be final. The result of the analysis could be to point the project in a different direction—the analysis may discover that the company is heading towards the right destination, but by the wrong route.

It's almost forgotten now; but when the Japanese firm Honda first tried to invade the world car market, after its stunning success in motorcycles, it made the mistake of moving as short a distance from two wheels to four as it sensibly could. The resulting product completely failed to meet the Japanese firm's high ambitions. Honda licked its wounds, rethought, and changed tack; aiming instead to produce the best family car possible within the price bracket available, rather than trying to create a new category of cheapness. Its management persisted with the ambition of becoming a significant motor manufacturer. It did not persist with the original errors.

It's quite possible that the Honda effect, rather than the man's sheer energy and commitment, explains the Case of the Awkward Subordinate—the man just mentioned who, though his plans were always "wrong," always comes out right. Maybe they really were wrong—originally; but maybe he has the priceless gift of rapidly adjusting his plans when he learns, from the hard teaching of events, that he's got it wrong. Which means, too, that the man must have the priceless fail-safe asset of never boxing himself into a corner, or so over-committing the business to one course of action that it's impossible to escape from the consequences.

That tends to happen when a big business decides, for one reason or another, that it needs to seek a new dimension of bigness. The managers of Singer Manufacturing did precisely this when, uneasy about the future for their main consumer lines, they decided to diversify into business machines, primarily by purchasing Friden. This isn't the kind of commitment from which a company—or a chief executive—can easily withdraw. The decision to sell out (as Singer eventually had to do) wasn't taken until, over many years, terrible damage had been done to the corporation—and to the careers of the top management.

On the whole, big companies and small firms alike are best advised to start projects on a controllable scale, to reinforce them rapidly in case of success, and to retreat at once in the event of unquestionable failure. Ultimately, the only supreme commitment is to the overall, measurable success of the organization. Every project needs the wholehearted enthusiasm of everybody involved—up to the point where it's clear that continuation would adversely and permanently affect the whole picture.

Then the truly committed man calls a halt. What he *never* utters are the deadly words "We've come so far and spent so much already that we might as well go on." In business, if you ever reach a point of no return with a project that offers no return—well, far more often than not, you shouldn't be in business.

The manager intent on winning searches for the Vital Fifth: the 20 percent on which four-fifths of the outcome depends.

Any management consultant, and any practiced manager, knows about the rule of the significant few and the insignificant many. It's the foundation of a vast amount of the (relatively speaking) small number of really useful techniques of "scientific management." But that's only what a believer in Pareto's law would expect: that, say, a fifth of all management techniques produces four-fifths of the worthwhile benefits attainable from application of the lot.

The principle certainly works in the cases of inventory problems, sales analysis, production engineering, product-line decisions and so on. Thus:

1. 20 percent of the items in any inventory account for 80 percent of all movements in and out.
2. 20 percent of the customers provide 80 percent of the turnover.
3. 20 percent of the parts in any assembly account for 80 percent of the total cost.
4. 20 percent of a product range represents 80 percent of sales, and so forth.

This knowledge points the manager's attention to the places where it can most valuably be applied. It helps to separate the essential from the inessential. Paretoism is also highly productive of the small insights from which large cash benefits can flow. Take good quality, which is very often a key characteristic of highly successful, long-term growth companies.

At Mars, for example, no expense is spared to keep the group's confectionery plants spotless and uncontaminated; and the quality of a candy bar is never sacrificed on the altar of cost. According to former Mars executives quoted in *Business Week*, the company takes pains to ensure that 51 percent of a candy bar's selling price is in food ingredients and packaging material (the latter must not exceed 6 percent of the total). If the price of sugar or cocoa fluctuates, so does the size of the bar—the consumer may get slightly less or slightly more. But it's always the same *quality* of bar.

Long ago, Forrest Mars decided that quality was one of the essentials on which his company had to concentrate. The formula described above is an elegant way of solving the problem of maintaining quality without sacrificing profit. In more complex manufacturing industries, the task is greatly complicated by the large number of variables. But manufacturing executives who want to achieve high, consistent quality at economic cost can turn to Pareto for the knowledge that only a few quality characteristics in a product account for the major number of quality and inspection rejects.

Given such information, the manager can begin to concentrate on the essentials of quality control and ignore the inessentials. The principle, not only logical, but scientific, is difficult for many people to accept. Their difficulty is one confronted by investors: if equity shares (common stock) account for only 10 percent of your total holding, doubling their capital value will only raise the worth of the entire portfolio by a tenth. Since such a doubling is a formidable target, beset with dangers, is the prize worth the risk? Plainly, it isn't—but that won't stop the average investor from pursuing the inessential.

Human nature, as it always will, given the chance, interferes with logic. But the manager intent on winning can't afford this luxury. Time being a scarce resource, he must respond to the logic (which says that solving a few key problems leads to major improvements) by identifying those problems. He searches for the vital fifth: the 20 percent on which four-fifths of the outcome depends.

The rule applies not only to inventory and quality control, but to people. At the humdrum, day-to-day level, the bulk of absenteeism is accounted for by a relatively small number of employees: within a department, section or unit, a few of the people do most of the effective work.

From all such observations, conclusions flow. If the absentees can be individually identified, then maybe a company-wide approach will prove to be unjustified; specific action could work better. Do the non-talkers at meetings really need to be there—is the silence a sign of superfluity? How far can you reduce numbers to the Pareto-efficient level without sacrificing the output of the outfit concerned, or should you link the pay of the ultra-contributors to their ultra-performance?

This kind of analysis becomes instinctive second nature to the winning manager. But concentration on essentials and relative disregard for inessentials are not enough on their own. There's no virtue, for instance, in cutting out the non-contributing products in a range if the whole offering isn't making sufficient return on investment, even after the chop. The instinct for the essential needs to be coupled with the direction of effort into rewarding channels.

A Pareto analysis can automatically lead to this wonderful end. After Honeywell had expended a decade's strenuous effort on altering its base to computers, moving away from instrumentation and its other more traditional lines, the company's managers faced the hard fact that computers never had and apparently never would yield returns proportionate to the effort. So the Honeywellers put their strategy into reverse—placing the emphasis back on the non-computer lines; and thus emulating, on the grand scale, the many, many managers down the line who have found that concentrating on the profitable products, and slinging out or de-emphasizing the unprofitable, is the easiest way to personal fame and fortune.

By much the same token, every operation needs a threshold: a level of sales or profit below which a business is too small to be worth any attention from anybody—*even if it is highly profitable.* When I visited Dunlop many years ago, its managers were distinctly proud of the way in which a relatively tiny fishhook manufacturer, which it owned, had to prepare its corporate plan just like the group's mighty tire division. But in truth, even the biggest fishhook firm in the country (as this was) didn't merit that level of management attention—and Dunlop has since, very properly, sold the outfit.

Like a logical investment policy, a rational attitude to the rewarding and unrewarding areas of business is hard for the typical executive to absorb. Selling a business or abandoning it entirely, simply on the grounds that it doesn't make a large enough absolute contribution, goes against the grain. But the opposite policy—diverting personal or corporate time to ventures whose existence makes a negligible difference to the corporate whole—goes against not only logic but the lessons of history.

John Brown, the builder of the *Queen Mary, Queen Elizabeth* and *QE2*, had its core in the shipyard on Clydebank. Whether or not the idea of disposing of this incubus ever occurred to the management, nothing happened until the British government took the horrible thing away. The group's pretax profit of £2.3 million in 1974-75, before the benefits flowed, gave a return on capital employed of 4.2 percent. The next year the yield nearly doubled to 7.9 percent. Then the figure rose to 18.3 percent: then to 34.3 percent—representing an increase in profits of nearly six times in three years.

Case after case of disinvestment, forced or voluntary, shows the same wondrous pattern of results. The analogy with the investor holds true. Again, the manager and his company alike hold a portfolio of resources (for which read money). It makes no sense to spread these resources over too many investments, or to have some investments which are too small in relation to the whole, or to excuse any investment from the same high targets set for the totality. Pareto wouldn't have approved—and neither should you.

PART 2

ORGANIZATIONAL BASICS

5

LOVE THAT COMPANY

Should you run a theory Y outfit or a theory X one? This algebra of corporate life was made famous by Robert Townsend in *Up the Organization*. The distinction, created by Douglas McGregor, is between easygoing, cooperative, permissive companies (Y) and hard-line, authoritarian operations (X, and bad cess to 'em). McGregor, Townsend, myself and almost everybody else think Y is good and X bad—though in all honesty there's no evidence to prove that the Y organization is any better than the X when it comes to winning.

But in today's society, that hardly matters. However victorious it may be in the marketplace, the X company has lost the battle for men's minds. In this contest, Y is winning all along the line. Would anybody even try to set up an X company today? He couldn't get good enough people to work in a Captain Bligh atmosphere; he could rely on getting terrible publicity; and, anyway, he probably wouldn't want to do it in the first place. We are all children of our times, and the times, in organizations from the presidency downwards, don't educate the young to accept being pushed around.

If you do run what Nixon's White House henchman Bob

Haldeman called a "tight ship," you'll find yourself—like Nixon and Haldeman—with a crew of sailors who, even if clever, are all of the same stamp: prepared, for one reason or another, to receive the odd lash with the cat-o'-nine-tails. Yes-men are bad companions for the authoritarian manager. They aid and abet his excesses, and in the end captain and crew are all likely to pay the price of failure.

Since most of Nixon's crew have made fortunes from books, including Richard Nixon himself, justice may have been cheated at the last. But the market for memoirs of fallen business executives is unlikely to be so brisk or so rewarding. The risks of that tight-ship management style have increased, and those of the loose boat have probably lessened, for reasons to be explained.

Still, it's idle to pretend that either extreme is an ideal approach, and not only because ideal approaches never exist. Every organization must find its own appropriate style somewhere along the line between X and Y; or, to define it differently, along the spectrum which runs from autocracy to participative democracy: *tell–sell–consult–join–delegate*. The winning manager must find his style, too; but he must also vary his position on that spectrum to suit his varying circumstances.

> *Only one question counts: does the organization itself, and the style which managers adopt within it, stop people from achieving their potential?*

The only real significance or value in the debate over X and Y lies in its contribution to getting the best/most possible from the almost infinite resources known as people. The propositions below are a test of your basic beliefs about these resources: mark them true or false.

1. The expenditure of physical and mental effort in work is as natural as play or rest.
2. The average human being has an inherent dislike of work and will avoid it if he can.
3. Man will exercise self-direction and self-control in the service of the objectives to which he is committed.
4. Because of their dislike of work, most people must be coerced, controlled, directed or threatened with punishment to get them to put forth adequate effort towards the achievement of organizational objectives.
5. Commitment to objectives is a function of the rewards associated with their achievement.
6. The average human being prefers to be directed, wishes to avoid responsibility, has relatively little ambition and wants security above all else.
7. The average human being learns, under proper conditions, not only to accept but to seek responsibility, etc.

The statements come from McGregor's pioneering work. Any agreement with an even-numbered proposition is an X attitude: the odd numbers are all Y. It could be that you hold some X and some Y opinions, even when they are inherently contradictory. There should be nothing surprising in that. Bazarov, the Nihilist doctor in Turgenev's *Fathers and Sons*, thought that the personalities of human beings were as alike as their spleens. But we know better: we know not only that personalities differ greatly, but that the same person can behave differently at different times. For instance, sometimes he will dislike and avoid work (X): at other times (Y), work seems the most natural thing in the world to the same person.

How does the practical manager adapt this theory to his needs? There's only one question that counts: "Does the organization itself, and the style which managers adopt within it, stop people from achieving their potential?"

It isn't an easy question to answer. For a start, what is somebody's potential? Neither you nor they may know. But you, as boss, should have an extremely clear idea of what you expect from anybody in the organization. If their potential doesn't at least match that demand, then somebody (you) has made a grave error. If, however, you, as subordinate, don't know equally clearly what you are expected to contribute, how are you going knowingly to deliver that contribution?

This question goes to the heart of the matter. The tug-of-war between theory X and theory Y is not an issue of human relations or "behavioral science." It's an issue of organization. Just as the old-style organization-chart enthusiasts, with their dotted and undotted lines and boxes, were wrong to assume that structure by itself solved anything, so the human-relations school is wrong to think that style and attitudes will achieve much in themselves.

It's a business version of the old Latin tag *mens sana in corpore sano* that you need; not a healthy mind in a healthy body, but healthy human relationships in a healthy corporate setting. The definitions of health will vary in both contexts, simply because different people are involved in different businesses. In nearly a quarter of a century, I've found no method of organization, no management style, that works universally. I have come to suspect strongly that at some time, somewhere, excellent results have been obtained with every conceivable form of organization, ranging from much tighter ships than Haldeman's White House to utter chaos; and with every style of management from Stalinist dictatorship to complete *laissez-faire*.

The supergrowth of Xerox outside the United States is a fascinating case. By a quirk of history, 51 percent of the non-American rights to the great invention (then a bulky document copier) were acquired for a song by the British-owned Rank Organization, a slowly subsiding cinema chain and film producer. The company was dominated by Sir John Davis, a demon for work, who acquired a reputation for detailed interference of a highly abrasive character, for a general lack of lovable theory Y qualities, and for hiring and firing. (The last act which signaled the end of Davis's reign was to fire his own appointed heir apparent in circumstances which caused major scandal.)

In spite, or because, of Davis's X characteristics, Rank-Xerox became one of the century's great growth stories. In 1969, Rank could boast a ten-year record of a 1,207 percent profit increase, after tax; achieved, what's more, on only a 274 percent gain in income from sales; and entirely thanks to the Xerox multiplier. The pre-tax profit represented a 51 percent return on the stockholders' investment, and Davis can fairly claim fabulous success for himself and his style. Nobody could argue that the potential of xerography wasn't exploited.

But—well, there are some big buts. First, the Rank-Xerox operation had some able senior managers (for whose selection Davis can justly claim credit); second, one of those able managers says that he spent half his time insulating his own subordinates from the stream of head-office memos; third, Davis in effect reserved to himself only key matters like pricing and financial direction, leaving the marketing and manufacturing (where the American joint owners were a powerful influence) to the subordinate executives.

So the X managment had a Y result. At the end of the day those in charge of operations had enough room and power to do their jobs; while the high voltage which X management can generate never ceased to drive powerfully through the business.

But the other enterprises into which Sir John diverted the Xerox millions were not well insulated by success. Move on to 1977, and his organization's ten-year figure for profit growth is only 246 percent, a quarter of its previous level, partly because of the dead weight of unprofitable diversifications. Businesses like hotels, scientific instruments and leisure were not inherently unprofitable. But the way in which Rank either acquired or managed them, or both, produced unprofitable results.

Whether you approach the problem on an X or a Y route, the solution must be the same. People and organizations alike will probably not approach their potential unless:

1. They know what they are supposed to be doing.
2. They are capable of doing it.
3. They are given the environment and resources needed for the job.
4. They are encouraged to succeed.
5. They are rewarded for their success.

The classic mode of organization (more X than Y in its orientation) may not meet these five requirements. That fact—far more than any humanistic objections—is why the classic form is now long overdue for overhaul.

In real-life business, as opposed to the vertical world of the organization chart, anything worth doing is usually a lateral achievement.

When I first became involved in business management, the textbooks were much obsessed (as some may still be) with limiting the number of people who "reported" to one man. The ceiling, if I recall correctly, was seven; whether any real scientific research lay behind the number is doubtful; seven always has been a mystical number for man—and not only mystical. One of the latest insights sent my way, from Sweden, insists that no decision-making mind can handle more than seven variables at a time; and research suggests that the memory cannot cope with more than seven "chunks" of information at once.

It must follow that, if the top man has no more than seven people "reporting" to him, and each of those has seven "reporting" in turn, and so on, it will require four layers of management to accommodate 400 executives, of whom no fewer than 343 would be in the fourth layer. If each of them made a point of speaking to one different lateral colleague each working day, he still would fall short of the total by 103 contacts, even if he takes only a four-week holiday each year.

Not only that, but the limitation of seven ensures that command will flow down in strict vertical channels; the operational lines are vertical. Any horizontal or lateral contacts have to be arranged separately. Of course, some of the groups of seven will be associates: a marketing department's senior people, say, all "reporting" to a marketing director or vice-president. But in real-life business, so opposed to that vertical world of the diagram, anything worth doing is usually a lateral achievement, linking people not by the hierarchical, vertical lines, but by the task.

Growth companies in their early days usually function in this flat, level way. The levels of hierarchy (not that the word means much in most of these situations) are seldom more than three. The boss (or bosses, if partners are involved), then his closest henchmen, with everybody else at the bottom. If any subject, project or problem comes up, the boss/bosses and henchmen all dive in and splash about until a decision is reached.

As many a growth company has discovered to its cost, the resulting dis-organization can become untidy. Sooner or later, somebody has to impose some semblance of vertical order, with properly defined roles and responsibilities. The natural response is to choose the Moltke model—the organization of a company according to the principles laid down by the great Prussian general. But a civilian company is not a battalion; the basic Moltke tenet—that you should organize in such a way that mediocre men achieve good results—needs some heavy qualification in the business world.

You need a framework (which will probably end up looking vertical) to keep the business tidy and to maximize the contribution of your mediocre managers. Moltke pointed out that God simply doesn't send enough men of genius along. However, almost everybody has his flashes of something akin to genius. And a strictly vertical organization structure tends to keep the creative fires burning too low.

To switch the metaphor from fire to water—if you pour water from a height, it falls in a narrow stream. People outside the stream only get splashed. If anything interrupts the fall, some of the water never reaches the lower levels. In contrast, even a small amount of liquid spreads alarmingly far if spilled on a polished surface. By the same token, horizontal organization in a company tends to encourage interchange and participation, and to make it easier to work towards the ideal: at every specific juncture, you have the best available people doing their best at their best task—irrespective of their formal position in the hierarchy.

Reverting to those 400 managers, though, the simple statistics show that you can't achieve the horizontal ideal with so many people. So you need fewer; a simple solution, like all the best answers. The horizontal organization seeks to break itself down into units in which people can relate as easily as they do in the small growth company. To take an Irish example, the packaging-based company Jefferson Smurfit has kept its layers of hierarchy down, even through a period of tumultuous growth in which sales multiplied 200 times and profits 100 times in a dozen years.

At the end of this astounding period, in mid-1977, *en route* to 1980 sales of £400 million, Smurfit consisted of 9,500 people in no fewer than seventy-five companies. Quick mental arithmetic will show that some of these firms must have been minute. The guiding principle, in fact, was that the biggest should never have more than 350 employees. Head office numbered no more than twenty-five, and the nine divisions—"strategic business units," in a phrase borrowed from General Electric—were kept on equally short rations.

As the next chapter will explain, this fragmentation, which might seem to make control more difficult, actually makes control easier—for the manager who knows what he's doing—while bringing the horizontal principle within the bounds of possibility. The fewer people you have, the fewer layers of hierarchy there should be. (It doesn't always follow. I came across one outfit with seven layers for only twenty-five people. It was, inevitably, a management consulting firm.) What's more, in a small operation *everybody* can participate, and it's natural for them to do so.

Managers are hooked on hierarchies for reasons which are so strong—habit, prestige, pay, *amour propre*, convenience—that the switch to flatter structures will take time and a major upheaval in modes of thought as well as organization. Anybody who's risen up a hierarchy has a vested interest in its perpetuation. It's true, too, that powerful personalities can dominate a flatter structure just as easily as a traditional pyramid. At Smurfit, for instance, the dominant force after the founding Jefferson relaxed control was a quartet of sons, strongly led by Michael Smurfit.

Like the water in the earlier analogy, though, power and drive can spread more widely on a flat surface. To continue the image, moreover, water flowing from a great height needs assistance (a pump) to rise back. In many vertical companies, the reverse flow never comes, even from levels near the top of the hierarchy. Top-down (as opposed to bottom-up) management becomes the only possible formula. Winning management, in contrast, always demands the possibility of alternatives.

> *"We're trying desperately to hang on to that early successful formula of a very small company."*

An executive in Jefferson Smurfit once put his finger on the nervous pulse of winning management. "We're trying desperately," he said, "to hang on to that early successful formula of a very small company." The formula he specifically had in mind referred to the time when "we got our orders by camping out on doorsteps and keeping very, very close to customers." But the point is a general one: size tends to create remoteness. Executives become distant even from their neighbors in the firm, let alone the world outside and the slaves down below. The task of preventing this deterioration is, just as the man said, "desperate."

It's even more agonizing, though, for the manager who wasn't even born in the days when the firm was small—and all companies, even General Motors, developed from small, sometimes minute beginnings. How do you find the "successful formula of a very small company" inside a corporation which is the size of a small nation-state? And has been since the Second World War, if not before? One thing is clear. You don't do it by putting young men in a boat called "Venture Company" and pushing it out to sea, victualed with a few big company millions. More often than not—as experience has shown—the venture vessel will sink.

That's because the principle is the antithesis of how small companies actually get formed and flourish. Nothing gets "spun-off." If a new idea is launched, all hands are on deck—just as they are in the main business. Any venture is too important, simply because the company is small, to be left to sink or swim untended by the captain and officers.

That's not all. Success in the small context has an impact in proportion to its extent. The prime architect of a $200,000 business is a hero in a back-street converted garage. In the big group, he earns a good mark on his record. True, that mark can be cashed in for later promotion and pay. But it's not the same as the reward that even a modest small firm can mine from a rich vein. If the operation is properly organized, everybody gets wealthy.

It doesn't necessarily make them amenable—Michael Smurfit once remarked, "Look, I have three highly aggressive, successful and very rich brothers. They need watching, too." But the immediacy of the reward is as powerful a factor as its size. Moreover, it has no bounds; in contrast, the vertical hierarchy, as much as anything else, is a system for limiting rewards.

Every manager who sincerely wants to win should have the name H. Ross Perot engraved on his heart. Not because, as founding and controlling stockholder of his own computer company, Perot could suffer the biggest single personal loss of money (on paper) ever recorded in one day. Far more important is what happened when I.B.M. limited the total remuneration payable to its computer salesmen in one year to an amount less than the salary of the chairman—Tom Watson Jr., son of the founder.

Perot, I.B.M.'s top Texas salesman, reached his annual ceiling on a few weeks' commissions and quit. (He followed the same logic which explains why a 100 percent tax must have a nil yield—nobody would bother to earn the income in the first place.) Maybe it was all to the good, possibly even for I.B.M., that Perot moved on to the new and expanding horizons of computer services. It was certainly wonderfully good for Perot.

Even in a much smaller organization, if you can't stand the loss of even your best man, something's seriously wrong. That's actually one more advantage of the horizontal organization—that it reduces dependence on the strategically placed individual on whom the vertical structure hangs. But you don't want to lose people simply because of some irrelevant vertical rule—like, nobody earns more than the Godfather. In the zone which ultimately determines all business rewards—the marketplace—the richest payoff goes to those who strike the richest lodes. Fluctuations up and down are the essence of the system. So should it be in companies: basic living pay can be as hierarchical and as closely linked to seniority as you like; but rewards for results above the norm should be linked only to those results.

The small firm doesn't have the inherent inflexibility which makes pay in large companies degenerate towards the civil service system of grades and "salary progression." Nor does it have the big firm's inertia—the difficulty of energizing a vertical hierarchy, especially when the firm lacks the pressure of duress. Under duress, though, a large firm will do almost anything. N.C.R. even demolished its historic buildings in Dayton, Ohio, in the desperate drive to complete a belated switch from the cash-register era to the new world of electronic systems.

The large firm does compulsory things well—often fantastically well. The coordination of effort that stocks the supermarkets of the West with fresh and packaged foodstuffs is, for example, a feat not to be thought all that inferior to landing a man on the moon. Where the big company fails, relatively speaking, is in the voluntary activities—such as innovation and improvisation. That's why, according to an American study, 80 percent of innovation comes from small companies, the next largest block from the medium-sized, and hardly any from the real giants.

It pays to be skeptical about such "facts"—since small firms vastly outnumber the rest, it follows that only a tiny percentage of the small companies innovate at all, while the handful of big-company innovations may well be much more significant in terms of the world economy. But there is a qualitative difference—easily recognizable in the following case.

One entrepreneur ran a private company which was a world leader in the gelatin business. His biggest customer was an American company which made all the world's gelatin capsules. After death had enforced a change in control, the gelatin supply contract was canceled overnight. The boss made his own capsule-producing machines and created some new customers. Later, when losing money in a Canadian factory, he went over to decide its fate. On a depressing journey via the

Great Lakes to Canada, he spotted a large number of new, unsold Chrysler cars, and was told these were surplus vehicles which the auto company (in sales trouble, as usual) was breaking down for assembly and sale in Brazil.

If you could ship broken-down cars to Brazil, thought our man, why not broken-down gelatin machinery? Which is what he did—building a new geographical offshoot that became one of his biggest markets. Unless a company (any company) and a manager (any manager) can react with that speed and vigor, they can't win. That means giving the maximum possible discretion to individuals heading discrete business units; who are judged and rewarded on their success; and who are encouraged to do likewise within their units—to develop their own horizontal modes.

That's where two strands come together: the Y organization and the entrepreneurial streak which lies in every manager. Without that streak, a company may be lovable, but it won't succeed. And at the end of the day, nobody loves a corporate failure.

6

COMMAND, CONSENT AND CONTROL

The old-fashioned vertical hierarchy had one sovereign advantage, which explains why it has lasted so long. The hierarchy looks so easy to *control*. Just as Moltke expected when drawing up his blueprint for the Prussian army, systematic hierarchical organization puts all the mediocre men in their proper places, where they can perform their tasks in the mediocre, planned manner laid down. Fit all the pieces of mediocrity together, just as the army or company manual ordains, and the whole collection of parts ticks as efficiently as an old-style Swiss watch.

That's a pregnant analogy. Clockwork is now an outmoded technology, as thousands of little old Swiss watchmakers have sadly learned. The Swiss have been sped past, in technology and in marketing, by the Japanese—and it's to the Japanese that the Westerner must now look for solutions to the problem posed by the breakdown of hierarchies. To state that problem in essence, industry and commerce need efficiency as never before, but can no longer rely on the discipline which efficiency has depended upon in the past.

A hierarchy without discipline is toothless. Yet the teeth of hierarchies are falling out all over the world: one wise man has cited the three most authoritarian outfits in the United States—the army, the Catholic church and the Mafia—as examples of change and decay in the matter of respect and obedience.

If the generals, the bishops and the godfathers can't maintain hierarchical law and order—though armed respectively with the military prison, the fear of God, and the icepick or garrote—what can the humble manager expect? The answer is obvious. He still needs authority, but it has to be a different kind of authority. The Japanese, of course, have a more tightly bound society than ours, and one which cannot be reproduced in the West. But the Western manager can go East—and that's very probably where he is going.

The winning combination, the old one-two of theories Y and X, is as follows: first, get their consent, then tell them what to do.

For all the weakening of traditional authority, people by and large do what they are told. Managers generally fall obediently into line with orders from on high; even when the injunction is "You're fired," they rarely refuse to go, or blow up the building, or sock their superiors. With varying degrees of meekness, they pack up their desks and depart.

Discipline is part of the human condition (or conditioning), an essential span of the necessary bridge between theory X and theory Y. Not only is the tendency to obey something on which managers can more or less rely in their mutual relationships; it's something that in most societies still makes the factory floor and the office respond to instruction. This relative docility has confounded many behavioral scientists, who reveled in what they took to be a blue-collar rebellion. But what such thinkers saw as an emerging confrontation between the worker and his job has so far failed to emerge.

The simple explanation seems to be that human beings like to work and to conform—just as theory Y says. The paradox is that this very self-discipline helps men and women to nestle comfortably within those X-like set-ups which demand and get strict obedience. But the paradox is extremely useful. It establishes a natural law:

> In any organization, no matter what its structure and social norms, effectiveness depends on *clarity* of purpose *clearly* conveyed to people who *clearly* understand what they are expected to do.

To put that in bad old theory X language: they know what I've ordered them to do, and they damned well do it.

The bad old language, though, conveys a misleading picture. The fear of the sack—a psychological phobia as well as an economic threat—isn't the sole force binding the authoritarian company together. The slavish obedience is more apparent than real. Conformity always rests on a degree of consent—and the history of capitalism contains countless examples, some of them bloody, of what happens when the consent of the workers is withdrawn.

The winning combination, the old one-two, of theories Y and X is as follows: *first*, get their consent, *then* tell them what to do. You must always bear in mind, however, that the command or instruction, the right-hand punch, had better be right. Consent won't extend indefinitely to botched instructions. Moreover, the consent is crucial. The old-time *implicit* agreement must now be made *explicit*. You can't hope to smother the opinions of managers or other workers in a blanket of paternalism; although the temptation is obviously still very strong

Few people have spotted the rich paternalist vein in the recent vogue for behavioral-science notions like job enrichment. Old-style Quaker paternalism concerned itself with the morals and welfare of the employee off the job—in the company house, with his children at the company school, with the company doctor standing by in case he fell ill, and the company pension waiting to support him all the way to the company undertaker. The new-style paternalist worries about the man's happiness and well-being in the *factory*: is his job "rich" enough? Is he perhaps (God forbid) bored? What can be done to save him from work that is not only boring, but "mindless, exhausting, servile and hateful"?

The words, from Charles Reich's *The Greening of America*, refer to car workers, and were quoted by John Thackray in a most perceptive piece in *Management Today*. The article mentioned some of the abundant evidence which shows that car workers don't share Reich's attitude toward their work, or anything like it. Thackray went on: "It is the discontent of the managers, not the underlings, which is possibly the problem. An American Management Association poll of managers has found that 52 percent of this population feel their work is, at best, unsatisfactory." These liberally educated men, in other words, are visiting their own discontents on their subordinates. It isn't a blue-collar revolt that has to be faced, but a grey-suit rebellion.

The symptoms of executive dissatisfaction are just as serious, though, as those of the blue-collar blues that faded. The ills that the professors and the progressive managers saw in the employees—like a higher level of education seeking a higher level of work—are real problems in the manager ranks. The problems can't be ignored; and they can't be solved within the old, hierarchical, military framework of order and obey. After all, any fool can obey an order after suitable training. But who wants to employ fools?

If you are seeking highly intelligent, highly educated managers, you will—or should—expect intelligent and educated contributions from them. You still want a form of obedience, true. But the orders that can be given have changed fundamentally—they generally have to be orders with which the recipient agrees. Most of the time, they will be the orders he would have given to himself. Often, they will be orders which he has greatly helped to formulate.

There's a technical reason for this. The military invention that will last longest in business is the distinction between line and staff. In the old days, staff were either part of the chief executive's entourage—his courtiers—or were the people in non-operational functions, which were either clearly defined (like finance) or impinged on the operating people (the line) across a broad front (like marketing). Very few of the broad-fronters in the Anglo-Saxon world were experts, and the same went for the courtiers.

Today, all has changed. Staff will help to direct product divisions or be expert in specialized fields like corporate planning or personnel. These experts form the boss's managerial entourage. Even the financial people are now expected to contribute far more to management than bookkeeping. But these professionals don't have the field-marshal's baton in their hands, even if it's in their knapsacks. They can't give orders to the line. The operating manager has to agree to their proposals, just as they must agree with his.

At the deeply troubled British Leyland car giant, chairman Sir Michael Edwardes has been forced to make crystal-clear definitions of this new-style relationship. He told a *Financial Times* interviewer that "I do everything by exception. If a top staff man and that line chap agree, I don't get involved . . . I will never interfere with a decision made, given that the top staff people agree with it, and that it is within the clearly laid-down limits of authority."

What has been forced on Edwardes, partly by the need to speed decisions in a never-ending crisis, enshrines a truth for all seasons. The exercise of authority is a whole new ball-game—and one which the enterprising, informed player can still win, without the whip of order and obey.

> *Within the organizational framework, people need the controlled freedom that "advise and consent" suggests.*

Advise and consent, the formula which defines the relationship of the Senate to the Executive in the United States, is the correct, the inevitable replacement of order and obey. It rests, though, on the foundation of command. As in the family, authority has to reside somewhere, even if it's only in the heartfelt cry of the playwright Moss Hart, when contemplating the indiscipline of his young: "Damn it, we're bigger than they are, and it's our house!"

The equivalent in management terms, these days, might be: "We're older than they are, and it's our job to preserve the company!" *Somebody* has to be the keeper, not only of the company's conscience, but of its *being*. Barring terrible accidents, the company will be around long after all present incumbents have retired from the scene: at the least, that drive for survival should be among the managerial objectives—more, it should stand behind all the others. There has to be a framework for any business into which people and parts can be smoothly slotted.

Within that framework the people need the controlled freedom that "advise and consent" suggests. In an ideal, closed system, the philosophy of the technique which is known as "management by objectives" (M.B.O.) would be perfect. The company would form its plan, which would be broken down into individual objectives, which would be agreed (consented to) by the individuals and which would (of course) be fulfilled. The plans would add up to a fulfilled master plan, everybody would live happily ever after . . . and pigs would fly.

The philosophy contains true propositions—that everybody and every company should have clear objectives; that people should take part in deciding what their aims should be; and that it's fair to judge them on how well they perform against target. But philosophy, from the time of Plato onwards, has been one thing, real life another. The neat formulation of M.B.O. just doesn't fit the errors and omissions within plans—not to mention the need for people to improvise, adjust and overshoot targets as well as hit them on the nose.

This truth presumably explains why American management consultant George Petitpas, explaining in 1978 why we've been living through something of "a period of disillusionment with 'hot' management concepts," put M.B.O. top of the list of has-beens. There's nothing particularly shaming for M.B.O. in that. As Petitpas says, "Over the years, managers have learned that these ideas tend to become fads." Addicts of California cults have nothing on management gurus when it comes to the ins and outs of fashion. The rigidity in the M.B.O. process in fact conflicts with the consent element, which is supposed to be a vital ingredient in the stew.

Bill Reddin, a Canadian guru, tells how he did a consulting job for a government department whose boss had "decided to introduce M.B.O. by participative means. . . . The top man's autocratic decision was hardly the way to introduce a participative approach! Even so, a meeting was held, which raised expectations above the delivery point . . . over the next few months, budgets were done the old way, and some key decisions were imposed autocratically." The result was apparently failure: you can't impose consent, and reality speaks louder than promises. An earlier remark by Reddin points to an even more relevant truth.

He notes that "M.B.O., certainly in the traditional format, is not suitable for most government departments, since power in them is so diffuse." In other words, again, the effective diffusion of authority depends on a strong central source of that authority. Being informal is no excuse for not being strong, any more than striking strong attitudes (like the civil service boss in Reddin's story) is an excuse for actually being weak; or any more than being decisive is an excuse for taking bad decisions.

In the Western company, though, decisiveness and decisions have come to have an almost religious importance—and the high priest is the decision-maker. First, he decides; then he sells the decision to those who are going to be involved in implementing the thing; or, if he is a participative type, he consults people before the decision is made, and *then* he sells it to them. This habit causes considerable trouble to Westerners negotiating with the Japanese. The latter will go on and on and on with discussions, seemingly for ages, long after the Western side has made up its mind. Then, all of a sudden, the Japanese decide—and expect immediate implementation, much to the shock of the unprepared West.

How come? As noted before, the Japanese decision process (remember Pearl Harbor) takes in everybody who is involved and covers how they are going to do something, not just what they should do. Thus, when the decision is taken, no further process of indoctrination, persuasion or information is needed; everybody already knows what's collectively decided and individually expected of them.

In the Western context, the same outcome can be achieved, but needs harder work. The difficulty can be exaggerated. The way to get advice is easy enough. It's the same answer that Roy Thomson, the acquisitive Canadian press tycoon (who once even made an offer for *Pravda*), gave to a British chairman who wanted to know how one found out if a company was for sale. "Simple," said Lord Thomson. "You ask."

Ask, and most of the time it (advice) will be given. That gift of itself makes consent more likely. We agree more readily with those who seek our opinions, but lasting agreement demands one stage more: results. The management that's only and soundly interested in gaining real competitive success will always get support—just like a winning coach in football. There's logic in this. If respect is going to the man, not to the uniform, then respect must be won. There's only one way in which that can be guaranteed—by professionalism that is only satisfied by professional results.

> **The true authority of expertise automatically carries with it both obedience and consent.**

Everything you hear about some foreign country which manages things better should be taken with a pinch of salt, about as much salt, in fact, as accounts of paranormal phenomena. It's difficult to obtain truly accurate accounts of what goes on in companies from your own land, let alone in countries many thousands of miles away—and even further distant in terms of manners and mores. But if accounts of how Japanese companies have wrought their wonders are not true, they should be; for the stories are too good to be false.

They could be summarized as the Tale of the Authority of Expertise. When one of the aforementioned huge committee discussions is going on (and on) in a Japanese firm, the chief speaker on any subject is the man, so the tale runs, who is recognized as the company's leading expert on the matter—no matter how young he is.

Moreover, if a young ace on ball-bearings has said his piece and the gathering has accepted his view, the expert will automatically be entrusted with executing the decision. Whatever his rank, he will arrange the contract, order the new machine, implement the change in technology. He won't, if an important foreign customer or supplier comes to town, take him to a geisha house. That pleasant task will fall to a much more senior manager. In other words, respect goes to seniority, but authority goes to expertise. Thus the Japanese, on this account, contrive to maintain a rigidly hierarchical system, but to avoid its rigidities.

In the West, authority and respect normally go to the senior man, irrespective of the situation. The error is evident from a commonplace experience in company turnarounds. Once the dead wood at the top is carved away, the existing second-line management proves perfectly capable of running (well) a company that (partly because of the very same second-line management) was running appallingly. The trouble wasn't that their seniors were all bums; the problem was that, bums or no bums, the seniors had all the authority.

The case of Rolls-Royce Motors is a wonderfully satisfying proof. For twelve years it made annual losses from producing the most expensive car in the world. When its aero-engine owner went bust, the car subsidiary was set free—free mostly from the fact that the parent board carried the authority and the responsibility. When both devolved on David Plastow and his colleagues at Crewe, and the company became independent and public, they chalked up the following almost geometric pre-tax profit progression: in round millions, four, five, six, nine, eleven, fourteen and a half.

This was achieved with the same cars, the same factory, the same work force, and much the same management. Plastow wasn't some genius hauled in from the great beyond, but a home-grown manager who had been there all the time. What would have happened (one wonders) to the motor division if the Rolls-Royce main board hadn't made so monumental a bungle of its affairs as to bankrupt the entire group? Instead of being worth £40 million on its merger with Vickers, the car company would very likely still be a loss-making subsidiary.

Would-be winning managers lower down can't always rely on a bankruptcy or similar catastrophe to set them free. The tough truth, though, is that just as the imminence of execution (in Dr. Johnson's words) wonderfully concentrates the mind, so, far too often, only calamity or its threat can crack hierarchical authority and liberate the people who can really run the company. No man likes to fire himself; although the old-stagers at G.E.C. did that, in effect, when they asked Arnold Weinstock to take over their ossifying company. For the veterans who were preserved on the board in the Weinstock era, that was only just reward for getting one particularly critical decision supremely right.

It's a type of decision which, according to the Japanese model, should come naturally; to step gracefully aside when somebody else is more capable of handling the matter than you are. That, after all, is one highly specific form of management expertise—selecting the right person for the right function. Skill at this demanding task will in itself establish the new kind of authority without which, in modern management, it's increasingly difficult to exercise any kind of command—let alone to win.

What passed in earlier days for authority of position, anyway, was nearly always founded on the authority of expertise. Edwin Land hasn't dominated Polaroid only because of his personality; but because nobody in the world, not just in his company, has surpassed Land's skills as a scientific entrepreneur. Time and again, when younger managers are complaining about some aspect of the behavior of an overbearing boss, perhaps including some undeniable piece of incompetence, they will pay tribute to the monster's uncanny skill—probably in the exact heart of his business.

So long as that expertise persists and stays relevant, the old buzzard is probably secure. But even a manager laden with skills and success has his blind spots. For instance, Heinz Nordhoff's building of Volkswagen, the most important single economic performance in postwar Europe, was a bravura demonstration of production engineering and control, investment planning, relating service to sales, unifying a worldwide operation around the product—and many virtues besides. Nordhoff's blind spots, however, included apparent total ignorance of new model development—an expertise which is commonly thought basic to running a successful car company.

It could be that Nordhoff's blind spot played an essential role in concentrating V.W. entirely on the Beetle in the first postwar period—a seeming master-stroke of genius, which a true car manager, obsessed with new models, might well have missed entirely. But Nordhoff, though he didn't miss the turning point when V.W. began urgently to need new models, missed the fact that his authority of expertise was non-existent in this area.

Still, the Germans, along with the no less victorious Japanese, have lessons to teach in this crucial area. The foundation of their extraordinary industrial achievement has been, not only the expertise supplied by formidable technical education (all the way from beneath the *Meister*—or foreman—to the *Doktor Ingenieur*), but also the enormous authority which such functional expertise confers. If the Germans had possessed marketing wizardry to match their technical expertise, they would have left precious few fields for the Japanese to conquer.

But in the more demanding business conditions ahead, nobody else will win who doesn't have expertise equal to the Japanese or the Germans—plus the authority without which expertise will always be castrated. The true authority of expertise carries with it both obedience and consent; and companies and managers need all three.

7

TO MARKET, TO MARKET

"Small is beautiful" is a marvelous phrase. Small wonder (you might say) that the late Ernst Schumacher's small book on smallness slowly became a world best seller. Schumacher's vision of industry broken down into units of nineteenth-century proportions is incomplete in many respects, notably in its deliberate failure to recognize today's reality of gigantic plants and colossal organizations. For the manager set on winning, however, the main defect is that smallness in itself gets you nowhere. The big battalions will still win if they are better organized, better financed and better led.

The same management principles apply to big and small alike. But "small" (in the relative sense of "as small as possible") does have an advantage when it comes to obeying one key principle: that *market responsiveness is crucial to effectiveness*. The beauty of smallness (for instance, in Schumacher's book) is generally extolled because of human-relations benefits, greater ease of communications, and consequent higher productivity. But, in my book, the main advantage of cutting the business down to size is to fit the unit to its market.

It might still end up very large by the standard of the

ideal production unit. This has come down in two decades from a 2,000 maximum to 1,000 to 500 and now to 200; and even that's twenty times bigger than the ten-man "hunting unit" which Antony Jay put forward in *Corporation Man.* Throughout this theoretical dwindling, though, large homogeneous businesses like oil or computers or cars have had to deploy armies of people. What determines their size isn't necessarily the demands of production; it's the demands of the market.

Matching the organization to the market is no more the final answer than, in the fifties and sixties, it was enough to appoint "marketing men." No matter how sensible a principle of organization, or theory of management, may be, that inevitable word "effectiveness" crops up again. Marketing techniques and a market-based structure are tools to be used for winning customers and keeping them. There's a well-known formula for remuneration: a good pay system should *attract, motivate and retain* good executives. That's what effective use of "small-is-beautiful" marketing should do for good customers.

> *What matters in marketing is whether a line drawn around customers and business envelops a coherent whole.*

Management pundits have always insisted that any manager worth employing keeps his eyes firmly focused on what's happening *outside*, on the customers, on the market. Whether they know it or not, all companies are market-oriented. That is, even if they are besotted with the product and production and never lift their eyes from their beloved machines, the survival and prosperity of the firm still depend on whether anybody out there wants what's being made.

Clearly, there's a trap here for the unwary (into which

many a British manager fell headlong when "marketing" was imported, like some new brand of chewing gum, after the war). The theoretical case described above fits in practice the majority of the middle-sized German engineering companies which are even more numerous in the Federal Republic than brands of beer. These German firms know only how to make the types of machine they've always made, and they cling to the old-fashioned notion that, so long as they make the machines as well as they can, producing improved models every now and then, the world will continue to buy their offerings—with price no particular object.

In this obsolete thinking, what's more, the Germans have been undeniably right. A user of industrial machinery wants, above all, a reliable piece of equipment that will give him the best performance in output terms—or at least the highest performance that he wants. Provided that his technical specifications are met, price is of secondary importance. The thing, after all, will be depreciated over several years—which is one very good reason why he doesn't want an improved version coming out every twelve months, like Detroit's new-model cars in their heyday. The interests of the producer and the customer coincide perfectly—and that's true marketing.

Those time-honored twins, the chicken and the egg, appear at this juncture. The producer can't satisfy the customer (market-orientation) unless he can bring to bear the concentrated attention on product which is anathema to the white-hot marketing man in some consumer-goods operation. It's no real puzzle. What matters in marketing is whether a line drawn around customers and business envelops a coherent whole: just as the shell which is the egg surrounds the embryo which is the chicken. The market isn't only outside the firm, it's also inside: how well the inside and outside fit together determines success or failure.

This explains the trend in many winning companies to move back in time to the days when firms like the German engineering heroes were formed. Typically, the German entrepreneur started from some technical process which had only recently been mastered, but for which the potential market was enormous. The business grew around this technical nucleus and was defined by it. Even today, most of the giants of German manufacturing are built around some nineteenth-century core.

The wise modern corporation seeks to find cores around which it can build businesses. It can be done in many different ways. At one extreme you can have tens, dozens or scores of little companies under any number of names, none of which give any clue about the ownership. Or you can imitate the American General Electric and divide the whole company into "strategic business units," which is how the kind of expert who devises S.B.U.'s tends to talk.

In truth, G.E. presents some problems for would-be winners. The company is always far ahead in the introduction of tomorrow's techniques; yet it's usually stuck tight in the middle of the pack when it comes to measurable results. There are organizations, just as there are athletes, who do everything the right way, yet never win. But what G.E. is doing with its S.B.U.'s seems incontestably right—and, in a sense, its management *has* won, since nobody doubts that, without the introduction of corporate planning built around the S.B.U. idea, the mud into which G.E. was sinking a few years back would by now have engulfed its many thousands of employees.

Michael G. Allen, then one of G.E.'s top planners, wrote in the *McKinsey Quarterly* that, at the start of the seventies, "Evidence of our vulnerability to competition was increasing. . . . In the computer business the strategy of a world-wide frontal assault against I.B.M. had failed. In the commercial aircraft engine business, a suicidal price battle with Rolls-Royce had deferred profits for a number of years." A three-month strike, too, had hurt: "It took us many years to regain the share and price levels lost." Sales, all the same, grew strongly. "But the profits on those sales were below expectations; earnings per share were flat, and return on investment was sliding dangerously."

That was the bad news. The good news was that G.E., under Fred Borch, had the sense to see that the answer lay in Chapter 2's theme of "competition." The old decentralized structure of ten groups divided into forty-five divisions and 175 departmental profit centers was scrapped; enter, instead, the strategic business units—forty of them. Some were as big as the old groups, some as small as the old departments.

But they all met the same criteria—and any manager contemplating the same route must ask the same questions:

1. Is this a complete business, including all functions?
2. Does the manager in charge (the general manager, in G.E.'s case) have the authority and ability to develop a strategic plan, balancing short- and long-range performance objectives?
3. Does the business have clearly identifiable external competition?

All the questions are important, but the third is an excellent aid in drawing the necessary line around the business and its market. For G.E., it set up Pratt and Whitney as the natural, clear outside competition for G.E.'s aircraft engine S.B.U.; the major appliance S.B.U. confronted Whirlpool, and so on. This new division of G.E. is the foundation of an intensive and highly sophisticated planning process. But its truly valuable contribution in this context comes from defining the business and the market in terms of the competition. Allen quotes a "competitive analysis drill" which is a catechism for the market-oriented manager:

1. Who is the competition now? Five years from now?
2. What are the investment priorities, objectives and goals of our major competitors?
3. How important is our specific market to each competitor, and what is the level of its commitment?

4. What are the competitors' relative strengths and limitations? (At least ten crucial resources are reviewed, including management, technology, finance.)
5. What weaknesses make the competitor vulnerable?
6. What changes are competitors likely to make in their future strategies?
7. So what? What will be the effects on the industry, the market and our strategy of all the competitors' strategies?

The business that can answer those questions has the best chance of winning in the marketplace. The business that has won without even asking them—because, as with all those German engineers, so far it has never had to—will be forced to ask them sooner or later. And, in these tough times, it's safest to assume in all matters that it's later than you think, when it comes to considering change; and sooner than you want when change you must.

"Prepare an order of battle beforehand. By this means, a methodicism is instituted which takes the place of art, where the latter is wanting."

No marketing operation makes sense without the emphasis on competition which animates G.E.'s latest organizational form. Competition in business can be linked to international sport: war without guns. A former Gillette executive in Europe, Alastair Sedgwick, has taken the metaphor further. Just as one Prussian general, Moltke, was the father of modern business structure, so another, says Sedgwick, should be recognized as the sire of modern marketing.

This unlikely thought rings immediately true when you

read what Carl von Clausewitz (1780–1831) actually had to say:

1. Apply the utmost exertion of powers.
2. In other words, apply the sum of all available means, plus all the strength of will which can be brought to bear.
3. Understand that "powerful motives increase the force of will."
4. Obtain "a preponderance of physical force and advantages at the decisive point."
5. Know that the result of "war is never absolute. . . . Follow up success with utmost energy."
6. Never forget that "We are inclined and induced to estimate the power of our opponents too high rather than too low."
7. None of the events upon which we calculate in war come to pass exactly as anyone would imagine.

Much else in the great Prussian soldier's advice is valuable, as shown by examples of tackling the competitive forces in the annals of Gillette—and Gillette is one of the great marketing armies of our times. Writing in *Management Today*, Sedgwick recounts how the Toni home-perm business, bought by Gillette for $20 million, was originally built up by Neison Harris. His first attack on the market flopped. "He withdrew the product, repackaged it and gave it a new name—Toni." That was Clausewitzian "force of will" exemplified. But Harris also reinforced his "available means"—he promised "to pay for cooperative advertising that would equal the value of the stores' initial orders." After that it took Harris only four years to reach his $20 million payoff.

As Sedgwick notes, "In marketing terms, physical force can be equated with the available budget." But even the mighty Gillette didn't have the budget to match its rivals when launching Right Guard deodorant on an unresponsive United Kingdom market. So it concentrated its spending on the launch period at a time ahead of the traditional selling season. By the time the enemy arrived on the battlefield, Gillette was home—but not safe. Concentration (as above) can lead to domination. But the formula needs another ingredient—repetition.

The triple threat—or the Clausewitz follow-up—is well illustrated by Gillette's darkest hour: when Wilkinson Sword's stainless blades threatened to carve up the American company's biggest and basic market. After a three-month concentrate-and-dominate campaign Gillette reinforced its efforts by getting free samples of the blade into nine and a half million British homes, even ensuring expensively, to avoid bad publicity, that the blades were handed over to an adult. Nothing less would have worked, though, given that Gillette was starting a full *two years behind* its competitor.

The truly competitive battler can overcome even longer lags. I.B.M. was four years behind Univac with the computer. But the laggard can't afford to make mistakes, especially the same ones as his enemy. I.B.M. didn't make Univac's error of selling *computers*; it sold business systems instead. Gillette knew that Wilkinson's main failing sprang from its very success—recurrent shortage of supply. When Gillette launched its rival blade, the abundant output it had taken care to ensure won the trade's good will and achieved the substantial share of the market which Gillette had to win.

But Clausewitz's warning that the battle never ends can't be ignored. He advised, "Do not make a venture with all our forces at once, because we throw away all means of directing them. It is only with disposable troops that we can turn the course of the attack." This advice—in marketing terms, always to keep something in reserve—helps to resolve the paradox of prudence and boldness. The Prussian comes down firmly on the side of boldness in choice of action and in planning. He adds, "In forming a plan of battle have a great object in view." The marketing general can be bold with prudence by maintaining a strategic reserve to throw into the battle if he finds that the inevitable unforeseen is running against his company.

The proviso is that throwing good money after bad, in the hope of turning the bad into good, requires as much systematic evaluation and method as the original attack. Clausewitz had this to say on the subject. "Prepare an order of battle beforehand. By this means a methodicism is instituted which takes the place of art, where the latter is wanting." There's an echo here of the other Prussian, Moltke, with his insistence on order as a substitute for genius. But there can be no substitute for rigorous advance preparation—which includes rigorous assessment of whether, this time, retreat isn't better than another expensive attempt to advance.

That was the course which G.E. (like R.C.A. and Xerox) ultimately took in computers. Large as the sums were which such companies had spent for the privilege of losing money against I.B.M., just as many dollars would have to be invested again, with no likelihood of an adequate profit materializing at the end of the rainbow. Had this not been so, maybe the computer failures would have been tempted by the marketing man's siren call: "O.K., it's cost us a million already. But another half a million will push us through to a hundred thousand a year—and that's a 20 percent return." It isn't, unless the first million has already been written off completely. If not, the return is 6.66 percent—and it isn't worth having.

The good head of a market-defined business will know that fact instinctively and shouldn't need to be argued out of a mistaken policy. He may sometimes need persuasion, though—and that's partly what central command in the management of a large, widely spread company is for, to provide something to push and to be pushed against. Clausewitz, as usual, had a word (or several words) for it: "Each corps or division commander must be given general control of his march. Each commander has the order to attack the enemy where he finds him, and to do so with all his strength."

To put this in business terms, strong central planning must be combined with localized execution. That way, the operation can be highly responsive to markets, highly stimulating for those who run the business, and highly rewarding for the ultimate owners, without any of the parties having rightful cause to complain about the others. The best way of ensuring that harmony, in peace as in war, is success—the perpetual "grand object" which, as Clausewitz so correctly said, should always be in view.

> *In marketing, whatever the truth about war, it's all too common to underestimate the enemy.*

The chief difference between war and marketing competition is that the marketing enemy seldom lays down his arms and surrenders. Even if he does, the odds are that (unless the victorious opponent pre-empts the possibility) somebody else will buy the loser's market share. If that interloper is really powerful and well armed, the opposing companies may ultimately be worse off—as the beer barons of America were after the Miller breweries fell into the hands of Philip Morris, the most successful of all the American cigarette firms.

That success isn't founded on the remarkable feat of hoisting Miller from nowhere to the second position behind beer leader Anheuser-Busch. While its larger competitors in the tobacco business were dissipating their energies in massive diversification programs, spurred by the cancer threat, Philip Morris followed the key word "concentration." It concentrated on building up its strength in the king-sized filter market, winning lucrative increases in overall share at the expense of the diversifiers.

When the Morris men moved into another business, too, they followed the rule of devoting their effort to an area where a worthwhile payoff could be obtained. They obeyed one of those Clausewitzian maxims of war, by having a "grand object" in view—nothing less than repeating in beer what they had done in cigarettes, but with the advantage, this time, that the competition was totally unprepared for an assault with the marketing weapons that were first and second nature to Philip Morris and the other tobacco firms.

The takeover of Miller was painful. The new parent had to suffer setbacks and to force through a management upheaval before the attack on the established brewers could begin. That's an obvious, essential corollary of any breakdown into self-contained, market-defined units. If Clausewitz's advice is followed, and the man with the responsibility is given the resources and the authority to run his business, he must be the right man: right not only in his general level of ability, but right for that business. He doesn't have to come from the same area of business, although there are some trades (notably cars) where total outsiders seldom succeed. But the manager must be able to understand and totally identify with his business. You don't want somebody who operates through remote controls—that's the job of a holding-company executive (and a crucial role it is, too).

When Philip Morris had rearranged the Miller management to its satisfaction, it found, thanks to the mistakes of its old established competitors, that the Morris approach had won a rare advantage. Clausewitz rightly insisted that "one of the most important principles in offensive action is surprise."

As Alastair Sedgwick pointed out in *Management Today*, it's not easy to achieve surprise if a company is methodically (and very properly) advancing from test market to national distribution, all of which takes time. He cites the extraordinary lengths to which Eastman Kodak went to achieve a completely secret international launch of the Instamatic camera. Given Kodak's commanding world position, won by many decades of tough, competitive marketing, it's doubtful if security leaks would have much damaged that particular launch. But Kodak's few competitors—conditioned like Pavlov's dog to react to its every move—would certainly have done their limited best to disrupt the Instamatic's advance.

In most industries, most established firms are conditioned *not* to react. That's why an aggressive competitor like the revamped Miller wins time to steal a march—and sometimes wins the whole campaign by reason of that fatal initial lag. As noted in Chapter 2, competition from smaller entries always confronts big firms with an acute problem: how much profit should they invest in repelling the opposition?

Clausewitz's observation, that generals customarily exaggerate the enemy's strength, doesn't always apply. It does sometimes. The *Financial Times*, confronted by Roy Thomson's takeover of *The Times* and launching of a separate business section, probably overreacted in the amount of spending it poured into the defense and counterattack. Since the final outcome was total victory (one fine day, Thomson's separate section sidled back into the main paper and has stayed there ever since), the *Financial Times* can claim justification.

Its market is in effect a monopoly. Since monopolies are unnatural, unusual means are often needed to protect them. Since monopolies are also highly profitable, the price put on protection will be high—merely insuring a Rembrandt will cost you more than buying a whole set of Andy Warhol prints, and you can't expect to protect an Old Master business on the cheap.

But in marketing, whatever the truth about war, it's all too common to *underestimate* the enemy. Since you want the new opponent to go away, that's how you wrongly view him—as somebody who isn't there. It's the same mistake as that of insiders who pooh-pooh the innovation which some outsider is launching into their industry, like top-loaders pooh-poohing the front-loading dishwasher. Wishful thinking isn't thinking at all. The correct response is to second-guess the competition—to place your company in its shoes, to make the most accurate assessment possible of the resources available to the enemy and of his weaknesses, to assess carefully his chances of breaking through into profit.

All this should be as meticulous as the examination of a

new product of your own. But even if the analysis shows correctly that the competitor will lose money heavily for years ahead, one key factor will still be missing. You probably don't, and can't, know how long the enemy will go on standing the loss.

I.B.M. had no means of predicting how long its competitors in mainframe computers would stay in a losing game. But since I.B.M. continued to make unheard-of profits, its ignorance hardly mattered. In other industries, the persistence of losses can matter a great deal. The basic rule of thumb—that any market will support two profitable across-the-board competitors and one profitable specialist—gets broken. The situation that results crops up again and again in the chemical industry in Europe. Nobody withdraws, so everybody loses.

Defending a market position, or preserving at considerable cost a business that has been properly structured around that market, is only right if the business makes money. Otherwise, it isn't a business—it's an operation with no justification outside itself; the antithesis, in other words, of the marketing principle. Either the interruption to profitability is temporary, and business as usual will be resumed reasonably soon, or the interruption is permanent, in which case the strategy and the business unit themselves must both be radically reappraised. The really strategic business unit is like the late film star and United Artists tycoon Mary Pickford: small, beautiful and amazingly rich.

8

THE HIGH-OCTANE OUTFIT

There's one trouble about describing, let alone recommending, the company with a flattened pyramid, no hierarchical hang-ups, informal relationships between all levels, high rewards and low bureaucracy: it all makes the company sound like a holiday camp. A business certainly can be fun—of a kind. Probably all good businesses are. For good people are being especially foolish if they spend so much of their lives doing something they don't enjoy in an environment they hate. That's not winning; it's serving a voluntary prison sentence.

But the cases of easy-going, experimental, lovely firms that have failed commercially are a warning. They are more or less identical in number, these cases, to those delectable concerns which have succeeded. Usually they are the identical firms—hailed with delight as shining examples to us all in their early days, and allowed to disappear into oblivion as disappointment and disillusion set in.

Many explanations of this decline can be offered: ranging from the same line used by Communists to defend abuses of the system (the ideas are fine, but the people aren't up to them) all the way to the Hawthorne Effect (the proposition, proved over and over, that people respond positively to any form of unusual attention, but that the response never lasts). I prefer to ask a simple question: "What was more important to the management: the experiment or the business?"

If the former was the real passion, it's no surprise if the business labored and lost. Part of the fun of a great business is success itself. As a rule, successful firms are much happier places to work in than companies where failure is staring everybody grimly in the face. A firm can do wonderful things for those who work there—only provided that it has created the resources and the means to go on doing so.

Thus an essential element of the environment, along with the permissiveness, the true decentralization and the rest, is that insistence on high professional performance and on applied effort which is known as drive or dynamism. Ideally, the insistence on the best standards will come from individuals themselves. If not, the system—and the colleagues who run that system—will have to apply it to the individual.

A useful analogy here is with the medieval gang system. The workers were collectively responsible for their output and worked, not under a boss, but a master (the foreman is still known as *Meister* in Germany). The master had the authority of expertise, but also that of the group: one bad workman, and they all suffered. Something very like this medieval system is used for making cut-crystal pieces at Waterford Glass in Ireland in our times. It works like a charm.

The same principle can be applied throughout a company: use the influence of peers as a method of achieving the results for the group which are wanted by each individual. But to say that is to echo the beginning of the famous recipe for roast wolf: "First, catch your wolf." The start is to focus the organization on objectives and intentions that anybody, from the greediest plutocrat to the sternest critic of capitalism, would recognize as worthwhile. The higher the ambitions, and the more developed the social form of the company, the higher the octane it needs in its tank.

> *If you decide that—
> come what may—you
> will always provide
> the market with its
> top quality, many
> beneficial results
> must flow.*

Money isn't everything in the setting of standards, although it can be the catalyst. In several cases, a sinking corporation has been saved by putting in rigid cash controls at once: cash being the quickest way into the heart of a business. Thereafter, cash becomes an everyday discipline; just as the budget is a yearly (or, better still, three-monthly) one; just as the overall target—like the return on investment discussed in Chapter 2—influences all the decisions of the company.

Chapter 2 sang the praises of R.O.I., which seems as objective a measure as a manager could demand. But the objectivity is in the eye of the beholder. Suppose your target is a 20 percent return. Why 20 percent? Why not 22 percent? or 32 percent? Even if you have (very rightly) decided to relate the target to the cost of capital, that was *your* decision. The choice wasn't an absolute, like the temperature at which water boils. In any event, you will want to exceed that cost of capital by a margin, which, again, will be subjectively chosen.

Any kind of financial objective, moreover, is inadequate in other respects. Sometimes money targets have to go by the board, either for the business as a whole, or for one of the sections you are trying to monitor and motivate, for instance, when the entire market collapses (like that for ships after 1973), or when new plant is coming on stream. Of course, budgets and re-budgets should allow for these circumstances; but the usefulness of the financial measure in judging efficiency in those conditions won't be great.

Still another problem is that in some businesses particular targets—R.O.I. especially—have no significance at all. An advertising agency or a magazine publisher may have virtually no capital. You can even find that the more "efficient" they are (that is, the more piles of cash they generate), the more their R.O.I. drops; that happens if retained profit boosts their capital by a percentage greater than their rise in earnings. In such businesses, though, there's no difficulty in finding other measures, some financial, some not; but they won't all be of the classic variety.

Even in a business where the classic R.O.I. applies, does it tell you anything about the company's standing in the market? Suppose a firm decides to cut every corner and cost—like Philip II debasing the Spanish coinage. For a while profits and R.O.I. may rise spectacularly; but the Spanish nemesis awaits, when the market recognizes, and reacts against, the debased goods. The same is true of deferring capital investment; that's what managers in multinational conglomerates often do in the last of their usual three years in a job—ending on a high personal note at the expense of the long-term future of the business.

Just as some businesses can't really use return on capital as a guide, nor can many departments inside a business. What financial measure, for example, do you apply to a personnel department? It's no answer simply to abolish it, as recommended by Robert Townsend in *Up the Organization*. The personnel work will still be done somewhere by someone, and will still cost money. Some misguided souls have shown great ingenuity in trying to prove that R.O.I. targets can be applied to overhead departments, but it's a futile cause. After all, you don't have personnel or finance departments to make money in the same way as a new brand or a new piece of plant. That being so, you should judge the overhead departments by what they *are* supposed and paid to do, that being the key to all objective, physical measures.

Finally, profit is an *outcome*. It stems from the company's success at providing goods and services. You cannot derive the outcome except from the input. So any measure by which you judge and seek to improve efficiency must apply to the input: the use of materials, labor, plant, and the rest. If a business has no targets for wastage, no standards for effective hours worked (in terms of output) as compared to paid hours, no targets for plant utilization, it is flying blind. All these measures and many more can lay bare waste and encourage saving. But one particular physical measure takes in so many of the others that it can (and, in many lucrative cases, does) stand for all of them.

That single measure is *quality*. That key word cropped up in discussing what has kept Mars so high in the growth and confectionery leagues all these years. Mars is not alone. Time and again, when a firm has kept up a profitable supremacy in the market for decades, the basic reason is the unvarying pursuit of the top quality.

Among those mentioned or to be mentioned in this book, the verdict is true of companies as different as Anheuser-Busch, the leader in American beer, or Porsche in German sports cars, or Waterford Glass. In other cases, the foundations of success can lie partly elsewhere; for instance, the success of I.B.M. and Xerox is inseparable from the brilliant financing arrangements which accompany the sale of their machines. But when did you last doubt that a Kodak film would be up to standard, or a Kellogg's cornflake taste as it should? In cases like these, every customer takes the quality for granted, nearly always with good reason; and that is the best of reasons for Kellogg's and Kodak's market dominance.

Perhaps the most convincing demonstration of the profound impact of quality is the rise of Peugeot in the world auto industry. Until quite recently, this family-owned firm was a minor force even in its home market of France. But its single model (allegedly made under the traditions of the Swiss watchmakers across the border) had a remarkable reputation for quality, which ensured a loyal clientele and a premium price.

The fact that quality usually commands a premium is complete proof of its power. Building on its premium reputation, Peugeot was able to extend its product line in both directions, into smaller and larger cars. It absorbed the troubled Citroën and then, by picking up Chrysler's European interests, it emerged (if unwisely) as the second-largest car company outside the United States and Japan—thanks, in the last analysis, to the quality factor.

In companies which have adopted the best product or "the best service" as guiding light, management attention is automatically focused on that pervasive aim. If you decide that—come what may—you will always provide the market with its top quality, many beneficial results must flow.

1. You are forced constantly to watch the market and all your competitors.
2. You are forced to assess and evaluate your own products and services constantly and critically.
3. You have a criterion to govern all design, product planning and production activities.
4. You have a built-in source of motivation and pride.
5. You have a distinct, invaluable identity in the marketplace.

It's true that a quality-first policy can look expensive. Many prime companies—Anheuser-Busch's breweries being one example—spend far more than they need on production. But the cost equation, in which production costs are only part of the total expense of getting goods into the hands of the customer, works in favor of these purists. Their price premium applies to a much higher figure: 5 percent more on the price will always vastly exceed 5 percent on the costs.

Not that quality has to be expensive. For many years Peugeot persisted with old-fashioned engineering, because it felt that change might affect quality. Its conservatism probably saved money. If higher quality wins higher volume, the top-line producer may even end up as the cheapest one, having his cake and eating it.

From any angle, quality must pay. But it pays most, paradoxically, when it isn't thought of as "quality" at all—not in the sense of hand-tooled leather or vintage champagne. Quality, like profit, is, rather, an outcome—the result of doing things the right way. And there's even a right way of doing that.

> *"If you start confusing quality with elegance, brightness, dignity, love or something else, you will find that everyone has different ideas."*

Since you cannot do better than achieve 100 percent of anything, any business, and any manager, can seek perfection by aiming at 100 percent performance. But that begs the most important question of all: 100 percent of what?

I've seen studies arguing that the only "acceptable" level of performance is the totally fault-free, and that programs for improving productivity should be geared to that demand. But there will always be drift. Machines will always have more or less idle time. Salesmen will never hit the jackpot on every call. Trucks will never carry the optimum load all the time. Even if mechanical or human failures didn't occur, complex systems (and the simplest business in the world is quite complicated) are bound to have inefficient gaps and overlaps.

Still, the attempt to operate with zero defects (Z.D.) has obvious power in fueling and directing a drive for efficiency. It has a direct connection with quality, too. If a product is made, or a service provided, with zero defects, its quality must be perfect, too. (It could be a design unacceptable to the market, of course, but that's another matter.) The American expert on Z.D., Philip Crosby, has emphasized this basic relationship in the very title of his book on the subject, *Quality Is Free*. It contains a questionnaire composed of ten basic propositions which have to be answered, true or false:

1. Quality is a measure of goodness of the product that can be defined as fair, good, excellent.
2. The economics of quality require that management establish acceptable quality levels as performance standards.
3. The cost of quality is the expense of doing things wrong.
4. Inspection and test should report to manufacturing so manufacturing can have the proper tools to do the job.
5. Quality is the responsibility of the quality department.
6. Worker attitudes are the primary cause of defects.
7. I have trend charts that show me the rejection level at every key operation.
8. I have a list of the ten biggest quality problems.
9. Zero defects is a worker motivation program.
10. The biggest problem today is that the customers don't understand.

The questions read as if all the answers should be "true." But only (3) and (7) are correct propositions, according to Crosby. It's absolutely true that good quality costs nothing. Scrapped and rejected articles are colossally expensive. Pity the industry where the costs of failure are remote from the factory —like the cars which keep on coming back to the dealers (at the manufacturer's expense) for rectification. Perfect quality, if it could be attained, would eliminate all the costs of what Crosby calls "non-conformance."

But you can't conform unless you know what you are supposed to conform to, nor check on conformance without data. The second "true" proposition is that charts must be kept regularly to show how well (or badly) quality performance is matching the laid-down requirements. The beginning and end of effective quality control is to have precise physical definitions of what you require from each operation and to insist that those requirements be met.

To quote Crosby, "If you start confusing quality with elegance, brightness, dignity, love or something else, you will find that everyone has different ideas." The essential discipline in the company is to have identical ideas on a prime issue like quality and to ensure that those ideas are followed through.

It isn't only a question of stopping slackness and eliminating episodic human error. Losers take persistent failure to reach predetermined standards as evidence that the standards were set too high. *Management Today* recorded one case where an automated production line, originally supposed to run at 80 percent efficiency, had its targets reduced, because of successive failures to meet them, to 65 percent after five years and 55 percent after ten years. That kind of under-performance always has a cause; it's far less likely to result from bad planning in the first instance than from bad management in the second, third and fourth.

One study showed that 45 percent of all machine-hours lost among several different companies resulted from slipshod management—and that was six times as many as the losses stemming from maintenance work or some action or inaction by the operators.

There's a battle going on all the time between the learning curve and the drift process. The learning curve means that with every cumulative doubling of output, you should get something like a 20 percent reduction in total costs (unless you foolishly insist on change, which, if it's excessive, can keep a company living on the learning curve forever). The "drift process" refers to the fact that, after a number of years, a close examination of any operation will reveal inefficiencies. Savings of a third are often there for the asking and, if you don't believe it, just look at the economies that are always found at some time of budgetary crisis.

The principles of a good zero defects program are a parable for efficiency generally.

1. Performing well is the responsibility of the performers.
2. Ensuring that they live up to that responsibility is somebody else's care—in the case of quality, it's a quality control department.
3. If poor performance apparently results from failure by the workers, somewhere in there lies failure of the managers.
4. Better performance isn't a matter of motivation and virtue, but of better technical methods better applied.
5. A lower standard than one you could achieve by better application isn't acceptable—even if you can find some goon of a customer who will accept it.

The realization that the pursuit of quality is the key to the storehouse of competitive efficiency has been borne out in America by the postwar rise of the Japanese. It's easy to see why this rise, based on quality, has especially disconcerted rival American manufacturers, since quality theory is an American invention. Yet a special report on quality in an April 1979 *Business Week* was hinged on the Japanese success in stealing American clothes. "American managers," said the report, "are beginning to recognize that product quality can be a pivotal, strategic weapon—sometimes even more than price—in the world-wide battle for market share."

What you can achieve, given the will and the know-how, is shown by one Sony plant—not in Japan, but in San Diego. It managed (or was managed) to achieve a Sony record of two hundred days without major defects. At I.T.T., where Crosby has wrought his major works, the cost of "quality" used to amount, he reckons, to more than 10 percent of sales revenue; that colossal cost was mostly the expense of correcting errors. The conglomerate now says that its zero defects program saved an estimated $700 million in 1978, compared to what quality would otherwise have cost.

That's the kind of iffy calculation with which winning managers have little truck: "would-haves" aren't facts. But you can't ignore the logic of defect-free performance: because it stems from design to eliminate defects; purchasing from suppliers that concentrates on the quality aspect of an efficient supply; insistence that there is no such thing as an "acceptable quality level," if the latter means a significant number of defects; recognition that money spent on rectifying supposedly finished products is money wasted.

The same logic applies to services of all kinds: quality is all the customer is paying for, and its provision is what has always separated the service sheep from the too-many goats. The winning advantage which good, long-lasting companies have gleaned from quality is so obvious that it shouldn't have required an invasion of Japanese goods to remind the West of quality's competitive power. But better late than never—for any company that has survived this far without producing, as excellently as it could, goods or services as excellent as it might: just think of the gains that lie in store.

All the boss wants to know is "whether you made what you said you would. If not, why, and what have you done about it?"

A company which is committed to physical performance standards—whether it's the time a car-rental firm takes to process a client, or the ten defects per million transistors which is all that one Japanese electronics firm allows—is committed to discipline. Not only discipline, but *pressure*: there will be failures of omission and commission, and rectifying these inevitably means that somebody must apply pressure on somebody else. The iron hand, it might seem, is back again, and the velvet glove of the permissive, collaborative, company, if that company is really efficient, is just a piece of fancy dress.

If that's the case, it shouldn't be. People discipline themselves willingly enough in their voluntary leisure activities; they strive to perform better, and get angry with themselves if they under-perform. In business, they behave no differently if given the chance. They don't have that opportunity unless high standards of performance are the norm, and unless they are expected to meet those standards on their own initiative, and in their own way. In the emergence of companies from the slough into the bright waters, plentiful clues to the right technique abound.

Just as, time and again, the common characteristic of the growth company with stamina is its emphasis on quality; so, in any collection of such corporate recoveries, a single common feature stands out. It's *the reduction of head office to a tiny size*. In the company described in the opening chapter—the sluggard whose renewal methods inspired the acronym **BACK TO BASICS**—a headquarters staff of six hundred became thirty. In another case, in which profits multiplied one hundred times in seven years, the operations of eight thousand people were masterminded by just twenty-five at the center—a handful of executives and the few personal staff who were needed to enable the executives to function.

The function is itself necessarily limited if only small numbers are available at the center. Sheer shortage of time forces the top management to manage by exception, to set the standards, to insist that the standards are met, to intervene only when things are going wrong, or when asked to, or when they simply feel they've let too much time pass since the last long talk with John—the independent boss of an independent subsidiary.

He, in turn, may have satellites of his own. They can be managed in the same way—on a loose rein which can always be pulled up tight. You can make this policy sound as gentle or tough as you like, even using the same words. Take this example from a vice-president of Louisiana-Pacific, whose monthly memo to headquarters has been cut back from fifteen pages to a single sheet since a millionaire entrepreneur took control. All the latter wants to know, says his subordinate, is *"Whether you made what you said you would. If not, why, and what have you done about it?"*

Those words could be made to sound quite threatening; but the speaker plainly thought of the change as a great relaxation ("We no longer have a thousand Nubian slaves with stubby little pencils"), and he's probably right. Head office holds the key in these recovery stories, partly because its reduction removes overhead costs at a stroke. These savings in costs can't easily be exaggerated. When a new chief executive arrived at Kaiser Aluminum in the early seventies, he turned loss into profit merely by cutting out the superfluous layers of management.

A badly run company can always be recognized by its number of executive layers. If everybody has a boss, and every boss also has one, the recipe for corporate failure is complete. One of the prime tasks of a high-octane headquarters, in fact, is to insist that managements out in the sticks don't start breeding executive layers themselves. It's no big deal to produce a lean head office by shunting all the superfluous bodies out of the center and loading them on to the periphery.

The right to insist on such philosophical principles is one of the disciplinary powers that the center must reserve to itself. It needn't seek to impose a common pattern within that philosophy. Apart from anything else, different businesses in different markets need different forms. Possibly even common financial reporting systems (usually the first essential of multi-division firms) can and should be varied to suit varying needs. As one highly successful boss of a conglomerate told a divisional head, "You can write your report in Chinese, if you like. We'll hire an interpreter."

That same company is a good guide to the principle of providing central drive without central overload:

1. The only unbreakable code is cash: all cash gets remitted at once to the center, and if there is no cash to remit, somebody has to explain why—and fast.
2. The talks between the centralists and the sharp-enders always take place at the latter's place of business—not at head office.
3. All divisions are expected to move their product lines and commercial status towards the top end of their markets.
4. Everybody is encouraged to devolve to sub-organizations; if the right size for an operation is six people, that's how big it is.

That last principle is the key to escaping from the trap of "top-down management," in the old sense, and entering the new "top-down" era in which managers in the plants (like the head-office executives mentioned above) go *down* to find out what is happening, and don't rely on anything but their own minds and work to maintain the vital contact with the places where the costs arise and the profits are earned.

It's easy enough, in applying central pressure, to discover if people know what they are doing; to find whether they add, to this basic mastery of their trades, the habitual use of logical, systematic thought; to check whether they are hiring good people and allowing them to produce good work.

Any competent journalist, without the advantage of the internal figures, can test these essentials. A competent central executive should find it much easier. But the answers even to these penetrating questions are not complete. They cannot tell the investigator whether this or that manager is running this or that business creatively: changing what should be changed, resisting change when he should, keeping up the pressure on himself.

Too often, losers convince themselves that whatever method they have adopted does answer these questions—because that's what they *want* to believe. At Litton Industries before the fall, Tex Thornton and Roy Ash used to pride themselves on the day-long "strategy sessions," at which subsidiary managers would be put through the intellectual wringer about their plans. Later, after the fall, one of the best managers concerned claimed that the sessions were useless, because Thornton and Ash couldn't know enough about the industries to ask the right questions.

The right questions are those you can ask of any manager in any business, without being fooled by the answers. David Mahoney, the chief executive of Norton Simon International, once told *Vision* magazine, "From an operating point of view Avis president Colin Marshall will forget more about renting and servicing cars than I'll ever know. This is not my job. *It is my job to understand how one finances it, what is good advertising, and whether we are picking the right people.*" Note the middle definition of Mahoney's job: he has built the company around businesses whose common theme is a rich consumer franchise built around advertising—which Mahoney, a former advertising agent, understands thoroughly.

The high-octane company, at all levels, asks basic questions from the position of basic understanding. But there's one thing more. It insists on getting the right answers. "When Canada Dry president Richard Beeson had trouble meeting his figures, Mahoney hissed, 'Make your figures, or clear out your desk.' Beeson made his figures."

Now, Mahoney is a rough and tough figure, whose style doesn't have to be imitated. But the insistent pressure is essential, and the person who should most insist on the pressure being applied is the manager himself. In fact, he'll apply it to himself—if he sincerely wants to win. Otherwise, he has a license to fail, and fail he will.

9

GROUP THERAPY

Talk to any group of British managers for any length of time about their art, craft or racket, and sooner or later someone will come out with the word "leadership." Americans have much the same tendency—that's why their elected officials, especially the president, are always being berated for lack of "leadership." It seems to mean one man solving the problems of society or a company by a dynamic exhibition of knowing what to do, and how to do it—and then seeing that it is done. Since the problems, certainly of society, are too complex for this to be possible, politico after politico is adjudged a failure —as "leader."

It's true that the company which wins does so because a dynamic management, or leadership, generates more and better ideas, turns them into more effective action and is satisfied only with excellent results. But in companies as in politics this package of virtues is rarely found in one person. In fact, ideas, action and results are the key words for three different and equally important management types. You could substitute the functional descriptions, marketing, production and finance, and get the same distinction. Managers seldom switch between these functions, because experience on the job confirms their natural, separate bents.

Both production and finance men, of course, need ideas. Marketing and financial people need to turn ideas into effective action. No manager can afford to be satisfied with less than the results which please an especially sharp and sharp-eyed finance man. But the qualities in the trinity are in some ways contradictory. Nobody can spurt out ideas like an advertising man; but you would rarely trust one with running a factory; nor, judging by the mess that many ad agencies have made of their business affairs (especially when mistakenly diversifying), would you let the ad men loose on the company finances.

There's an instinctive answer to this regrettable but natural separation of talents: the formation of management partnerships, marrying together talents which are complementary and which mutually supply the deficiencies of the other marriage partner. It's "partnership" that's needed much more than "leadership"—at least in the latter's traditional sense.

The traditional meaning is taken from the military models which underlie most conventional management theory. But disappointment is nearly always waiting for anybody who seeks the commanding figure, the take-charge guy, the man on horseback who will lead the management troops into victory by the force of his personality and vision.

Here people confuse style with substance. We're habituated to admire the visible qualities of a General MacArthur; we respond warmly to the very words "supreme commander" or "chief executive." But the history of warfare and nations is littered with the corpses of men led by incompetents who looked and even sounded magnificent—like Nicholas II's uncle, the towering Grand Duke, whose hopeless blundering did far more damage to the Russian army in 1914 than any German brilliance. MacArthur's memory lives for his achievements, not just for his panache; and the achievements, although style certainly contributed to them, can be analyzed, explained, weighed and measured in concrete terms by the military historian.

In modern, peacetime conditions, a good leader is somebody who gets good results. How the paragon gets those results will and should vary from place to place and time to time. But he will seldom work simply by the exercise of a mystical bunch of qualities that could be identified as "leadership." In any event, as Chapter 3 emphasized, the five-star company evolves into plurality.

Leadership in this context might well demand cheerfully taking second place, or even third, when the running must be made by the man with the ball. The strong leader must know when *not* to lead—when to be, not merely a partner, but a junior one. Partnerships are *groups*, and groups, from pairs upwards, are the building blocks of modern winning management. Making groups work well, in today's circumstances, almost defines the management role.

> *Successful groups need members to play several different roles, and successful top managers must play all of them themselves.*

The theory and practice of group management demand that the "leader" should play, not a single role, but many of them. To make groups work, and nothing else in the company will work if they don't, the leader has to adapt both his style and his function to the different membership and purposes of the various bunches of people who form and re-form around him.

For instance, at certain times he'll have to be the man with the *ideas*: fitting into the traditional mold of the "heavy" boss, spouting ideas, some bad, some great, but all his—and all exclusive of anybody else's. A vital ploy in this kind of environment is that of persuading the Great Man that your idea is actually his; otherwise, it has little chance of being accepted, let alone applied.

Ideas which are not thus modestly and deceptively packaged bring out the Great Man's strong propensity to play *critic* —always in a destructive sense. But no manager can escape the critical role. The higher he rises, the more constantly the critical faculty needs to be applied. Without self-criticism and the power to be fairly critical of others (remembering that praise is also a form of criticism), the "leader" won't lead in the right direction; he probably won't even know the difference between right and wrong.

The basic concept of delegation, though, is that while the leader may dream up ideas and criticize the ideas and actions of others, he won't *implement* actions himself. He sits above the battle, in Olympian comfort, while the lesser gods do the dirty work down below. But the ability to do, and a practical fascination with how it's done, are inseparable from getting others to operate effectively. The boss from time to time takes his jacket off and proves (to their satisfaction, not his) that he can still outdo any man in the place. He is doing more than showing his prowess; he is symbolizing that business is about action.

By moving down to the level of the "team" (as overworked a word as leader) the boss also helps to create the individual and group *motivation* ("team spirit" in the cliché) which genuinely does make the whole more powerful than its parts. The human desire to serve a common cause is extremely potent; if mobilized, it increases the general strength of motivation. An inescapable role of the boss is to pass among his people reassuringly, like Henry V before Agincourt; or thunderously, like General Patton before Palermo.

These days, a manager will need more than Agincourt's "a little touch of Harry in the night" to inspire him. The chief executive, or whatever other title he goes under, needs more than charisma, more than his internal management powers. In addition, he can't help but be the first *external* link between the organization and the outside world. Without his example, moreover, it's less likely that others will develop that power of "outsight" which alone can forestall the perpetual threat of excessive inbreeding.

These four roles still don't exhaust the costume changes required of the true leader. Not only is he the critic, he's the *inspector*, too. If he doesn't insist on "zero defects," will anybody else? Nor is it any use insisting on fault-free performance unless you look to see if it's being obtained. The inspection job is often tedious to both inspector and inspected: one man's inspection is another man's nit-picking. But nits are there to be picked; perfection has no exemptions.

None of these roles, even that of inspector, is specifically associated with leadership; but there is a group role which only the "leader" would normally be expected to play—*coordinator*. Somebody has to gather up all the strings in one hand, to make sure that objectives, tasks, responsibilities are clear to everybody, that the plans make collective as well as individual sense. Few situations can allow the head of a group of people to avoid the duty of coordinating their efforts—that, above all, is what earns him his salary.

The role demands "self-control, decisiveness and trust," in the words of Michael Wellin, a practicing manager with B.O.C. International. Writing in *Management Today*, Wellin gave psychological profiles to the other roles as well: "Creativity, intelligence, imagination and innovation" (for ideas); "Intelligence and a serious and shrewd outlook" (for criticism); "A practical, conventional and controlled outlook" (for implementing); "Social awareness and understanding" (for team building); "A stable, extrovert and inquisitive outlook" (for external contacts); and "An anxious, meticulous and controlled personality" (for inspection purposes).

A brisk run through these contradictory pen-portraits is enough to show why highly successful top managers are so hard to categorize. They have to play-act, to switch constantly between such different roles that the real personality becomes elusive. Very few leaders, however, succeed in being all things to all men. They are better at some aspects of these seven star parts than others, as you would only expect to find. But Wellin didn't expect to find this seven-star manager. Quite the opposite: these are the seven roles which, he suggests, have to be played by *some* individual in *any* successful group of people.

Wellin reported on research that is manna from Heaven for anybody forming or operating groups—task forces, say. *While you need the seven roles to be played, you don't need seven people.* The super-manager with the seven interchangeable personalities doesn't exist, but the research indicates that people can effectively play two or even three parts. The minimum group, says Wellin, is five, the maximum twelve—but unless the seven "behavior patterns" are balanced, the group won't be effective.

As summarized, the theory looks mechanistic. But think carefully about any management team you know well. Do the personalities slot easily into the seven key roles? If they don't, you may suddenly spot why the group is a failure. In Wellin's own company, a general manager, upset because his so-called management team wasn't one—it showed no team spirit—had a two-day workshop arranged. They discussed a real-life business problem, and from that discussion it quickly emerged that the group had one "critic" too many.

The surplus critic was behaving in a highly aggressive and hostile manner towards the other group members. Maybe this was connected with the fact, which the general manager was forced to face, that he wasn't playing his "coordinator" role well enough. The group took an inordinate time to solve its problem, too: a failure which sprang from the absence of an "inspector." In any ineffective group, always look for the possibility that some vital group function isn't being performed.

Group analysis can be useful in another way. A perennially tough problem in hiring is to know just what you want.

If the job is seen, not in the usual way, as a marketing man, a plant manager, etc., but in its true light as an addition to an identified group, the missing role should appear. Are you looking for a coordinator, an ideas man, a critic, an implementer, a team builder, an external contact or an inspector?

The answer will lead to the question of whether the candidate trundled before you fits the missing role. Real life seldom works out so smoothly. But a sound rule is never to hire any executive without checking his fit against Wellin's roles. Apart from anything else, you may find that the man cannot play any of them. In which case . . .

> *Given that every person is imperfect, who's the partner to supply his deficiencies?*

A powerful reason for seeking effective groups is shown by the history of many great businesses. The early formation of groups which can still be seen running the show decades later is the source of the company's strength. These bundles of people won't have a complete set of all the required patterns of behavior—partly because the numbers of partners are usually too few. Partner is the right word, since often these management teams evolve rather like a genuine partnership in, say, law or accounting—an assembly of equals with an equal voice in the enterprise.

But partnerships of unequals can work marvelously. A feature of even the most tyrannical tycoons is the lesser, invaluable figure lurking in their shadows. Henry Ford I's success—the greatest in all manufacturing—as a founder-proprietor can't be understood without knowing the part played by subordinates like Charles Sorensen, a genius of mass production. The function of these unequal partners is no different from that of equal members in a group: that is, to supply the missing parts, the inadequacies, in the make-up of the great man, as in the membership of the group.

Sometimes the tycoon's deficiency is technical. Some founding fathers, like Polaroid's Land or Intel's Robert N. Noyce, are technologists through and through; others, like I.B.M.'s Tom Watson, are not technicians. One Watson-type dynamo called his technical *éminence grise* "my day-wife." The phrase is excellent (whatever the night-wife may have thought). Not only does the strongest-seeming manager need support, but that support, if his strengths (as is likely) are predominantly masculine, will have to be essentially feminine.

Male-female makes by no means the only complementary contrast in human affairs. It follows that, when appointing a senior executive, one question—usually ignored—has to be asked. Given that this person (like all of us) is imperfect, who's the partner to supply his deficiencies? In Plato, there's the fascinating theory that male and female are two halves of the same personality, which incessantly seeks to join up its separate halves: hence, coupling. Without going as far as that, you can say that each management personality is stronger for combination with a complementary type.

The concept of partnership is essentially different from that of "teamwork." The correct analogy is with the very peculiar English game of cricket. There are "partnerships" between batsmen, meaning that two men happen to be batting simultaneously, and even between bowlers, meaning that one hurls the ball from one end of the pitch while the other does so from the opposite end. But there is never (or very rarely) any idea of partnership in the sense of the two doing the same thing at the same time in the same way, together.

The true partnership, in modern management, is the relationship between two people whose skills are complementary, and whose personalities are mature enough to accept this fact —whether the partners are equal or not, and whether they number the minimum of two or more.

The most famous combinations tend to be duets, like

Wilson and Johnson, the Holiday Inns pair; or Marks and Sieff, the real names behind the retail revolution of Marks and Spencer; or Hewlett and Packard, the biggest personal numbers in the calculator business. Maybe, as in marriage, a *ménage à deux* is the easiest kind to form and run.

Certainly, the close harmony and durability of such pairing beats most marriages. David Packard and William Hewlett have, for four decades, exemplified the familiar type of combination mentioned earlier: the marriage of the technological (Hewlett) with the managerial and administrative (Packard). At the same time their executive habits are strikingly similar (modest salaries that don't match their immodest $800 million personal fortunes; simple offices; shirtsleeves; dislike of hierarchy; conservative finance). They can sound like Tweedledum and Tweedledee. "The problem with debt," said Hewlett to *Management Today*, "is that you eventually have to pay the piper. It's more comfortable to have zero debt." Echoed Packard, "My philosophy goes back to the Depression. I don't want to be in debt if a downturn comes."

Theirs is the classic type of two-man growth—in the 1970–80 decade alone, with a 26 percent annual advance in earnings per share, Hewlett-Packard outstripped I.B.M., Polaroid and Xerox with vast ease. But the same principles can be observed in most *untypical* circumstances. For instance, what chances would anybody give for a company set up to make a product for which it has no labor force, no technology, no factory, and no markets, and which also hasn't got much money?

From those apparently impossible beginnings, a large group of managers has created what looked at times to be the perfect company: able to sell everything it produced in advance and, within reason, at whatever price it liked. The company is Waterford Glass, whose fine crystal pieces, much in demand for American brides and others, appear to have sprung from a centuries-old tradition. But only the designs do. Waterford's handful of Irish investors decided as recently as

1947 to revive an activity that had been stone dead since 1851.

The joke goes that in 1947 their infant company had only three production problems—how to make the glass, how to blow it, and how to cut it. But as the "partners" arrived, one by one, year by year, each task was tackled in turn. The technical director brought in glass blowers from Germany and Italy, cutters from there and Czechoslovakia. The personnel expert trained Irish workers. The finance man saw that the losses (once as big as the turnover) were reduced. The administrative man, finding no organization worth the name, installed one. The salesman in 1952, when at last some crystal glass worth offering was made, legged it over to New York, a market which finally paid and took off six years later.

Only then did Waterford arrive at the marketing man's promised land—permanently oversold, and able to allocate supply to its hungry customers. Profits passed a million in 1971, and were £9 million six years later. Just as remarkably, the self-grown men who had attended and escaped from those desperate beginnings were mostly still running the company thirty years after its feeble start. As with Hewlett and Packard, long partnerships of this nature breed both deep familiarity among the personalities involved and a profoundly imbued, shared knowledge of the business, its history and its practicalities.

Not many businesses, true, offer the chances for development of a Hewlett-Packard or a Waterford. But the principles of partnership work wondrously in all management. It can't be done by mere institutional changes—nothing can. The attempt to build the partnership idea into the super-large company, usually with a three-man "office of the president," was a right-minded but ham-fisted reaction: ham-fisted because the president, the chief executive, couldn't put his own responsibility into commission—not so long as the hierarchy stayed intact in all other respects.

True partnerships can't easily evolve in a pyramid. That's why tycoons can take partners so readily: their dictatorships are flat structures with a single towering peak. The other side of the coin is that a true partnership levels the structure, spreading authority and sharing information more equally among the executives. The question "Who are my partners?" is too rarely asked. But without the answer, and without knowing what the partners have got that he hasn't, even the best manager can't manage at his best.

> *The idea of subordinates voting down their superior—even one whose name is on the label—shouldn't be strange.*

Family businesses are partnerships by and of nature. The natural process of reproduction provides the top executives, and in most cases the fact that they are heavily loaded with stock guarantees that they will have a partner's (more or less) equal voice in the business. All the same, the family firm, a Victorian creation, has supposedly been in the doldrums for several decades. Yet just like the Victorian virtues—such as abhorrence of debt—the family in management has shown glorious resilience.

People still sneer at nepotism (along the lines of the celebrated gibe at the Universal Pictures tsar, "Uncle Carl Laemmle," who had "a very large faemmle"). But historical fact suggests, on both sides of the Atlantic, that procreation has been as good a method of executive selection as any. Take American beer. Nothing in brewing, you might suppose, could match the high-octane growth of Miller, the Philip Morris acquisition, which multiplied volume six times in eight years by aggressive marketing and production techniques (quoted approvingly in an earlier chapter). But Miller's rise to Number Two is no more remarkable than the staying power of Number One, Anheuser-Busch, headed by the founder's great-grandson, and still out-selling Miller by a decisive four barrels to three in 1979.

August Busch III spent seventeen years in the company, run sternly by his father, before being handed the presidency in 1974. It's hard to fault Busch III's subsequent record in expanding the market share to nearly a quarter, and dominating the more profitable, higher-priced reaches of that market. Describing the regime, *Fortune* magazine refers to "the Teutonic persistence of August Busch." The ethnic reference is telling, because no nation has outdone the Germans at turning the old-fashioned family business into an engine of modern economic growth.

It's these firms, rather than the great multinationals, which are the main source of West Germany's rightly famous business stamina. They dominate the economy, especially in the medium-sized sector: and middling in Germany can be very large. For example, Porsche, whose ten shareholders are all descendants of the great inventor Dr. Ferdinand Porsche, now achieves sales, mostly through its sports cars, in excess of a billion D-marks annually: until the end of the sixties, five Porsches held five key places as executives, headed by Ferdinand II (Ferry).

Steeped in the business from their own beginnings, the members of an owning, executive family, just like a haphazard band of founding executives (such as the Waterford Glass directors), develop their specific strengths and that knowledge of each other which is the invisible cement of the management structure. The interrelationships will never be a perfect fit. Because men and women come in such varied psychological shapes and sizes, even in families, ideal matches are never possible. But people can be made to fit by shared experience and objectives: and both are easier to share if the partners also share genes.

The rules for a family of business partners, though, must be exactly the same as if all were unknowns plucked from the Harvard Business School. The only favoritism shown to a manager—if the company wants to succeed—is to consider him for a job in the first place. Whoever he is, thereafter the apprenticeship must be the same.

True, there's only symbolic virtue in making an August Busch III start his career shoveling malt in the warehouse, when everybody (including the malt-shoveler) knows that he's the heir apparent. But symbols in management have much point—even if that point is only to show the company at large that being born into privilege confers no privileges.

The wisecrack which some wit at R.C.A. directed against Robert W. Sarnoff still rings true. "Bobby joined the company at the bottom, and then his father [founder General David Sarnoff] took a fancy to him." Many years later, after a woeful series of disasters ($490 million lost on computers, a 40 percent slump in profits), Sarnoff got removed from the board, despite the family name.

That must always be the rule—rewards for success and penalties for failure. Perhaps it should be applied more severely to family members, and for much the same reason that August Busch had to shovel malt: *pour encourager les autres*—or, rather, so as not to *discourage* the others.

Even in a flat company of little hierarchy, example has to be set at the highest level. Anyway, the "others" in business become more and more important with every modern day; so much so that the ability to recruit good outsiders is almost the acid test of a good family management. The test was passed in grand-prix style by the Porsche family, in one of the most extraordinary acts of abdication in business history.

One adverse quality was shared by all the Porsches: the fact that they *were* all Porsches. In a billion-mark concern, the Porscheness of the top executives was a potential disadvantage, since it restricted the quality of the partners or fellow executives who could come into the company. So the entire top family echelon stepped down to let outsiders in—with results that, despite the 1973 oil crisis, have been financially gratifying to the self-same Porsches as shareholders.

There's an immediate analogy with one of the first moves by August Busch once he took command of his beer empire. At one level he hired a bunch of youngsters, all armed with MBA's from the business schools, and staffed a new planning department with such recruits. With new, critical intelligence inserted into the core of the firm, Busch, at the top level, formed a management committee, whose seven non-family vice-presidents had an average age of under forty in 1979—a fact which alone should guarantee the succession, if not the success, of the brewing giant.

In theory—and, according to *Fortune*, it happens in practice—the seven outsiders can outvote Busch. It's a nice point whether a boss who lets himself be outvoted, but who could choose otherwise, is being truly democratic. Where the family holds the largest block of shares, it holds the ultimate power. Yet the idea of subordinates voting down their superior—even one whose name is on the label—shouldn't be strange. It's a logical response to the recognition that rank confers nothing save responsibility: rank doesn't equal right or might, and it is wrong to employ able people unless their ability can carry the day.

The correct approach is found in common business speech in the Porsches' native land. The West German chief executive (although he can sometimes domineer as heavily as any Anglo-Saxon boss) is described as the "spokesman" of the board. He customarily sees himself as a *primus inter pares*, a man whose subordinates are in a sense his equals: a very senior partner.

Many words have been spun about experiments in forming working groups in the factory. But the development of genuine co-management is probably far more significant for the future of firms. Possibly that's what has given the family firm its spectacular lease of late twentieth-century life—the fact that family members, secure in their shareholdings, have been readier than insecure corporation men to bring equal partners into the heart of the company, giving them power and responsibility, without necessarily going as far as the Porsche abdication.

In the same country, Reinhard Mohn, whose family has been in books since 1835, has built Bertelsmann to a £950 million publishing turnover, which may well be the largest in the business worldwide. As Mohn says, "When a business becomes as large as ours, it's no longer just a personal affair. . . . It's no longer good enough, in the fifth generation, to think only in terms of the family and tradition. One has to be more concerned with how to ensure the continuity of an economic unit."

The best way to do that is to turn the family into a working group—just as the best way to weld a company into a lasting, coherent success is to turn an executive group into a family: a working one.

PART 3

WHAT MANAGERS DO— AND DON'T

10

THE MANAGERIAL POTENTIAL

The manager cannot be considered apart from his relationship with others; he also cannot be considered as anything but himself, all alone and unsupported. Some companies are trying to recognize the individual in the bunch of bananas by serving up, as fringe benefits, items like biofeedback and meditation, so as to improve individual function. Whether the company is providing therapy or not, though, the manager clearly needs to make the best of himself if he wants to get the best out of others—and out of the organization.

He has the advantage, compared to earlier generations, of the boom in the self-help industry. There is now hardly any aspect of human performance which lacks its attendant gurus —and most of the goods they peddle work well enough to justify the time and trouble. Self-help (even jogging) does consume both, but it's as great a mistake in management as in any other human activity to assume that the best results flow to the gifted amateur who takes no trouble to prepare for the contest.

You cannot avoid the necessity of self-management. It can be taken too far, like the sad case of one bright financial star:

he quit a top job, one he had been fantastically lucky to get so early in life, because his "career plan" demanded that he become chief executive of a public company by the age of forty. He joined a large firm as heir apparent. But before the mantle could fall on his shoulders, the business collapsed, and with it went the star's career plan and his stardom.

All self-management, like all management, should be flexible and cautious. In the above case, the disappointed princeling was following the well-known principle that the selection of objectives increases the likelihood of achieving them. It's technically known as "set": the choice of specific objectives helps to focus the mind on spotting the opportunities which, if taken, will lead to the chosen target. But each opportunity has to be evaluated afresh. The question he should have asked was not "Will this job offer make me a chief executive by forty?" but "Is this company the right one for me to join?"

That particular man had so high a judgment of his own qualities that the thought of a mistake, either in the career plan itself or at stages along the chosen path, may never have occurred to him. Here, too, effective self-management can help. It depends, above all, on the proper organization of thought, and no thinking process deserves the name unless it includes the possibility of error.

It is wrong, for a start, to think that being physically unfit, or suffering diminished mental capability, or wasting time are conditions that either do not matter, or are simply incurable. The only difficulty about self-management is not where to start (even though there's so much to be tackled), but where to stop. The ten key areas, however, are ones that only the lucky, the very lucky, managers can afford to ignore: fitness, reading, reckoning, analysis, intuition, simplifying, planning, communicating, self-direction and relating to others.

> A healthy executive mind in a healthy executive body requires a healthy company.

Managers will not perform at their best unless they are physically and mentally fit. The only puzzle about that obvious statement is that many executives either don't believe it, or act that way. The answer probably lies in unwillingness to admit, even to themselves, that self-neglect has a harmful effect on their performance. The delusion is easy to maintain, too, because no measure of performance exists to prove that one man's exceptional success relates to his fitness, while another (perhaps even more triumphant) won *despite* his flabby physique.

It's unlikely that you will find an exceptional success with a flabby mind or personality. But that, too, is a physical statement. One of the more compelling arguments for physical fitness lies in the medical evidence which indicates that physical conditioning improves basic mental performance; and that regular exercise, as well as physical benefits, has psychological ones, largely in reducing stress levels.

The logical starting point is thus the body: not its ability to pass the standard medical check-up—on which many companies insist, with somewhat less good reason than they think. That is one criterion of fitness, true: but as with measures of management, there is some controversy about what the correct measure should be.

Most doctors, however, would at least include cardiovascular performance, meaning the ability of the heart and lungs to process oxygen and pump blood about the system. You can pile upon that all manner of tests of strength and agility, which the middle-aged manager may well fail abysmally. That, too, can be put right by a course of yoga or calisthenics. But a better lead-in must be the now-famous twelve-minute test (you have to complete a one-and-a-half-mile run, or thereabouts) devised by Dr. Kenneth H. Cooper, as the key, not only to a man's current state of fitness, but to Cooper's best-selling aerobics program.

It's hard to remember now, in the age of jogging, with places like Central Park crawling with happy exercisers, that a decade or so back the running executive was all but unknown. Running is by far the simplest way of achieving the thirty points total (equal to four of those twelve-minute, mile-and-a-half runs) that is Cooper's recommended weekly dose of exercise.

Managers who swallow that dose and little more are unlikely to develop the assorted ailments, from Achilles tendinitis to black toenails, which afflict those whose competitive urge drives them to greater heights and whose wounds give running a bad name. (The lure is that at ninety points a week, according to some more medical research, you are so conditioned that, because of the law of diminishing returns, only a quite ridiculous level of extra training will get you any fitter.)

Nobody has to run, although running, as every champion knows, is the best general training for any other sport. Swimming, however, vies with running as the top exercise choice. Much less effective in use of time, swimming is possibly even better for the heart and lungs, while far less apt to result in injury. However, it is much less convenient—unless you have a pool, sea, river or lake in your backyard.

Walking, too, is excellent, but more extravagant still on time. A very brisk walker would need to cover three miles five times a week to reach his thirty points. Squash or handball and cycling also get Cooper's approval—but devotees of golf or tennis are in for shocks if they believe that a round or a set, no matter how competitive, does much for their cardio-vascular condition.

Both these popular managerial sports, of course, can be powerful antidotes to stress: taking the mind off business to concentrate on the game. However, vigorous exercise, with its burning up of adrenalin, is even more effective. All managers who are winners by nature (and maybe even those who are not) require some outlet for the stressful feelings that are inseparable from their work.

Not that managers are *especially* prone to stress, as many comparisons of blue-collar and white-collar workers have shown. But if managers *think* they are under stress, the prophecy can be self-fulfilling. And since stress is common to all those engaged on any ambitious task, it makes sense to arm yourself with stress protection.

Taking regular adequate exercise for granted, the right approach to mental ease is mostly a matter of Eastern magic and Western sense. Donald Norfolk, in his book, *Executive Stress*, has spelled out this response:

1. Use proven relaxation techniques.
2. Live for the moment.
3. Take many, ample breaks for relaxation.
4. Slow down when danger signals appear.

The specific relaxation techniques in this list are those which cause most trouble—but only to the uninitiated. It's a stark, useful fact that anybody can relax at any time by following what sounds like an absurd, almost childish routine.

Simply sit or lie comfortably. Breathe in, long and comfortably, making the abdomen rise and fall deeply and easily. Direct your mind to your right foot as you breathe in. As you breathe out, tell the right foot to relax. Repeat the process, right to left, ending with the facial muscles. If you have not already relaxed into quasi-sleep (which may well have happened), continue to relax while breathing as before; only, say "one" to yourself every time you breathe out.

This routine is child's play, both in itself and in comparison to the highly developed exercises of the Eastern mystics. But it should work like magic. For instance, taken before an important, testing speech, the dose will often produce a better, calmer, more dynamic performance than any drug: even the beta-blockers. Many people "meditate," using the above technique or something similar, every day—and it is certain that everybody needs a daily switch-off in order to achieve their best during switched-on periods.

There seems to be an analogy between this need and the evidence showing that many short holidays or breaks are more effective than one long vacation. The mind and body are not designed to maintain peak performance for indefinite, continuous periods. All human beings have a breaking point, which can be reached relatively quickly—although the danger signs (such as disturbed sleep) usually appear well before the ultimate crisis.

From the individual's point of view, that's the moment to slacken off the daily routine, even if a complete break is not possible. From the organization's viewpoint, that's the moment to review the circumstances which have brought the stressed individual to the risk of breakdown. The good company "stresses" people in the sense that it expects and gets the best that they can achieve. It does not "stress" them in the sense that their efforts burn out the psyche.

Apart from the humanistic angle, any such policy is self-defeating: people who are burning out will not be able to provide their best. Any company where stress-breakdown symptoms are commonplace will not solve the problem by linking its suffering executives to a biofeedback machine which enables them to monitor and control their stress responses. It is the organization itself which needs the biofeedback. A healthy executive mind in a healthy executive body demands a healthy company—and one of the manager's prime targets must always be to build an organization fit for fit people to work in.

All managers, like it or not, are in the business of words.

A fit company is one where it pays to think and to be intelligent, but not necessarily hyper-intelligent. Great mental powers, on the face of it, should be more valuable in management than any other attribute. Since managing is strongly intellectual in character—all to do with ideas and plans, methodology and alternatives, articulation and communication —great minds should by rights be its greatest practitioners. But it's a piece of folk wisdom that brilliant minds seldom make first-class executives, and that highly effective businessmen (especially the entrepreneurial type) often have only mediocre intellects.

The confusion is similar to the popular misconception about I.Q. tests. The standard tests measure a broad range of ability, heavily weighted towards literacy and numeracy, and all abstract, not applied. The supreme examples of human intellect (like the theoretical work of Einstein) are also abstract in nature, even if their results are concrete. Business management is practical: there is seldom any equivalent to the "elegant" solution of the physicist or the mathematician.

Making things and people behave in the way you want is often an inelegant process. The successful, apparently none too intelligent manager is probably highly accomplished at some key aspect of his work—just as there are many people who score hopelessly on an I.Q. test, but who can run rings around any intellectual when coping with an internal combustion engine.

The manager does not need mental pyrotechnics. A marvelous memory is not wonderfully useful, although simple memory training provides a valuable tool and a convenient way of showing adults that their brain capacity did not begin to die with childhood. Ask a manager if he can write down ten objects on a piece of paper and simultaneously memorize them so effectively that he can recite them backwards or forwards, and any way around. It sounds a tall order but is actually an easy trick: the technique is simply to associate each object with the numbers one to ten, either by a visual link (one = stick) or a verbal one (one = gun).

The point is not only that the associative method is an

excellent way of remembering anything from telephone numbers to lecture keynotes (which it is); more, the exercise proves that mental powers, no less than a golf swing, can be improved by coaching at any age. Good memory is managerially useful because it keeps in ready access the information which the manager needs; it capitalizes on his reading, since what is read is no use unless either remembered or recorded; and it is the key to the understanding of figures, on which all business measurement depends.

When the mind is analyzing a statistical report, it's the short-term memory that establishes the comparisons between the figures presented, and the longer-term memory that tests them against previously established criteria. That's why the numerically educated manager with a scientific, accounting or engineering background has a flying start over an arts graduate, who has never been familiar with the language of numbers, and whose memory is not trained to register them.

Hence the "figure-blind" manager, who may be exceptionally able at his job, but has a mathematical memory so defective that he cannot add columns of figures and cannot recall the right number of zeros in a sum of money. People like that suffer not from inability, but atrophy, "lack of exercise." Force them to master figures and eventually, if only with much pain, they will do so—especially when they learn the easy short-cuts (like, that rounding off even the largest numbers to two digits causes only a tiny loss of accuracy in addition).

What's true of reckoning is true of reading and, to a lesser extent, of writing: fear and unfamiliarity cause problems which better techniques can overcome. Reading (especially of reports and letters) is a substantial part of a manager's work, and most managers complain that they do not have time to read still more—the magazines, books and papers which land on their desks and then disappear unread. Yet only a minority of managers even know how fast they read (which is a truly vital statistic), or have ever done anything to raise that speed (500 words per minute, or twice the norm, is easily within range).

Since higher speed, experiment shows, goes hand in hand with better comprehension and retention, sloppy reading is an unforgivable omission. Proper training works quick and painless wonders. Even simple elimination of bad habits, like going back over passages or words already read (known as regression), will raise reading speed by as much as a third.

In *The Brain Book*, the consultant Peter Russell gives, in addition to eliminating regression, several other hints which will help to produce spectacular gains in reading speed. You can train the eye to take in more words at each of the so-called fixations, or halts on the line, which are the only way of taking in written information. But you don't have to get a fix on every word; peripheral vision will absorb several words to right and left of the fixated ones. Use a guide—a pencil, say—and run it down the center of the page. By following that guide, you not only avoid regression, but you will also make full use of the peripheral effect.

The loss of comprehension will be far less severe than most people would suppose, partly because much of the wording on any printed page is redundant. As Russell writes, "every fifth word . . . be omitted from a . . . without losing the meaning." You will have grasped his meaning perfectly, thus proving his point. Another useful piece of advice is to preview —to go over the material swiftly beforehand. One benefit of this swift survey is to identify the passages which can safely be left out entirely, thus producing the fastest conceivable reading time: none at all.

The more useful written information the mind can cover, the more material it has for use in the basic intellectual work of the manager, which is to apply rational thought processes to verified data in order to establish the logical procedures that will lead to rationally chosen results.

The mechanics of that process will be discussed in the

next chapter. But thought is inseparable from words. Thinking cannot be shared, nailed down or communicated save by language. *All* managers, like it or not, are in the word business. One difficulty in picking men for jobs, indeed, is that verbal dexterity, on paper and in conversation, passes for talent. Few selectors find it easy to believe that any manager who talks well is incompetent. But words can be used very well to cover up lack of thought (all too many newspaper editorials confirm the existence of this verbal Watergate). Many articulate managers are only good at articulating.

Not that fluency is useless. On the contrary, it's a skill of great value to executives, provided they are genuine managers, and a skill which it pays to develop. Just as reading speed can be improved by exercises and techniques, so can speaking and writing performance. There are tricks of the trade, like using a simple form of speed writing, which can raise longhand speed to that of a highly competent typist.

Dictation, however, is far faster than any manual method, and the technique of writing with the voice, if developed by practice with a tape recorder, kills two birds with one stone, helping the writer and the speaker alike. You start with a target well above people's normal speed of report writing—say, 250 words in a quarter of an hour, and build up from there. In theory you should be able to manage 400 words in *two and a half minutes*—that being the speed of a broadcast—provided the tongue does not start to run ahead of the mind.

Good management writing obviously has to keep the mind in conscious control. The writing must "say" exactly what the author means. A natural style, keeping close to normal speech, using short words and direct sentences, and as few words as possible, is the best style. In correcting what you have written, start by trying to cut words: the cuts always improve style and usually clarity as well.

The bosses who demand that reports and replies be kept to one side of paper have the right idea. Some subjects cannot be covered with brevity. But the effort to be brief is a well-tried method of bringing mental faculties under control to improve their effective use. As a mental power, it does not rank with total recall, or the ability to complete complex long-division sums in the head. But concentration on what the mind is doing and why is much more important than any such pyrotechnics—and it is the beginning of that successful organization of the internal self which is the source of external success.

> *How managers organize their own time and the work done within it is the biggest single determinant of their success.*

The basic management techniques have nothing to do with the organization, but everything to do with organizing. How managers organize their own time and the work done within it is the biggest single determinant of their success. A whole book could be written on the subject of time—and many have been. But few authors have added much to the terse, wise advice of Peter Drucker, a thinker whose own time has been expertly deployed for decades.

Time is a precious resource whose use should be analyzed like that of money (which is time), or energy (which is time). Time's future use cannot be planned without accurate knowledge of the current usage. That means keeping a time-log, or having someone do that tedious job. With your actual days spread on the table, Drucker's three questions, which were the basis for the organization quiz in Chapter 3, can be applied to the individual.

1. What am I doing that really does not need to be done at all—by me or anybody else?
2. Which of the activities on my time-log could be handled by somebody else just as well—if not better?
3. What do I do that wastes the time of others?

The answers self-evidently lead to action. Everything unnecessary is scrapped. What should be delegated, or passed on, is. What wastes the time of others—like demands for reports that are redundant—is dropped, too.

Large areas of the day are almost sure to be misused. That is a matter for rejoicing (since you can now redeploy the wasted hours) and for understanding (because the reasons are universal). Just as all corporate activities silt up with inefficiencies over time, so do human lives. The only real difficulty springs from the involvement of others in Drucker's questions. You may be wasting *their* time—but somebody will be wasting *yours*. If that means a hierarchical superior, how can you stop the waste?

The evidence shows that the question is relatively unimportant: far more of the typical executive's time is wasted and interrupted by those *below*. This problem can be dealt with in two ways: by setting aside specific times of your day or week for specific individuals or general access; and by developing your skills in answering Drucker's second question—the delegation of needed work to others. The sleeper in that question, though, is the condition on which it depends: that the delegatees be as good at the job, or better, than you are.

First, it is hard to admit that anybody is your match. If not, should they be? Are they the wrong people, or have you trained or developed them inadequately? Is that because subconsciously you do not want to let go? If so, that is no way to win.

These questions take the use of time right to the heart of management. The English expert Mark Brown has pointed out that mental "set" considerably affects the chances of successful delegation. If when giving somebody one of "your" tasks (actually, it does not *belong* to you at all), you doubt that he will do it to your satisfaction, the delegatee's faults will leap out at you—and you will ignore his success at, say, getting to within 5 percent of your standard. Perhaps nearly is not nearly enough—but the learning curve, the improvement gained by experience, given time to operate, could well take that man to 100 percent as the number of times he attempts the task increases.

Conversely, when necessity demands handing over a job, the mental "set" immediately sees the man's virtues and ignores his blemishes. Often, in these circumstances, the man handing over boasts how much better than himself the new fellow is at the job. It is a harmless enough brag, reinforcing the egos of both parties. But delegation is unlikely to succeed unless the delegator has the determination, or "set," to make it do so.

If the disposable work includes meetings, so much the better, for meetings are great thieves of time. To succeed, they require more careful planning than any other use of the day: they rarely receive it. No meeting, even a regular weekly or monthly conference, should lack a precise objective, an answer to the key questions: (a) Why are we meeting at all? (b) What should we have achieved by the end of the meeting?

If the reason and objective are truly vital, then time is not of the essence: if an all-day or all-week meeting is needed to decide the company's whole future, so be it. But if the matter is routine, always limit the numbers to those who really have to be there, and always fix and stick to a clear, short timetable. Do not treat the meeting as a debating society, either. Since everybody attending is there for a reason—if not, it's a bad meeting—*use* their time. Get a contribution from each in turn, and fight the Pareto factor—which means that one of the people at a meeting of five will be doing four-fifths of the talking.

If the schedule has so many meetings that other activities are put under pressure, something is badly awry. The system must contain slack. Emergencies and other unscheduled events are sure to occur. The efficient schedule always contains elements of flexibility in order to cope. The schedule should always be built around your own basic time unit: that is, the span over which you can maintain unbroken concentration without hitting any kind of fatigue.

Experiments with students show that this span can be as little as twenty minutes and is rarely longer than forty. Managers find this difficult to accept, although their time-logs probably show that uninterrupted periods of twenty minutes are most uncommon in the typical day. Whatever the span, that's how to divide the day: allowing short breaks between time units for doing nothing at all, for reasons to be explained below.

To that first rule of a well-managed schedule add these:

1. Fit timings to yourself and the necessities.
2. Stick to the timetable where possible—but not slavishly.
3. Reduce interruptions, by making appointments for regular interrupters and scheduling "not to be disturbed" periods and *"to be disturbed"* ones.
4. Allocate time for the unexpected.
5. Allocate time for the undone.
6. Expect backsliding.

The sixth point is easily ignored; the new, tight schedule will silt up just like the old. It's human limitation rearing its head; the fact, again, that the mechanism cannot be run flat-out indefinitely. That's part of the function of the little breaks for doing nothing at all. They can act as buffer zones for work which is unexpected or overruns. But their most important use, as the work with students has shown, is to increase the number of high points of concentration and to allow the brain time to sort itself out after a concentrated period of attention.

By a break, as by a short holiday, the strain on the human machine is removed, and the mind, by relaxing and shifting its attention, can prepare for a new bout of activity. That way the manager can hope to achieve the most with the least expenditure of his personal capital, which is as excellent a definition of good management as can be found.

II

QUESTIONS, ANSWERS AND PROBLEMS

Tom Watson Senior, who broke away from National Cash Register to found I.B.M., had many right ideas. One of the brightest and best, enshrined on the placard he had placed on every desk, is that the essence of a manager's task is to think. An excellent head of a thriving corporation, famed for the pressure he applies to his managers in face-to-face sessions, likewise protests mildly that he is only trying to make them *think*. The whole import of managing to win is that constant thought is required, or constant questioning, or the use of the word "why?"—the launching pad of all wisdom.

There are other short probing words: what? when? how? where? and who? Unless these words are constantly in the manager's mind, he is not managing—merely responding to events. He is not thinking. Since thought, or the imposition of order and organization on events, is hard work and sometimes hurtful (when you prove that you have been a fool), reluctance to think is understandable. *It is never excusable.*

The process of asking questions and getting answers is wrongly regarded as a method of solving *problems*. That, in itself, is bad thinking. Effective thinking prevents problems arising. Frequently, a business problem is the direct result of inefficient thought. Good thinking starts by distinguishing between a question and a problem. What system of management accounting will give us effective control of profitability and cash flow? That is a *question*. If the company does not ask, or does not get the right answer, and the cash outflow leads to a liquidity crisis, that is a *problem*—and how!

Real problems, in this sense, can always be averted. In addition to the inevitable internal failures, suppliers or customers can cause havoc outside; out there, too, the actions of competitors, or the impact of economic forces, can upset the most carefully stacked apple cart. But the thinking manager constantly seeks to find reality: what is *happening*, outside and inside the firm. He builds contingency planning into every decision. If he is sometimes caught unawares, he does not stay ignorant for long.

One large company, according to the consultant and author Simon Majaro, is so obsessed by the negative effect of "problems" that it has banned the word. Its executives are exhorted to think positively; they are only allowed to think about "opportunities." Majaro, finding one executive in this corporation in a dismal state, brow furrowed with anxiety, asked if the man had any problems. The executive shied away from the forbidden word: "Hell, no. But, God, do I have a lot of opportunities."

It is a story full of morals. You cannot make problems go away by calling them something else. But it is right (as in this company, as in I.B.M.) to stress the power of positive thinking. By question and answer, and their partners, trial and error, the success-ridden company can turn even its most severely negative "problem" into an opportunity for moving forward. Sakura, the Japanese company mentioned in Chapter 1, made an apparently daunting problem, the fact that its marketing image and market share alike were hopelessly inferior to those of Fuji, into the springboard for a superb rethinking of its product strategy. Accentuate the positive with sound enough thought, and you eliminate the negative.

> **The definition of the perfectly right question is one that answers itself.**

In my book *The Naked Investor*, I postulated a few years ago that the most profitable quarry for the private investor was the nice, fat anomaly. An anomaly is an exceptional event with no evident explanation. In the world of investment, find the explanation and you may find a fortune: like Douglas Pope, the obscure Canadian investor who wondered just why and how an even more obscure railroad was able to pay a $6 dividend year in, year out, although it never made a profit.

The answer turned out to be that in 1884 the road had leased to the Canadian Pacific 800 miles of right of way—forever. Pope's further inquiries revealed that the C.P. directors had fallen into the easy, but bad, habit of regarding their landlord's property as their own—even selling land that did not belong to them. At the last count, Pope's discovery had made the shares in his control worth some $23 million; and his successful lawsuit had landed the C.P. with a possible liability of a cool billion.

Anomalies in commerce can be worth as much for those who, like Pope, ask the right questions. As in his case, any good question springs from good observation. Most scientific advance has stemmed from exactly the same source. The process of asking profitable questions starts from noticing what is going on: what might be called the Pope phenomenon.

This explains in large measure why the Japanese have been so successful in penetrating Western markets. They have never been afraid to ask and answer big questions beginning with Why? For example, "Why has 35mm photography not become a mass market?" Today the question sounds stupid. But long after the Second World War, 35mm was still a specialist's market.

Since all film, not just 35mm, had to be developed and enlarged, there was no answer to why—except that the established manufacturers (the Germans and Eastman Kodak) had failed to realize that camera systems capable of taking up to thirty-six exposures on one film had an immense advantage.

Chapter 1 of this book suggested that the Japanese as a nation had an immense advantage, too—that of being outsiders in the world economy. This may explain why an excellent work on using questions as a competitive tool comes from a Japanese author—Konichi Ohmae. This McKinsey consultant wrote a local best seller called "The Corporate Strategists." He gives two easy examples, in the same article from which the Sakura case came, of questions leading to profitable answers.

The first involves an electric-appliance maker, whose blankets carried the familiar warning "Do not lie on this blanket." An engineer asked the obvious question (it's one which had in fact occurred to me, with no profit, several times): "*Why* can't we design a blanket that is safe to sleep on?" It turned out that the firm could: what's more, since the safe under-blanket was insulated by the other bedclothes, it wasted far less heat.

That question is similar in nature to one asked by a camera firm: "*Why* don't cameras have a built-in flash, instead of a separate, troublesome attachment?" As Ohmae points out, "To ask the question was to answer it." Just as in the case of Mr. Pope. *The definition of the perfectly right question is one that answers itself.*

In the case of the camera flash, the consequent innovation, says Ohmae, "swept the Japanese medium-price single lens market." But another of his cases is more typical of the situations—or, rather, the questions—that firms customarily ignore. The company made trucks. Somebody in its management noted an anomaly. The salesmen made most of their calls between three and six in the afternoon. "Yet analysis showed that this was precisely the period when their success rate—i.e., the number of calls resulting in a sale—was lowest." In other words, the salesmen seemed to be working hardest in the very hours when they were least likely to succeed.

Why?, in this case, didn't have to be answered, because the observed anomaly suggested its own response. The company decided that salesmen no longer had to report to the office before and after work. Instead, they were told to go straight from home to their first calls and to take their free time in the unproductive afternoons. The result, says Ohmae, was "a significant share improvement for the company," though he does not say *how* significant. All the same, the real significance of the anecdote lies in the incisive questioning of an everyday activity that went on without anybody ever wondering if it made any sense.

Such wondering can be built into a company by a process akin to zero-based budgeting. The original form which so captivated Jimmy Carter when he was Governor of Georgia is not too promising—which explains why, according to one report, its main positive result was to narrow the width of grass mowed along the state's highways. Z.B.B. has its main application in overhead activities, but if overheads are too high in relation to other costs then much more is at fault in the company than its budgeting procedure.

All operations, especially the products and/or services offered, should be systematically submitted to questioning. Why are we doing it this way? Do we have to? What alternatives are there? Do we have to do it at all?

Flashes of entrepreneurial insight can arise without systematic inquiry. No better example exists than the question asked by Kemmons Wilson, one of the Holiday Inns founders, in his private funeral venture: "*Why* are bodies buried horizontally?" There was no reason; vertical burial proved a far more effective use of space. Such inspirations do not often come to corporate managers. But systematic questioning will often yield the same kind of benefits as those experienced by Wilson and recounted by Ohmae. Inspiration, however, is not in the nature of the process: it's *inspection* that gets the results.

Good questions spring from intelligent, acute analysis. There's a marvelous, sad story about the dying Gertrude Stein, who, on her deathbed, asked her constant companion, Alice B. Toklas, "What is the answer?" Struck dumb with grief, Alice could only shake her head. "Well, then," said the indomitable Gertrude, "what is the question?" Her remark deserves to be as immortal, in management terms, as I.B.M.'s "Think."

> *A problem is far more likely to find a solution than a solution is to find a problem.*

The statement that the right question is the one that generates the right answer sounds like a tautology. But the basic sense comes across sharply from two contrasting cases in the automotive industry. The first is that of the Chrysler Corporation. Year after year, Chrysler has been a dismal third in the American car industry. You could argue (following the researches of the Boston Consulting Group) that Chrysler's normally poor profits directly reflect its low market share; just as the normally high profitability of General Motors reflects the opposite condition.

But the Boston explanation is not good enough. If it were, Sakura would never have increased its share of the Japanese color-film market, and Peugeot, only recently a one-model firm, would not, as mentioned before, be Europe's second-largest car company, having got there, in part, by absorbing Chrysler's unhappy European operations. The latter activities were miserable because the American management, abroad as at home, had never asked the right question, which guaranteed that it could never achieve the right answer.

Chrysler thought of itself as competing across the board with General Motors and Ford. In reality it was so far behind that *specialization was the only possible answer.*

If Chrysler cars had earned a higher price and cachet than Fords or Chevrolets, or Buicks, Oldsmobiles and Pontiacs, the penalty imposed by a lower market share would have been overcome. Peugeot, starting from a much worse market share, arrived at its present strength by stressing quality—as noted in Chapter 8—and by steadily extending its image on each side of the original, solitary, medium-price, middle-class model.

Chrysler never appeared to ask the right question: "How do we differentiate ourselves from G.M. and Ford?" As it happens, the latter's best-remembered products, the Thunderbird and the Mustang, both as valuable in upgrading the whole Ford image as in themselves, were exactly the kind of answer which Chrysler should have sought. But Chrysler kept on chasing a mirage: the hope of competing successfully against the two domestic giants on the same terms, when a much smaller base doomed it to failure. Even Chrysler's European purchases of Rootes in Britain and Simca in France seem to have had a similar mistaken motive. Ford and G.M. had two-country European operations based on down-market models—and Chrysler decided to buy itself the same.

Suppose that Chrysler's management had set out, instead, to have the most profitable car company in the United States and in Europe. From that objective—a feasible one—a wholly different series of questions and answers would have flowed. (The Americans then might not have bought Simca and Rootes, but might well have tried to purchase Peugeot.)

The history of invention shows this same phenomenon of right objectives leading to right answers. Profitable inventions have customarily arrived through seeking a means to an end (or a route to an objective). World-beating ideas seldom arise from seeking a use for some material or application that has arrived out of the scientific blue.

The fact that a problem is far more likely to find a solution than a solution is to find a problem has innumerable illustrations. The idea is not fashionable. Modern thinkers about thought (like Edward de Bono) have tended to emphasize the unstructured ways of finding answers: the lateral, or sideways, route, as opposed to the linear or straightforward one. The reasoning is that thinkers become prisoners of their past thought patterns. Had the Chrysler executives, in other words, been asked to draw up a plan for a quite different company and industry, but in an identical position, they might immediately have escaped from the confines of their own corporation and reached the right answer.

There is truth in this. What would the results have been if Chrysler executives had been asked to dream up a corporate plan for Number Four, American Motors, and vice versa? Would both companies have done much better—or failed again? Whatever the answer, the thought is truly lateral—the idea of two sets of competing executives swapping problems. But the lateral leap has validity only in the light of a strictly orthodox analysis and objective. Since neither company had proved capable of posing the right questions or finding the right answer or choosing the right direction by a logical route, an apparently illogical one was the only choice left.

Staying with the car industry, the most lateral answer that could be asked for was provided by the designer Sir Alec Issigonis when working on his Mini—a design principle without which the major part of the British car industry would long since have been dead and buried. Unable to fit the engine into his target dimensions in the normal, straight-line mode, Issigonis turned the power unit *sideways*. Yet whether he arrived at this solution by lateral inspiration, or by conventional engineering logic, is not the real question.

First, Issigonis would not have found the answer without the objective—keeping the car to a given overall length. Once the question was phrased in those terms, the number of possible answers was rapidly reduced to one. But life and engineering alike offer very few perfect solutions. The one which Issigonis found was no exception to the rule that no pearl is without price. A sideways engine meant extra cost, since the unconventional drive to the front wheels was considerably more complex than a conventional layout.

The logic of this fact pointed in inexorable, linear fashion to making the Mini *more*, not less expensive than its competitors. But the mundane managers who employed the genius Issigonis thought that his new, revolutionary car would never sell unless it was cheap. *They asked the wrong question*, as events proved, because, at its low price, the Mini, despite excellent sales, never made an adequate profit.

That criticism presupposes, in turn, that the Mini-makers had decided on a corporate target from which a profit objective for the new model could have been derived. That, of course, was the opposite of the case. In the Mini, those managers had a once-in-a-lifetime opportunity, the answer to a question which had long plagued them and was to plague their successors in all the years ahead: how to establish a clear, profitable identity in the European volume-car market. They missed the opportunity for lack of objectives and objectivity alike—just like Chrysler in the United States. Managers who do not know which questions to ask, even when they have stumbled across the right answers, surely deserve to lose.

> *It always pays when confronted with an apparent problem to ask: "Is this a problem or a question?"*

Airline managers are lucky in one respect. They have glamour—or at least their business has. Also, it is relatively straightforward: a single product, a known cost structure, and a self-contained market. There is no real competition, save from other airlines, and no rival is likely to steal a competitive march for more than the briefest moment. Their biggest marketing problem is thus how to differentiate between their identical services—if it is a problem, which is doubtful.

Several studies have indicated that, when homogeneous services are offered in competition, choice tends to be dominated by convenience, not by personal preference. So it probably makes little difference, in the long run, whether a Braniff paints its airliners in assorted colors or some Asian line dangles Eastern promise in its ads. The airline which is flying where you want when you want wins nearly every time.

That still leaves how you can differentiate between such products as an interesting and, if answered correctly, profitable question. But it pales into total irrelevance beside the real and horrendous problem which the airlines have faced periodically—an alarming inability to make money.

It is a fatal defect in any industry, but especially one where the items of plant come in such expensive dollops: like $75 million, the going rate for a Boeing 747. The root of the problem is buried there, in the fact that each new plane not only represents a massive financing cost, driving the companies still further into the arms of the banks, but also produces a large increment in capacity; one Jumbo can carry 240,000 passengers in a year. Every airline's business revolves about its break-even point. If passengers take a given percentage of capacity, the flight makes money; below that certain point, it loses.

Increase the airline's capacity by more than the rise in passenger traffic, and its managers have a cruel problem. Each wave of re-equipment with new and bigger jets has exacerbated the problem in the past, to the point where the major American airlines have often had the greatest difficulty in showing any profit at all—even though, as the jets have grown bigger, the break-even point has fallen lower and lower.

The three possible answers to a problem of this nature, as any experienced plant manager knows, are inescapable. If any factory is underloaded, you can (1) take machines out of commission (i.e., restrict capacity); or (2) take extra business at any price that more than covers the direct costs of labor, material, etc.; or (3) effect some combination of the first two.

The crux lies in marginal costing. If the machine is breaking even, with all capital costs and overheads covered, piling on more business at lower prices makes basic (but only basic) sense. It does so even if the fixed costs are *not* being covered by the existing load, so long as the extra, marginal business makes some contribution to those fixed costs. Now, marginal costing can create problems as easily as solve them. Used to excess, it can undermine a whole market. The limiting factor is what *average* price the manager is prepared to accept. But the established airlines, while they talked frequently about their marginal difficulty, and the revenue lost by flying empty seats around the world, did precious little about it.

Their favored, unthinking solution was to maintain the highest possible average price under the protection of a government-backed cartel. This ran counter to all the evidence. The facts showed that, like every other form of mass consumer market, air travel is highly sensitive to price. Lower the price and you raise the demand: higher prices, by the same token, reduce demand.

In the case of air travel, practical proof was provided by outsiders—and at the airlines' great expense. Every cartel creates outside it a posse of venturers eager to seize the business which the cartel is restricting. Charter companies, genuine and phony, began to take advantage of the airlines' unused capacity. By providing cheap travel, the charterers earned some fast and impressive fortunes (until they made the fatal mistake of providing the travel too cheap and buying too much air and hotel capacity in advance).

The inroads of charter travel—even though the airlines joined the game themselves—still failed to make their executives face the basic logic of their new equipment. They thought of the wide-bodied jets as lowering the break-even point, and thus enabling flights to make money with fewer passengers at the same high prices. *The logic of lower costs is lower prices.* This is what Sir Freddie Laker proved when, against bitter opposition from governments and airlines alike, he made money flying people across the Atlantic at a mere £59.

Since it cost only $38,000 to take a DC-10 across the Atlantic and back when Laker's Skytrain service began, he did not see that any great risk was involved. As he expected, the established airlines could not allow a rival scheduled—and crowded—service to undercut them. As he also expected, the combined result of all the cheap fare schemes that immediately burgeoned was a general, huge increase in demand, not only across the Atlantic, but on any route where lower fares were tried.

As the wide-bodied jets changed from comfortably empty to uncomfortably full, a wondrous thing came to pass: the airlines for a while made the abundant profits that eluded them in the past. The crisis of competition proved something which perhaps was not obvious: that people could be charged markedly different prices for the same seats on the same flights. But something which should have been very obvious was also demonstrated—a plane carrying 400 people at an average 40 percent below tariff earns more revenue than one carrying 200 people at tariff—and any extra revenue must fly straight through to the bottom line of profit.

The poor profit performance of the airlines thus was often not a problem of excess capacity. *It was a problem of excess price*, and a self-created one. It always pays when confronted with an apparent problem to ask:

1. Is this a problem or a question?
2. If it is a problem, what makes the matter so grave?
3. Are we doing anything of our own free will that is contributing to the problem?
4. Can we undo what is aggravating the difficulty?
5. If competitive factors are involved, are all the competitors taking the same view of the market or industry?
6. Is it possible to take a different view?

The car industry, which has provided many texts for this chapter, has a beauty here. Like all car manufacturers with plants in Britain, Ford Motor has had appalling trouble getting continuous strike-free production and acceptable quality and volume from its assembly operations. The problem appeared clear—the interruptions lost output (and thus customers and profits) and caused endless diversion of management time. Nothing could have sounded graver. But Ford finally saw that *the problem would disappear if the company stopped attempting to solve it.* Whether or not the assembly operations could have been raised to Continental levels of efficiency (a very doubtful proposition), Ford didn't actually have to achieve this result.

So the company shifted its emphasis. Where its British competition continued to see a problem—that of getting higher productivity from United Kingdom car assembly—Ford saw a question: "How do we get high profits from our overall British operation?" The answer was to manufacture car components in the United Kingdom, which is profitable business, and to import cars from Europe to fill the United Kingdom supply line. In both 1977 and 1978 Ford consequently made unheard-of profits: roughly a quarter of a billion pounds in years when it lost thousands of cars through breakdowns in labor relations—which stayed just as bad as ever. It is commonly said that you cannot run away from trouble. Nonsense. That is exactly how to convert a problem into a question, and the question into a winning answer.

12

THE DAYS OF DECISION

Management purists don't in general love the pressure of European trade unions and Social Democrats for more worker influence on corporate affairs. But the particular objection is that labor's insistence on a greater say in "decision-making" doesn't fit the management realities. The phrase suggests a periodic meeting of top executives at which, one by one, the big decisions are taken, perhaps by vote—a vote in which the anointed representatives of labor could easily share.

Even if some companies do sometimes proceed in this way, they shouldn't. Decisions should evolve in a continuum. Most of the things which really matter in companies are continuous, anyway. The discontinuous decisions are very few and far between (and often, the more discontinuous they are, the more disastrous). Where unions intervene, they are likely to try to impose discontinuity for their own purposes. This happened at Volkswagen when the union representatives on the supervisory board opposed a management plan for large layoffs. The plan was inevitable; it had evolved as a logical response to the awful straits of Germany's leading car maker—stuck with an obsolescent, largely single-product range in the middle of the worst world recession since the thirties.

The result of union intervention was one of the largest one-year losses in industrial history. At this point, the Federal government made it clear that V.W. either sank or swam through its own efforts. The alarmed unions dropped their opposition, and a duly slimmed-down V.W. completed a phenomenal turnaround. The management cut back the Beetle from the major part of its output at the start of the year to a minor share at its end, and made up the difference with a wholly new and highly successful range of models.

The decision to launch those new cars shouldn't have been difficult. For years, the Beetle's unavoidable demise—it was old-fashioned, slow and cramped—had been drawing uncomfortably near. V.W.'s unprecedented plant conversion, a superb management feat, came at the eleventh hour—and eleventh-hour decisions, however well executed, are bad ones. Decisions should be taken in good time before crisis forces a crash program on the company.

The well-managed firm builds its probable next decision into the one just taken. The day a new model is launched as the brightest and best, the company should already be thinking ahead to the next modification or elaboration; even as far ahead as eventual replacement of the new wonder. The plans, of course, may have to be modified as time proceeds and circumstances (like competing products) change; but the company still goes on making its decisions as continuous as possible.

In appointing personnel, too, the question isn't only who to place in the job *now*, it's also: "Who should follow?" and "When?" Correct decisions are reached more certainly if they are anticipated, and if the choices spring from a continuing, challenging appraisal of everything the company does—especially the activities nobody has questioned for years. If somebody hadn't had the wit to inquire into the anomaly, that Japanese truck company mentioned in the previous chapter would still be sending its salesmen out in force during the very hours when they are least likely to make sales.

When managers leave some aspect of a company alone, they are taking, often unthinkingly, a decision: that no significant benefit can be obtained by looking at the activity with critical, fresh eyes. That's unlikely to be true. But you can't win—or do—them all.

Omissions, accidental or deliberate, and failures, partial or complete, are inseparable from any human activity. Where the winning manager differs is in making priority choices about what degrees of failure are tolerable and in what areas.

The loser never makes any such choice. If he succeeds, it's often unnoticed. Planning is about altering the odds in favor of success. Fortune favors the prepared mind and the prepared company; and better decisions flow—continuously—from better preparation.

> *Any worthwhile routine will include the PROBE elements—Plan strategy, Review, Operating plans, and Budgets Evolved from the latter.*

Man can't foretell the future. This doesn't and shouldn't stop him from trying, but it should prevent the folly of treating an intelligent best guess as a fact. Disenchantment with unreliable forecasts, and realization of the increasing uncertainty of all prediction in a volatile world, was one reason why General Electric decided on a major reform of its planning. An earlier chapter explored G.E.'s procedure in terms of organizing each "strategic business unit" around its market. But there's more to it than that.

Every planning effort worth the name hinges on some central aspect of the company. A car firm probably plans around its new-model launches (if it doesn't, it ends up like

British Leyland, with no new models and not much of a company either).

In G.E.'s case, the hinge is capital allocation among the units, which is a cardinal aspect of a multidivisional, multiproduct holding company. The units at G.E. were forecasting so inaccurately that "the malfunction," wrote John Thackray in *Management Today*, "was ruining G.E. capital-allocation decisions."

He mentions the "constant occurrence of what at G.E. is derisively called the 'hockey stick' forecast. A business forecasts its imminent recovery, to justify the spending of more development capital; but every year the recovery is postponed again and the same arguments are made for fresh funds, with the result that the hockey stick gets longer and longer, and the upward hook further away in time." Hockey sticks are of the same ilk as "We've spent so much already, we might as well carry on." Unless challenged, managers will produce the forecasts that serve their interests—not necessarily the company's.

Even from their own point of view, managers are much better off for seeking an accurate understanding of where the business is now and where it is heading. The tool G.E. chose for this worthy purpose can be used by any business, large or small. G.E. thinks its version is the best. But other users of the tool, like Shell, and two firms of consultants, McKinsey and Boston Consulting Group, have equal faith in their variations on the theme. This proud possession is the matrix. Its nine boxes at G.E. analyze the attractions of an industry along with the strengths of each individual business.

The matrix fans use the boxes to sort businesses into three groups. The ones that rank high, the good guys, are reinforced with more investment. The mediocre affairs are supported only with enough capital to keep them going. The dogs are candidates to be sold. If these poor growth prospects (to change animals) can be milked of earnings before divestment or closure, milked they are.

It sounds a trifle mechanistic, and Boston's version, which

equates rates of return with a company's market share, was too mechanical for G.E.'s taste. G.E. goes further and rates the attractions of an industry by things like:

1. Overall size.
2. Market growth and pricing.
3. Market diversity.
4. Competitive structure.
5. Overall industry profitability.
6. The role of technology.
7. Social, environmental, legal and human aspects.

Individual businesses are measured by

1. Relative market share.
2. Product quality.
3. Profitability.
4. Technological strength.
5. Vertical integration.
6. Distribution.

And so on—you can make your own list and your own matrix. That's what Shell did in improving (so it believes) on G.E. It's to be hoped that this device saves Shell from future major embarrassments like its past decision to go into nuclear reactors in partnership with Gulf Oil. Shell now admits that its analysis of the nuclear game was perfunctory. It didn't even realize that the business had four distinct segments, of which Shell (of course) had chosen, with masterly innocence, the least profitable. That mistake cost $250 million, which even for Shell was a major misallocation of capital.

Successful planning avoids such errors by making rigorous analysis part of the routine of the business. The G.E. model won't suit everybody. But any worthwhile routine will include the four PROBE elements:

1. A strategic Plan.
2. Review and challenge of the above.

3. Turning the strategy into short-term Operating plans.
4. Budgets Evolved from the latter.

None of this PROBE procedure, as all budgeting managers know, can be done without effort. In the case of companies as huge as G.E. (with its army of 200 planners) or Shell, the effort and expense can easily be provided. That scale of planning is far beyond most firms' capabilities—but fortunately it isn't needed. What is needed is to overcome the resistance of people in the business (often including the boss) to putting any of their assumptions about the future on paper, to evaluating the products or operations objectively, just like any other portfolio of investments, to testing and criticizing proposals, and to having them tested and criticized in turn.

Don't think that big company pros enjoy the process any more. As G.E.'s top planner, Mike Allen, admits, "When you get to the fourth, fifth and sixth planning cycle in a year, there's a tendency for them to groan, 'not again!' " In fact, many American corporations have said "not again" to the whole business of planning, because of its past disappointments. But the recent results at G.E., which powered through the turbulent period from 1970 to 1977 with doubled sales, plus a strong rise in return on shareholders' investment (from 13.4 to 19.4 percent), show at the least that planning needn't impede better performance. The mistake of the disappointed and disappointing planners, though, was to place too much emphasis on "The Plan." It became a Bible full of fancy figures and unfulfilled promises, which was bound to be falsified by unforeseen events.

A plan is no more than a platform for managing a business more effectively. As with a good budgeting system (which is, of course, a plan), managers should update their thinking periodically as changes in real life validate or invalidate their assumptions. Only a bad manager congratulates himself on "beating the budget" or coming out "ahead of plan." The better performance is what would have been in the plan or budget if a better assessment of the business and its prospects had been made.

What matters most is not whether planned figures have been met or missed, but whether the *absolute* level of performance is satisfactory. That is a basic planning assumption: somebody has to decide, before any approach to the future, just what the company wants to achieve. What *is* satisfactory? In the end, all the sophistication of the G.E. model only supports the simple process of deciding which parts of a business are worth keeping and developing, and which aren't. The next stage is deciding how to develop what's worth keeping.

In the 1970s G.E. slung out its computers, educational equipment and materials, its European consumer outlets, and medical operations in Belgium. Many, many lesser companies have for years kept many even more unsuitable products going for want of systematic thought. If planning only prevented that from happening, it would earn its keep. Properly used, as a way of making managers think, planning can do more still.

> *Even if the idea passes all the tests, the decision phase involves answering a more difficult question. Can we do it?*

Every now and again a company is confronted with a new and totally unpredictable decision. There's no better example than a remarkable saga—now, alas, complete—involving E.M.I. The company had reaped whirlwind profits from a single decision before, when it decided to back an unknown pop group called by the silly name of the Beatles.

But the decision presented few extraneous problems. The Beatles' music was similar in business nature to many other opportunities which E.M.I. had taken with greater or lesser (in this case, much less) success in the past. The music side of the company was geared to exploit pop success. That was its job. The Beatles decision and the organization were one and the same.

Not so with the product called the brain-scanner. This invention sprang from work done by an E.M.I. researcher named Geoffrey Hounsfield, who had been working on the commercial development of automatic electronic pattern recognition for office equipment. In 1967, though, Hounsfield saw that his ideas were highly relevant to the problem of the X-ray. He knew that conventional X-rays conveyed to doctors only 1 percent of the information that was potentially available. The result of Hounsfield's insight was his revolutionary diagnostic machine.

The brain-scanner was a Very Big Idea, not only in technological terms, but commercially. It passed all the preliminary idea-scanner tests with flying colors:

1. Is the product/service an improvement on what is currently available elsewhere?
2. Are there enough people who will pay enough money for the advantages being offered?
3. If we succeed in bringing the product/service to the people at the indicated level, can we expect to make money?

The idea-scanner, however, is only the beginning. Even if the idea passes all three tests, the decision phase involves answering a more difficult question. Can *we* do it? In the case of the Beatles, E.M.I. had no fundamental problems. It could certainly handle the recorded music of a worldwide hit group. But when Hounsfield had his brainwave, E.M.I. was all but non-existent in the field of medical electronics—and even in the field of medicine.

So the question which Hounsfield's technological success forced on E.M.I. was altogether different from anything the group had ever faced: whether to set up a new medical electronics operation, built initially around the single product of the brain-scanner, and competing on an international scale—from the start—with the established giants in the field.

E.M.I. was possibly damned if it did, since the go decision would take it into uncharted territory; and damned if it didn't, since, as one director remarked, it didn't come up with world-beating ideas every day. Not surprisingly, some of the directors wavered unhappily.

My *The Naked Manager* identified a like turning point in the history of two British companies: the Rover car firm and the Beecham Group, famous mainly for consumer products like toiletries. Rover's idea was to launch a new range of saloon cars with a more sporting image, as antidote to and replacement of its existing staid models. The catch was that the investment came to more than the entire shareholders' equity (as did Lockheed's not dissimilar attempt to crack the civil airliner market with the TriStar). Beecham's decision was to explore fermentation chemistry, and, having found a synthetic penicillin family, to launch itself into the prescription drug market in force. Unlike Rover (and Lockheed), Beecham could afford the entrance fee (even though it grossly underestimated the amount).

Both cases differed significantly from E.M.I.'s in nature. Rover, a firm in cars up to its neck, and Beecham, which had begun in medicines (admittedly of the patent, non-prescription variety), had, in the absence of a car like the new 2000 series, or of a strong prescription drug business, serious deficiencies that any ambitious corporate strategist would have sought to correct. E.M.I., like any company, could always have done with a major new division, especially a world-beater; but it didn't have to be *this* particular world-beater, a big idea which was largely unrelated to any aspect of E.M.I.'s current business.

Hounsfield's idea *was* relevant to the company's purposes, capable of being implemented, likely to produce results which would make a measurable difference. That much was certain. But the brain-scanner was also sure to create many entirely new problems, if only because the market was entirely new to E.M.I. It had in the driving seat Dr. John Powell, who, having come from Texas Instruments, knew all about the impact of the big idea in electronics. But medical electronics is a law unto itself.

E.M.I. had to decide between its big idea and a relatively small one—either licensing its invention, or developing the scanner in partnership with another company, presumably a partner established in both the medical and the American markets. The obvious precedent is the Rank-Xerox partnership outside the United States—although it's highly doubtful whether the American side of the Xerox deal would ever have signed had the tiny Haloid Corporation known at that moment what later became clear: that it had a money-printing machine on its hands.

E.M.I. *did* know what it had. It's said that the company also knew that a scant two years were available before competition would enter its market and possibly compromise its pitch. Moreover, only by setting up expensively in the United States could that vital market be developed. E.M.I. knew that the effort to meet demand (hard to assess in advance, but certain to be large) would stretch, possibly overstretch, the available management resources.

The strain on cash resources was relaxed more readily. Once E.M.I., despite all misgivings, had passed the go/no-go point by going, hospitals buying the scanner had to deposit $300,000. That they did so showed the unnatural strength of E.M.I.'s position—unnatural in that it couldn't last. While the going was good, it was better than good: fabulous. After a loss of only £67,000 in the first year, E.M.I.'s brand-new medical division made £23 million of cumulative profit in the next three.

In the next two, alas, it lost all the previous three years' profits, and then some more. About the only warming financial news was settlement for £7.5 million of a patent action against the medical products giant Johnson and Johnson—a suit ending in the kind of reciprocal deal which E.M.I. might have arranged in much earlier days, before trouble pole-axed its profits.

What was that trouble? One, competition in considerable numbers arrived exactly on schedule as had been foreseen by E.M.I., and as was inevitable. *Except that,* two, the competitors offered a technical advance of greater scanning speed, which had (perhaps rightly) been rejected by E.M.I. on grounds of lower image quality. *Except that,* three, the brain-scanner led straight to the whole-body-scanner, foreseen by E.M.I., but where scanning speeds are much more important. *Except that,* four, the body-scanner is less essential than a brain-scanner, and was thus more susceptible to the restraints on capital spending by hospitals, especially in the United States, which were not foreseen by E.M.I. but which, five, dealt a savage blow to the whole market; in which, six, E.M.I. had lost its lead to the competitors, who started later but with formidable advantages in a market they had served for generations.

That surely is the point to which E.M.I. gave insufficient weight. In creating a new market, especially when the whole product field is new to the company, you must be able to afford the cost of staying Number One; remember the rule of thumb that most markets can support only two profitable mainline contenders and one specialist. Rover stayed Britain's largest maker of executive saloons. Beecham established and kept its lead in synthetic penicillins. But E.M.I. wasn't in a position, through no fault of its own, to maintain the same command technologically, geographically and in hospitals.

Managers should pray to be spared these do-or-die, make-or-break, on-off decisions. The natural dynamism of growth will favor the go-ahead all too often. It's hard to check that kind of momentum, but there's an extra question which must be asked before the go. *Will this decision raise more questions than it answers?* After its first three triumphant years, that's what the brain-scanner did for E.M.I. The unanswered questions about its medical division became problems, and any problems that lose £25 million in two years and end up with the company's takeover and the sale of its medical side (by Thorn) can't be described as small.

> *Making the decision guilty until proved innocent is an excellent way of avoiding voluntary defeats.*

Why did E.M.I. (fatefully) go it alone in scanners? Why did Shell (mistakenly) take the decision to plunge into nuclear energy? Why did V.W. (rightly) decide to change its entire model line-up in a single year? Why did Dunlop's board (disastrously) decide to merge with Pirelli? In some of these instances, it's tempting to add, "Why on earth?" But in disasters and successes alike, there's always a reason for decisions being taken, or even considered at all. *Cherchez*, not *la femme*, but the motive, and you have a better understanding of the crime or the victory.

Why, for that matter, did G.E. decide to intensify its strategic planning effort? It wasn't only because the sight of G.E.'s profitless growth gave the board of directors acute indigestion. It's because energetic men who rise to the top of great companies don't like to sit there twiddling their thumbs. They want to be "active," and active intervention isn't easy in a decentralized company which has placed operating power where it should be—with the operators. The reins can be grabbed back, though, by the imposition of a powerful, central planning apparatus.

A quote from G.E.'s Mike Allen delicately expresses the point. "Companies our size aren't directed. You don't sit at the top and issue orders. They're led by the authority of ideas, not position and rank." As a motive, the desire of top managers to find a positive, useful role is respectable enough. In their eagerness to prove that they really are useful, G.E.'s headquarters men have pinched a phrase from the new accounting discussed in Chapter 3: each level of the corporate hierarchy is supposed to "add value" in the planning process.

Every boss in every company must, from time to time, reconsider what role to exercise, and how. But G.E.'s central reassertion sprang in a sense from decentralized failure. The fact that the divisions hadn't delivered the financial goods gave the central barons the excuse to haul back power from the periphery. Not that central barons need an excuse. Their power is virtually what they choose to make it. No power on earth could stop Shell from signing up for its nuclear disaster, nor Dunlop from exchanging wedding rings with Pirelli. In neither case, however, were the boards reacting to failure. They negotiated from strength to create weakness. Why? What was the compelling motive?

In each case, and in nearly all such instances, large and small, the company is taking a bold step into what it imagines to be the future. At once, there are two possibilities of error: the company may be wrong about the future (as most of us are), and it may be wrong about its own position in that future. The bigger and bolder the step, moreover, the more careless the company becomes. Shell would have taken far more trouble over a small refinery in Chile than it did over nuclear power.

Often, the careless action is covered up with careless language. The president of Xerox told a shareholder that "we had to" develop or buy a computer capability. Shell thought it "had to" get into nuclear power. Dunlop, no doubt, thought it "had to" develop multinationally. Volkswagen *really* "had to" turn its factories upside down in a near-total model changeover. It was that or bankruptcy—the company was looking down the barrel of a gun. But nobody was holding a pistol on Shell or Xerox or Dunlop. An entirely voluntary decision was cloaked in the language of compulsion.

These managers had far less excuse than E.M.I., which

didn't "have to" push ahead with the brain-scanner, but, if it didn't, might never have found such an opportunity again. All the same, if you don't actually have to take a decision, there's a prima facie case for not doing so.

Making the decision guilty until proved innocent is an excellent way of avoiding voluntary defeats. It ties up with standard decision theory; that doesn't mean the pseudo-scientific type, which seeks to arrive at the best decision mathematically, but in fact does so spuriously, by combining (expected) financial outcomes with (estimated) probabilities of their being achieved. For normal decision-making purposes, the manager:

1. Decides *quickly* if it's clear that a decision must be taken.
2. Takes his time if the decision needn't be taken immediately.
3. Forgets about it if the decision needn't be taken at all.
4. Always, if taking a decision, applies the fail-safe test. If the worst comes to the worst, can the company stand it—and can I stand it myself?

Fail-safe demands a pessimistic attitude. Seeking new opportunities calls for optimism. Disasters in both directions stem from reversing the mental attitudes—taking an optimistic view of the likely outcome, on one hand, or being too pessimistic about ventures on the other. The emotional balance isn't easy. I've written elsewhere in praise of the onward-looking philosophy in Peter Drucker's priorities in this context:

1. Invest in the future, not the past.
2. Seek opportunities, not problems.
3. Choose your own direction—don't jump on a bandwagon.
4. Aim high.

But I had to point out that many disasters, including Du Pont's Corfam synthetic leather, met all four criteria; so did E.M.I.'s brain-scanner. Indeed, sometimes the past (subsonic jets, not supersonic) is the better investment. Sometimes excellent opportunities do arise from considering apparent problems (the assembly troubles in the United Kingdom which Ford side-stepped). Sometimes, a bandwagon can provide a wonderfully comfortable ride, as several entries in the digital watch and calculator businesses have found. Sometimes, aiming low is as wise as aiming high is dangerous (specialized computer makers were much smarter than those competing across the board with I.B.M.).

The more down-to-earth, prosaic, concrete and limited the motive behind a decision, the better. *Business Week* quotes the five-year goals that Gulf Oil formed for 1976 on: maintain Gulf as the Number Two producer of low-density polyethylene and push the company up from third to second in the high-density market. From this sober strategy flowed the tactical decision to "price competitively and add capacity as the market grows." It grew—but by two percentage points less than Gulf expected. Then, in 1978, came a hammer-blow—a new polyethylene process from Union Carbide. At this juncture, with the gun at its head, Gulf decided on a crash program to boost its own technology.

If its crash research and development paid off, Gulf would add capacity to reach its market-share goals. What if the r & d failed? If the Union Carbide process covered only one product, then Gulf would naturally concentrate on the other. If Carbide covered the waterfront, starkly and shortly the strategy said "abort the chemical program."

Whether such difficult decisions actually do get taken as the logic indicates is another matter. Decisions are no more all logic than they are all successful. Emotional force and also hunch (which is accumulated knowledge, experience and judgment) have powerful parts to play. But a framework like

Gulf's—of logical, interrelated steps following from a clearly identified and realistic motive—is the trellis on which decisions, continuous and discontinuous alike, should always be hung.

PART 4

THE HUMAN FACTOR

13

MAKING PEOPLE PAY

In the ideal company, perhaps, every member of the organization would feel equally and fully involved in every decision and action. The operative word is "feel." If those members *think* that full and equal involvement is the norm, then the result is just as desirable, whether the "feeling" is justified or not. That may sound unduly cynical, until you reflect on how subjective the question of involvement must be. The object of the manager, quite inevitably, is to encourage positive emotions, not necessarily to encourage participation.

The Italian adviser to princes, Niccolò Machiavelli, would have understood the distinction perfectly. An excellent book has been written, by the English author Antony Jay, adapting Machiavellian precepts to modern management practice. Machiavelli earned a notorious reputation for exalting the ends above the means. But once you have accepted that only virtuous means are permissible, the pursuit of desirable ends still demands and allows a great freedom of maneuver of the Machiavellian type.

The effective manager, in other words, must learn to manage (or maneuver) first himself and then, having achieved the necessary degree of self-mastery, other people. The key to controlling others is to control yourself: to know, at all times, what you are doing and why you are doing it—both much harder requirements than might appear. They lead on directly to understanding what you expect of others, and how you intend to see that they deliver the goods.

The techniques of controlling people are not especially complex. Some center around "identification"—leading people to identify their own interests with those of the company. Other methods range along the spectrum from inducement to punishment, from the dangled reward to the wielded cane. These two, the carrot and the stick, have played their part in every company that ever flourished, no matter how philanthropic its managers felt themselves to be; or, in a later age, how dedicated they were to the principles of behavioral science. Thus, some jobs are more desirable than others, and the possible climb to such positions is the carrot. Failure to achieve promotion is the stick; a punishment much more frequently applied than the outright fall from grace.

But some patterns of behavior are unacceptable to any company. That's the ultimate stick—behave that way and you're out. Other patterns are highly acceptable; behave that way and you're in—that is the carrot. "Making people pay" has a double meaning: getting the most out of them, so that, in turn, they can get the most of whatever it is they are seeking from the organization.

Many of the newer insights about what people want are valuable. But they share the common defect of telling managers that money isn't everything. That is true—but money is *in* everything, and if money isn't right little else will be right. Conversely, if the pay is good enough, people may put up with other conditions which are not.

That seems to be the key to people's willingness to work on the boring old assembly line: they like the high pay. Logically, of course, if you combine high pay with work which people actually enjoy, results will be better still. But it has been discovered again and again that happiness and effectiveness are not cut from the same cloth. Contented cows may produce more milk, but contented men may not produce more cars. All you can say is that, if the results are excellent, and are seen as such by the manager and the managed alike, then both must be doing *something* right.

> *"He's the worst sort of boss, because he makes you forget the basic injustice of capitalism."*

No big company in the Western world has produced more excellent results than Texas Instruments. Its success at the twin, tough tasks of combining old-fashioned growth with new-fangled innovation has been phenomenal. Had any of its founders been able to write a blueprint for T.I.'s future expansion, in the cast-iron certainty that the plan would become reality, they would surely have accepted—but might not have believed—what actually came to pass. The company's sales first exceeded half a billion dollars in 1966. Twelve years later, turnover had multiplied by five.

Still more important, T.I. could claim, as few major American companies can, to beat the Japanese in the very markets which the latter have done their best to saturate—like calculators of various kinds—while keeping up at home with the Silicon Valley Joneses in the crucial matter of producing microelectronic components. No company, what's more, has devoted more effort to making its people pay. While wages and benefits advanced by 9.2 percent annually in the five years to 1978, and prices fell by an average of 6.4 percent, productivity (according to *Business Week*) rose by just enough to compensate for both prices and wages.

Of course, productivity measurement is hazardous at the best of times. And, while there's no questioning the strength of

T.I.'s people performance, it must be true that a steep sales curve generates high productivity. To which a T.I. defender might well argue that high productivity generates a steep sales curve. Separating chickens from eggs isn't a profitable exercise, however; the two are inseparable, in theory and in practice. No chicken, no egg, and vice versa.

However, T.I.'s concern for people has been a theme from early days. If it didn't coin the phrase, it certainly spread the gospel of T.L.C.: tender, loving care. The initials stand, among other things, for a very high level of employee benefits, from gymnasiums and baseball diamonds to medical care and pensions. But possibly the most important aspect of T.I.'s care is the absence of firing and redundancy, and the complementary emphasis on tenure and seniority: T.I. people even wear badges whose different colors denote how long they have worked for the company.

Ambitious managers, who always keep one eye cocked for opportunities elsewhere (and T.I. has spawned a great many corporate globe-trotters), may find it hard to identify with the average man's yearning for security. But the lesson of untroubled firms in Britain's notoriously troubled labor-relations landscape is further evidence in support of the T.I. approach in America. Firms which promise no redundancy, and no layoffs, and which keep that promise, have the firmest foundation for making people pay.

The promise shouldn't, in fact, be difficult to keep, since natural wastage, coupled with other forms of labor turnover, will substantially reduce numbers employed over time. Also, the cleverly managed firm uses subcontracting and other devices to deal with variations in the work load above trend. These devices, however, won't work unless the company succeeds—as T.I. has—in generating so much demand for its goods and services that maintaining employment is seldom or never a problem.

Back to the chicken and the egg, in fact. No people policy will help a company if it's doing the wrong thing in the wrong way at the wrong time. But even the winning company with a surging, T.I.-style growth rate has no passport to the easy life. Expansion at such a pace, especially if it depends on rapid generation of new products and lines, places tremendous demands on people. How do you make them toil like galley slaves, but with no whip, and with the slaves actually liking it as they ply the oars?

One-off manipulative techniques are no help. The surest method takes many years to develop; in fact, the years are an essential part of this recipe. To quote T.I. executives in *Business Week*:

> "Everybody [in T.I.] is either from Texas or just out of school. And they honestly believe . . . the *company* can do anything."
>
> "The T.I. *culture* is a religion."
>
> "The *climate* polarizes people—either you are incorporated into the culture or you are rejected."
>
> "The employee is subservient to the success of the *corporate entity*."

In these quotes, the italicized words—"culture," "climate," "company," "corporate entity"—are key words. All organizations, like all social forms, have a culture. It varies in both its nature and its intensity. The winning company can't exactly seek a winning culture, in the same manner, say, that it can strengthen its marketing or research. The culture develops from the company's beginnings—or from some fresh start— and from the character of the founders, the environment of the actual location, and so on. (There's little doubt that the work ethic of Texas has been deeply embedded in T.I.'s behavior patterns from the word go.)

The culture, then, is something that's given; good or bad, it exists. What the winning manager does, though, is to recognize the key elements in the corporate culture and reinforce them: to *accentuate the positive* (and counteract the negative). Thus T.I. has put 83 percent of its employees into "people involvement teams," whose task is to improve their own productivity. Moreover, if people don't meet their targets (which they are supposed to set for themselves), they get moved briskly—but not, remember, right out of the company.

The targets emerge from T.I.'s famous "O.S.T." system—standing for objectives, strategies and tactics. The company has a separate, orthodox budget system for controlling day-to-day operations, while O.S.T. looks ahead via the T.A.P.'s (tactical action programs) which work on new products and processes for the eighty-plus P.C.C.'s (product-customer centers), into which the thirty-two divisions are divided. The jargon and dividing-up are designed to tie the managers to written goals within a system that provides extremely clear visibility for the managers looking down from the top—even though the whole approach is supposed to be "bottom-up": flowing from the under-managers themselves, rather than handed down from on high.

The contrast exemplifies the principle of using a culture to dominate by stealth. The boss of a T.I. competitor, quoted by *Business Week*, is probably right when he says that "the middle manager [at T.I.] often finds that the system is really a tool to manage him, not the other way round." That may sound fairly mean. But even if a T.I. manager were to suspect or know that he is being used, in this sense, would he mind? Presumably not, since the middle managers, too, share the culture from which O.S.T. sprang, and rejoice in the innovation-led growth which it produces.

Even the "people involvement teams" mentioned above have their place in O.S.T. The teams (yet more jargon) are part of P. & A.E., or people and asset effectiveness, which is designed not only to raise direct and indirect productivity, but to assist in maintaining good labor relations. Note that the three largest non-unionized companies in the United States are I.B.M., Kodak and T.I.—in that order. It's no coincidence that all three have immensely strong and clearly recognizable cultures, even though I.B.M. (unlike Kodak, based in Rochester,

N.Y., or T.I., the pride of Texas) lacks the advantage of a single geographical center.

You can't hope to keep the unions out—with all the advantages in operating flexibility and management freedom that follow—unless the employees are convinced that they are better off without unionization. That, too, can be made to sound Machiavellian—keeping the workers satisfied so that management won't be confronted with a rival power center. But it's difficult, if not impossible, to persuade people that they are well off when they are not. The executive who gives his employees what they want by getting what he wants isn't a mere manipulator; he's a very good manager.

The matter was summed up by a Communist union leader, working for the Lip watch business in France, which was saved (though only temporarily) under the direction of a left-wing advertising executive. "He's the worst sort of boss," complained the Communist, when Lip seemed to be riding high again, "because he makes you forget the basic injustice of capitalism." That's the people task of management in a nutshell.

> *"It isn't necessary to give them a veto or even a vote, but it is wise, indeed, to hear them out and to try to accommodate their wishes."*

What's just or unjust, honest or dishonest, depends, in many business contexts, on your point of view. Imagine this situation—which in the Europe of the eighties doesn't take much imagination. A manager wants to install a new machine that will radically alter working practices in his plant. He anticipates the usual difficult reaction from the men, especially their union representatives. So he takes a working party from the shop floor on a tour of all suppliers to choose a new machine—knowing full well that they are bound to endorse (without knowing it) the choice which he has already made. They do so, and because they think the decision is partly "theirs," that manager gets full cooperation in installing the new machine.

Is that dishonest? Is it morally superior or inferior to the old style of simply announcing the decision and expecting the men to implement it? Moral or immoral, the manager may have little option if he wants to be honest in the key respect of doing well what he is paid to do. It's nothing less than abject, immoral failure if the factory doesn't have the best plant used in the most economic way.

The virtuous end, as noted before, only justifies reasonable means, of course. But what's reasonable and what isn't depends on circumstances and—again—the eye of the beholder. For instance, which of the following techniques, listed in *Management Today* by marketing expert John Saunders, are a reprehensible use of the Machiavellian approach, and which are not? He sums them up with the mnemonic I-DOCTOR, which stands for intimidating, documenting, obscuring, confusing, timing, organizing, rigging. Here are examples of each.

You can *intimidate* by the authority of your position, by sarcasm, by deliberate loss of temper—and many other methods.

You can use *documentation* in many ways—controlling the nature, amount and flow of information to ensure that only your decision can be taken.

You can *obscure* and *confuse* issues by diverting attention away from what really concerns you to other matters calculated to absorb so much time that you will be left to cope with what was always your prime concern. (A familiar example of meeting technique cited by Saunders is to call upon somebody who you know has nothing to say—either because his views aren't relevant, or because he isn't paying attention. "Well, I think we should call upon Hubie to speak, at this point, because I know he has particularly relevant views on this problem.")

You can *time* meetings or actions to suit your purposes—like the chairman who always puts the matter dearest to his heart under "any other business," and leaves just five or ten minutes for its discussion before the lunch adjournment.

You can *organize* committees so that the membership is highly unlikely to take a different line from your own.

The latter, of course, comes close to *rigging*, which is so to arrange matters that the outcome can only be what you wish—like that manager, mentioned above, who wanted to ensure that the labor force wouldn't obstruct his plans for new machinery.

If you didn't regard *all* the I-DOCTOR devices as reprehensible, perhaps you should have, because they presuppose that your company is a long way from the winning behavior patterns recommended in this book, far from a company of equals, in which relevant expertise is openly and fully applied to answer questions in the light of full and intelligently selected information. The catch is that you will *never* find or be able to create such an ideal company this side of Paradise. Because of human fallibility, any manager who wants to achieve results with people will from time to time be obliged to use elements of I-DOCTOR to perform his job.

The more the manager is expected to share his authority, the more such techniques will come into play. Probably, in fully consultative labor-management set-ups, such devices are of the essence of the situation. For consultation, like any other form of relationship between people, needs management—or manipulation. The manager seeking his ends in these cases may even find that the means have been provided by his opponents.

In worker-democratic Sweden, for example, the unions succeeded in pushing through a new law enhancing the workers' say in matters like rationalization (the euphemism for throwing people out of work). The employers opposed the law, but have since proved adept at using its legalistic procedures to obtain just the cuts they want. The *means* can then hardly be attacked by the unions. But the managers are doing their own job, which centers around maintaining a viable enterprise for the majority of the work force. These managers are manipulating a union law—and why not?

The manipulative opportunities in consultation, which have to be seized if it (and the company) are to operate effectively, have an obvious bearing on the vexed matter of "participation" (see Chapter 16). In this context, note the logical outcome of Saul Gellerman's definition:

> Participation means simply that people should be consulted before moves affecting them are made. It isn't necessary to give them a veto or even a vote, but it is wise, indeed, to hear them out and to try to accommodate their wishes—or, at the very least, explain why you can't.

Since the manager need not supply "a veto or a vote," he is in command of the situation, provided that, in the first and last instance, he "hears them out." In other words, even if the boss knows exactly what he intends to do, he arranges for those affected to discuss the matter—for all the world as if his mind were undecided. If you don't give people a hearing, that alone can cause counter-productive resentment.

It may happen—and this should always be possible—that what you hear will change your mind; but that isn't the main object of the exercise. The aim is to get your way, preferably by making "their wishes" identical with your own; in which case, accommodation to "their wishes" will be extremely easy.

Where "their wishes" can't be accommodated, again there are ways and means of avoiding the stigma of outright rejection. One manager, forced to make economies, wanted to drop the free biscuits provided to office staff with their morning coffee. An awful row resulted. His successor craftily offered a choice—either no free coffee or no free biscuits. The staff voted for free coffee, and honor was preserved on both sides.

It's the gentle "offer-they-can't-refuse" technique: an invaluable tool.

What about the less gentle "Godfather" methods? Nobody with any authority, even the authority of expertise, can avoid some measure of intimidation of somebody—sometimes. There are always cases when rank has to be pulled, threats have to be made, and tempers have to be lost. The manipulative manager, though, having won, invariably follows the hard line with the soft touch—even, perhaps, an apology, carefully composed, designed not to weaken his action, but to sweeten its taste. Paradoxically, this often strengthens the memory, and thus the lasting effectiveness, of the original firm stand.

Nor is it possible, even for the most participative manager, to avoid the other tricks in the I-DOCTOR repertoire altogether. Somebody must decide what reports to request, who should sit in on what committees, what their agendas should be, how they are conducted, and so on. A manager would be extremely foolish not to use these necessities in a way that, in his opinion, will achieve the best outcome—best not only for him, but for the enterprise of his heart (which probably comes to the same thing).

That enterprise will function best if the people in it feel secure not only in their jobs, but also in their self-respect. This supplies a criterion that must be applied to any proposal affecting people. Does it truly endanger their security or their self-respect? Or does it only *appear* to be a threat in their eyes? Either way, the proposal requires built-in devices to offset the damage or counteract the imaginary fear. This demands cool calculation from the manager—the very behavior which Machiavelli enjoined on princes.

To be objective at all times is the ultimate aim (never achieved) of self-knowledge and self-control. The conscious discovery of which working methods work best for the individual executive is the basis for his conscious use of the techniques and approaches which help to achieve the best results through other people. It's impossible for most men and women, of course, to keep that degree of cool at all times—which is why it's a useful technique, when hot under the collar, to have a colleague who can be trusted to put ice down the back of your neck.

In a dispute, for example, the natural response is to get excited—anger being a form of excitement, of stimulation to action. The purpose is to gird the loins for battle against the threat. The adrenal flow helps to overcome the feelings of insecurity which might otherwise overwhelm your capacity for action. But adrenalin is no aid to judgment. The dispute will be better resolved if the threatened executive has the self-mastery to remove himself from the equation; to approach the issue as if it were a formally posed problem (which, of course, it is) happening to somebody else (which it isn't). That way, he is better placed to answer three vital questions:

1. What are we trying to achieve?
2. How can we achieve it?
3. Having achieved it, how can we consolidate our gains?

Building a set of objective and workable answers to such questions will strengthen, not weaken, the security of the management—and that of the whole firm.

> *If managers can't "take the initiative," aren't stimulated to "pride in performance," don't have their "self-confidence" built up, and aren't allowed to be "open-minded," everybody loses.*

Genuine threats are not required for the creation of insecurity. Anxiety as a human condition may well begin from the moment the child enters the world, and anxiety finds plenty to feed on at all subsequent stages. Nor are blue-collar and white-collar workers down the line the only people whose attitudes and efficiency are affected adversely by generalized insecurity. Among managers, insecure feelings seem to be the dominant mode.

In Michael Maccoby's *The Gamesman*, by far the most interesting material (to me at least) came in a brief section reporting on 250 interviews with corporate managers. Under "difficulties," and the heading "fear," 58 percent said they were "often restless," and nearly half were "anxious." Most of these people, too, presumably thought their fears were justified, since only 28 percent admitted to "unwarranted fears." Then, 61 percent said they kept their feelings to themselves, and 59 percent confessed to difficulty in saying what they meant.

There were 59 percent who thought they gave in too easily to others, and 46 percent who didn't know what they wanted. Half tended to blame themselves too much, and 44 percent admitted to depression. Considering that these are not images that an executive would willingly project to an interviewer, the results probably understate, if anything, the degree of managerial confusion and anxiety in the American company. Counterparts in other countries may be more confident, but surely not by much.

Maccoby's other researches may throw some light on these unhappy results. His managers seemed to be exceptionally dependent on the job itself for their productivity: 58 percent said that "the work itself stimulates interest, which is not self-sustained." Yet there seemed to be a large gap between what these managers thought to be "very important" for work and what was actually stimulated by the job. For instance, 91 percent rated "ability to take the initiative" as very important; 88 percent did the same for "pride in performance"; 86 percent for "self-confidence"; and 81 percent for "open-mindedness."

The percentages who found these traits to be stimulated by work were respectively only 58, 35, 50 and 30 percent.

Much the same gulf appears in what Maccoby describes as "qualities of the heart," as opposed to those of the head. In fact, only one "heart" quality was given a generally high rating: honesty, with 72 percent thinking it "very important" for work (for comparison, almost exactly the same proportion voted for "coolness under stress" under the cerebral qualities). Against that 72 percent figure, a shatteringly low 12 percent thought that honesty was stimulated by their work. Maccoby asked about several other "heart" qualities, getting very similar reports of human failure in response. Even though these other "heart" qualities were rated low in general importance compared to those of the head, there was still a large gap between the importance attached to the "heart" qualities and their actual stimulation by work.

The implication of these findings is that American corporate jobs do not allow the full expression of the personal and professional characteristics that managers themselves value most highly. To put it another way, executives have an extremely clear idea of the professional requirements of their jobs, yet they themselves (since they control the corporation) are incapable of matching the jobs to the requirements. Plainly, something must be wrong somewhere—and a good place to start is the personnel department.

Much of the complication introduced into advanced forms of corporate life has stemmed from "personnel"—such as organization development, or O.D. to its practitioners, a detailed program for changing the company and the executives within it as they go along. If personnel experts don't try to develop the whole company, they are likely to have a plan for developing individual managers. At its simplest—in the very successful West German style—this involves moving budding bosses from job to job, and possibly country to country, to build their experience, which is supplemented by in-company courses, with the "high-fliers" screened out and given special treatment as they climb the corporation.

But just as quality is much too important to be left to a quality control department, so the work content of a manager's life can't be left to "personnel." The shifting around is less important than the actual job, in particular the relationship with actual superiors and subordinates. If managers can't (as they complained by implication in the Maccoby interviews) "take the initiative," aren't stimulated to "pride in performance," don't have their "self-confidence" built up, and aren't allowed to be "open-minded," any development program is bound to be frustrated.

Hence the appeal to personnel experts of O.D., which attempts to ram home the manager's responsibility for developing his own subordinates, and which (of course) always contains the ritual exhortation for the "chief executive" or "senior management" to become fully involved as a prime condition of success. Every specialist, from computerization experts to cost-cutters, makes the same demand on top management; although, in truth, it's a prime example of the very fault that O.D. is supposed to cure; putting an impossible overload at the top of the structure, and trying to impose from above some common mold which can stamp out ideal managers.

Of course, it's true that "senior management" must be involved. The issues are, "How far?" and, "How far should *junior* management be involved?" People still get pushed around too much, and consulted too little, both in the matter of their own careers and in the conduct of their work. The answer is to provide as much freedom and flexibility as possible, within the context of seeking and rewarding good performance.

In that respect, climate is all-important. And, as Saul Gellerman points out in his *The Gellerman Memos*, whoever handles personnel policies, whether it's a department or line managers themselves, has a profound general influence on climate. Gellerman singles out:

1. *Recruitment*: if people of poor caliber are hired, nothing much else can be accomplished—and Gresham's law will work: the bad people will drive out the good (or cause them to deteriorate).
2. *Pay*: good pay motivates and bad pay demotivates; moreover, the number of full-time people on the payroll directly determines productivity; thus, to pay what Gellerman calls "longevity" increases, earned simply for another year of service, must be counter-productive.
3. *Treatment*: how kindly and sensibly "management" reacts to requests, for anything from days off to changes in job, has a profound bearing on how people regard the company. Even minor matters can make a major difference to climate and thus to cooperation. Going beyond that, treatment of the managed by the manager is a matter of management style, and style produces the kind of work and workers that the adopted style would lead you to expect.

Gellerman calls this process "self-fulfilling" and pairs these opposing stylistic qualities: "formal or informal," "helpful or harassing," "approachable or disinterested." Any intelligent company would select and train its managers to be "informal, helpful and approachable," so that these qualities become built into the management tradition of the company. But, says Gellerman, "some companies consciously select managers for their coerciveness, and many do so unconsciously." As he points out, either way you guarantee a rebellious and resistant work force.

If such basic stupidities are part of the tradition, nothing placed on top of their foundation is likely to produce much good result. But the following Gellerman tips will work effectively—if circumstances are right:

1. Get small groups of managers with interrelated jobs to meet from time to time to examine the way they manage and to set short-term goals for modest changes.

2. Have attitude surveys conducted to check on employee morale. And form an unbreakable commitment to act on whatever the survey reveals.
3. Avoid frequent management meetings—the managers attending become inaccessible, and rumors, aroused by the fact of the meetings, start to awaken people's insecurity.
4. Keep the organization simple, with the minimum number of levels. "Oversized, top-heavy organizations make for foggy communication, and all the costs that entails."

On that kind of foundation, a company should be able to make its people pay. But how does it pay *them* in turn? By sharing profits? Or incentive schemes? Or straight pay? All of these systems have worked brilliantly somewhere or other, and all have also failed abysmally. The universal rules are few: (1) pay must be seen to be fair and good; (2) as the company prospers, so should the people within it; (3) the system must be constantly reviewed—it should never be allowed to degenerate to the point where money no longer has any stimulative effect.

This has happened in many—perhaps most—large American companies, where huge bonuses and lucrative share option schemes have become part of the woodwork (and possibly the woodworm) in the executive suite: like fringe benefits in the United Kingdom. Men are supposed to take braver decisions for the sake of the company if they know that a fat financial cushion is there to receive them if, having risked unwisely, they fall from grace. This is a nonsense view of human nature. The fatly cushioned man (manager or worker) who hasn't really worked to earn his fat will continue that way—not really working.

The gulf between his rewards and his merits, moreover, will feed, not ease, his insecurity. This dividing line between incentive and coddling, like so many boundaries in management, is difficult to draw. But the important principle is to know that the line exists, and to make a continuing effort to ensure, first, that people do pay, from the employer's point of view, and, second, that the way in which they are paid as individuals encourages that vital payoff for both themselves and the corporation.

14

THE COMMUNICATION TRAP

In theory, communication should be the easiest of all management activities. You can only communicate in five ways —by words, pictures, deeds, ear and eye: and most people only think of the first two. That, perhaps, is where the trouble starts—in the failure to realize that actions *do* speak louder than words, and that attention to what others are communicating is an essential, integral part of the whole communication business.

This is very clear in labor negotiations—for example, on pay. The management needs, often badly, to tell the employees exactly what is being offered and to persuade them that the offer is sincere ("the best we can do"), fair and definitive. If the employees are deeply suspicious of the management, though, or convinced that more money is available, management's message simply won't be heard. If that happens, the automatic conclusion will often be that "militants," or "extremists," or "left-wingers" are exercising a malign influence on the men.

Even if there are Reds under the bed, or right out in the open, that never ends the story. Ask, rather, why do the workers believe and follow the "trouble-makers" rather than heed and agree with the management? If the battle for hearts and minds has been lost, it's the manager who has failed. Part of his job, in some respects his most important role, is to carry all the employees with him.

If they don't understand that the boss is sincere, fair-minded and means what he says, of course, that may be because he isn't and doesn't. Respect of this kind has to be earned, and that can only be done by actually showing that words and deeds are one, and that people can believe both to be broadly in their interests. Even so, slip-ups and foul-ups will occur, less often because of incompetence or malice than because of the two-way peril of any kind of communication.

The first danger is that the communicator may not actually have said what he meant. The British Prime Minister Edward Heath surely didn't mean, when he referred to "the unacceptable face of capitalism," that half the economic order which his Conservative Party was pledged to defend was indefensible. In fact, it's been suggested that somebody mistyped the word "facet," which was probably much nearer to Heath's feelings about the particular company scandal that was on his mind.

The second risk is that the receiver won't get the message as it left the sender. The message can get distorted at either end. For instance, there's a strong tendency to hear only what you want to hear, in management as in private life. So an unpalatable message may be totally blanked out—like the worried warnings that a man down in the finance department of Britain's Crown Agents vainly transmitted as the organization blundered on to a £200 million catastrophe.

But fortunately all is not lost. Much more is known today about techniques of communication, and use of that knowledge will help to avoid the traps, to put sound principles into practice, and to reach the increasingly large numbers of audiences with which managers have to communicate today. But the most basic audience, and maybe the most neglected, is management itself. Unless managers understand each other, and talk to each other effectively, how can they hope to get across to anybody else?

> *If you don't know what you're saying, nobody will ever understand you.*

Failures in communication between managers are not only common; they're commonplace, nearly always following much the same pattern. For instance, one manager brought a new project to his immediate boss; not as a tentative plan, but as something to which the manager was strongly *committed* and which the boss *felt* he couldn't reject. In fact, the project impinged on the concerns of two senior executives, who should have been consulted—along with the chief executive himself. But the plan instead went straight to the latter.

He quite naturally *assumed* that the other two men had been consulted, as usual. The fact that the project was more or less fully worked out *implied* that they had indeed been involved. He noticed, though, that the missing part of the project, where the planning was incomplete, was important. He discussed this with the manager and the latter's immediate boss, and gave his go-ahead, on the *understanding* that a satisfactory solution would be found, both for the unsolved problem and for one serious defect that he had spotted in the completed part of the plan.

The result could have been predicted by any experienced manager. The plan went ahead without the problems being solved, and the consequent shambles distressed nobody more than the chief executive. He felt it was his fault—especially since the unconsulted executives, once they learned what was going on, pointed out exactly (and, as it turned out, correctly) what disasters would follow.

The failure was entirely one of communications, since, if

everybody had known what was happening, the project would never have gone ahead. That's where the trouble began. Because Manager One was emotionally *committed*, he didn't want to hear from anybody that his plans were wrong. Because his boss, also for emotional reasons, *felt* he had to agree, he, too, shied away from inviting opposition. So, rule one of effective communication is to watch out for emotion. As in personal relationships, it can blot out sense. If you are receiving an emotional message, ask whether it is one you are really prepared to accept.

The chief executive didn't get around to this because of a different kind of error. He *assumed* something had happened because it was *implied*. The second rule is always to make sure that any message you think is implicit is actually made explicit by the supposed sender. The first way, by assuming things, you can arrive at a serious misunderstanding. The second way, by checking your assumption, you can't.

But this second type of error was compounded by a third. The only way that the chief executive could ensure that the conditions of his approval were met before the plan proceeded was to receive a report back. The third rule, if you want a message to be properly received and acted on, is to insist on playback, to make the reception of the message active as well as passive.

This technique, making the recipient repeat the message before proceeding any further, is recommended by Mark Brown (the expert mentioned in Chapter 10) as a method for negotiations—say, in a pay-bargaining session. After finishing its presentation, management asks the labor side to state management's view—and vice versa. As Brown says, the effort to express clearly what somebody else has communicated, putting yourself in their shoes, is a marvelous way of turning potential misunderstanding into understanding.

It doesn't follow, though, that to understand is to agree, or to accept. Many forms of communication are designed to *persuade* people to think or do things differently. That may mean reversing rule one—in other words, mustering emotion to your side. In negotiations, that could involve something like the good old American police game of Mutt and Jeff, in which two men deliberately take different roles, one sweet and conciliatory, the other tough and bullying, in order to confuse the other side, and to win their submission as a result of this psychological unbalancing act.

One man can use much the same technique. If that sounds too reminiscent of the Gestapo, it's really no more than a jazzed-up version of what the pundits call non-verbal communication (N.V.C.). Certain ways of behaving can either reinforce or negate a message. An extreme proof is what happens when an offending motorist is stopped by a policeman. If the offender leaves his car at once, it's a gesture (N.V.C.) of submission, vacating his territory for the policeman's, and is almost guaranteed to produce a better outcome—even amnesty.

In management, there's a whole library of N.V.C. devices. Putting a large desk between you and your visitor is calculated to give you a psychological edge—which you may not happen to want. Nodding and making noises of assent (even if you don't actually agree) will help to put the other person in a receptive frame of mind. Looking attentive will be taken as being attentive, and so on. The object of effective N.V.C. is to win over the person or people with whom you are communicating verbally.

That's why the best public speakers have an armory of *silent* weapons. They use gesture to reinforce their points, pauses to strengthen their words, the eye to supplement the voice—just looking at an audience can make an enormous difference to the impact of a message. Note, though, that a single message has a multiplied impact. The *less* a speaker tries to communicate by his words, the more likely he is to succeed. The mind absorbs less than we expect, especially if spoken words are unsupported by pictures or writing (which is a form of picture).

That explains both the importance of audio-visual techniques and, in part, the wisdom of the famous maxim of political oratory—stand up, tell them what you're going to say, say it, tell them what you've said, sit down. The simpler the message, and the more it is repeated, the better the chances that it will be understood and retained. If that simple spoken message is repeated in pictures, the chances are better still.

The principles of writing—either reports or letters—differ because writing involves the eye, which has much greater powers of retention than the ear. Even so, the fewer the points made in writing, the greater the impact. All good reports, like all good stories, have a beginning, a middle and an end (which correspond to the three stages of a good speech). Part one sets out the subject—what the report is about. Part two gives the relevant facts. Part three sums up the conclusions.

All this, what's more, is kept as brief as possible: any supporting information which demands length can be placed in an appendix. There's clear evidence that above 1,250 words or so (which happens, by no coincidence, to be roughly the length of most sections in this book), attention tends to flag, even if the writer (which is unlikely) is a master of the language.

Even non-masters, however, can master the central concept of good writing, which is to avoid ambiguity—the purpose, in fact, of most communication (ambiguity is only essential if your purpose, like a politician's, is to avoid an answer without appearing to). Few words can ever be as precise as the user wants, because words mean different things to different people. But managers are almost as prone as academics to use words as non-verbal gestures—to use, say, intellectual words to make the speaker or writer seem intellectual. Take this sentence from an English writer (if that's the right noun): "The role of personal pride in political polemics is certainly one of the Steinerian gaps in our knowledge or, in simple language, an urgent hermeneutic stasis."

I don't know what that means; nor do I care, even though that makes the author seem much cleverer than I am—which may have been his objective. I'm not even sure that *he* knows what it means. That's the most important point of all. Clarity of language and thus of communication follows from clarity of thought. The starting point of communication can only be in the mind of the communicator. If you don't know what you're saying, nobody will ever understand you.

> ***Tell the truth and act accordingly, and you can't go wrong.***

It's amazing how often winning management hinges on the same point—the choice of objectives and the direction of effort towards hitting those targets. In communication, everybody instinctively makes some kind of decision about what he wants to transmit, and why. The trouble is that the decision is usually fuzzy. The effort to clarify fuzziness, in this field as in any other, can make an enormous contribution to effective management.

A terrible case of failure makes the point. The Bank of America had actually based a major public relations program on coming clean, on revealing more to the public than it had to. But when one of its topmost officers, expected to succeed to the highest job in the world's biggest bank, got entangled in a questionable transaction with a customer, the bank put out a blatant lie to explain the man's resignation.

Because the lie was so blatant, it was easily and humiliatingly exposed. The fuzzy objective behind the lie was to save the Bank of America from embarrassment. But which was the lesser evil? To be embarrassed by a single incident that had, in truth, happened? Or to have several years of intensive image-building branded as a fraud? Put that way, the grossness of the bank's error is self-evident. Whether it can recoup is doubtful, for much the same reason that the South African government's hypocritical efforts to build a more liberal reputation were sabotaged by its 1978 clamp-down on the press.

The reason, as noted before, is that actions speak louder than words. Thus, all car companies boast about their care for the customer's safety, and most customers (since they want to think themselves safe) tend to believe the boasts. So Ford's American management, when it decided on a more dangerous, but cheaper location for the Pinto fuel tank, not only, it was alleged, incinerated some unfortunate Pinto drivers, but scorched the company's reputation so severely that there was a significant loss in home market share and profits.

There's no more important principle in communications than to *tell the truth and act accordingly*. If the truth is painful (as it was for the Bank of America), that's all the more reason for facing up to that truth. Otherwise, the damage when the truth comes out (as it usually will) is liable to be even greater than if the reality had been immediately revealed. Truth, of course, has many shades, and it's possible to influence opinion in favor of the shade which suits you best. But try to influence by untruthful means, and you risk the whole operation.

Appearances, in other words, must match reality. Actually, appearance and reality can be one and the same thing. I can't remember ever visiting a clean, bright, superbly equipped plant that wasn't part of an excellently run company with excellent results—and excellent labor relations. A *Time* reporter, visiting a northern English plant whose awful them-and-us divisions led to its eventual closure, correctly observed that the dirty conditions and clapped-out equipment told the men all they needed to know about the management's attitude towards them.

It must be true that the major influence on labor relations in a company (pay apart) is the continuous behavior of the management—just as the most important determinant of the attitude of consumers to a store chain or a brand isn't the advertising, but continuous perception of quality and value. Consequently, no management is in a strong position to win unless it knows what such perceptions are; unless, to be precise, there is some kind of feedback.

A falling market share, or some similar statistic, will provide that information, all right. But it's better to learn what your audience thinks, and why, *before* the damage is done. Yet there are still managers who authorize enormous budgets in order to advertise products or build a corporate image, without bothering to spend the relatively little money required to check on the results.

All such research findings are open to question. It's all too easy for bad researchers to tell the client only what he wants to hear. But research techniques are now perfectly good enough to give strong and clear answers. In one case, a new feature in an established product was the management's pride and joy, and the source of wonderfully favorable publicity. But quite unsophisticated research, which the company had long conducted as a matter of routine, showed incidentally, and without any shadow of a doubt, that the new and expensive feature was of virtually no interest to almost every customer. The management, naturally, took not the blindest bit of notice, and this much-praised innovation, in hindsight, looks like the beginning of the company's later decline.

In the two-way process of communication, that particular management had engaged in wishful hearing, which is just as easy as wishful thinking. The managers thought they knew better than the customers what the latter wanted. That will rarely be the case, although the possibility is one of the reasons for treating attitude research with care.

For instance, polls in both the United States and Britain in the late seventies showed that people wanted cuts in public spending and taxes, but were equally strong in favor of public services. The explanation is that most people do not relate a splendid new school, which they think of as "free," with taxes, which they pay, but for which they appear to receive nothing. The latter are bound to be unpopular, at almost any level, whereas nobody will ever want to lose a "free" benefit.

Thus, the results from polls and surveys need to be interpreted, by a non-wishful manager who is prepared to hear the worst. It is important to find out how the work force seems to perceive the company and its management, in case the perception is one the latter wants to change, or something to which it must adapt. Listening, and acting on what you hear, are essential for good communications. But it's a mistake to jump from that fact to the conclusion that making your actions speak effectively means doing what others want. That's only superficially the easy way out—easily taken because of the intense human distaste for confrontation.

A manager who doesn't mind (or doesn't appear to mind) confronting others with downright opposition, and who knows how to get his own way by the most direct route, is liable to be called "abrasive"—and the reputation may do him harm. But remember the importance of telling the truth. Even if you use non-abrasive ways of saying what you think, that's the only way to win—if the matter is of enough importance for the truth to be necessary.

But if you persistently shun confrontation then you are communicating a vital and destructive message—that of fear. There's a quiet and gentle man whose efforts to install a sound scheme for raising productivity and incomes at a depot were being frustrated by the opposition of a small militant group. The frustration came to a head at a mass meeting of employees, at which the militants' catcalls stopped the boss from even being heard. That quiet and gentle man lost his temper, jumped into the crowd, grabbed the ringleader and told him to shut up—or get beaten up.

I don't recommend that as a standard communications technique. But the work force then voted overwhelmingly for the scheme, which actually was in their interest as much as the company's. The overriding principle is not only to say what you mean, and to listen as carefully as you speak; you must also be prepared to back up what you say to the end of the line.

> *When the pervasive good image matches a pervasive truth, it's the ultimate in excellent communication.*

The work force, for all the failures which managers have experienced in trying to communicate with it, is one of the easier audiences. To begin with, the audience is captive: you know where its members are every day (if they are still turning up for work, that is); you have many means of reaching their ears; and they don't lack means of instant response if they dislike what management is doing or saying.

Other audiences are far harder to tie down, even to identify, let alone to reach, and it's even more difficult to put things right if a mistake has been made. For instance, the president of a pharmaceutical company, learning that one of its minor products had harmful effects, and would have to be withdrawn, decided to play the matter down, knowing that the authorities would only be putting out a routine announcement. But that routine news was picked up by the media. The embarrassed company, forced to respond, looked as if it was trying to cover up a major health hazard.

That kind of error in the arena of public opinion can only be slowly outlived. But the executive concerned had no experience to tell him beforehand that all drug withdrawals are big news; although he should, perhaps, have been aware that, in a consumerist age, and in any matter affecting consumer welfare, management is liable to be found guilty until proved innocent.

There are two possible reactions to this hard fact of life. The firm can choose to have:

1. A continuing policy, in which it seeks to project an image of concern for the consumer and for everything in the environment, from daisies to dinosaur bones; or,
2. A contingent policy, in which it reacts to trouble, as and when it occurs, treating each incident as a serious issue, and building a technique and procedure for dealing with questions as they arise.

What can't be afforded is to have *no* policy—or to be careless about the kind of activity which could bring down the wrath of consumerists, environmentalists, the media, politicians, etc. on the company's head. The offense is seldom worth the risk—especially since some of the critics whose wrath is risked are in any event hostile to business (big multinational business above all), and will never be persuaded into a verdict of innocent.

Any of these communication/confrontation areas can have a profound impact on the prosperity of a business: dealing effectively with lobbies, treating with politicians, trading with consumers or users of the company's goods and services, coping with bureaucrats, dealing with other managers inside the firm, negotiating with other managers outside the firm—all require a different vocabulary and a different technique.

But no words, however well chosen, and no technique, however skillful, can indefinitely plaster over an unpleasant truth. In the end, the company must be communicating a message that can stand close examination. If it can't, then the tests of good communication aren't worth applying. Here they are:

1. Is the message being addressed to the right people?
2. Are the latter receiving the message?
3. Are they responding to the message as we want?

The toughest cases are those which involve many outsiders at once: like the closure of a plant, or major and permanent reduction in the number of jobs. Both the affected and the unaffected workers may object. They will be supported by the politicians and bureaucrats, who usually have nothing to gain from a closure, and plenty to lose by appearing indifferent to it. Public opinion may help to make the instinctive opposition so powerful that the firm is apparently in a no-win position: condemned if it closes the plant, because of the odium it will incur; damaged if it doesn't, because of the financial losses that will follow.

The firm, though, has a stronger case than it may think. First, no management closes a factory or an operation just for the hell of it. Therefore, ninety-nine times out of a hundred, it must be telling the truth, even the whole truth and nothing but the truth. Second, nobody can force (as opposed to bribe) a company to continue operating a plant it no longer wishes to own, or to employ people it can't afford—at least, not in Britain (nationalized companies apart) or the United States.

Even on the continent of Europe, where closures are even harder to achieve, the laws of economics are ultimately allowed their inevitable victory—as happened in the case of Lip, the watch firm, once occupied by its protesting workers, as mentioned in a previous chapter, but now defunct. Such thorny problems, however, are more easily solved if the company—and each manager within it—starts from a foundation of public acceptance.

Like it or not, every business communicates all the time. Even the wholly secretive firm is conveying a message—for a start, that it *is* secretive. The message can be interpreted in different ways: that the company has something to hide, at one extreme; or, at the other, that it's run by strong, silent men who prefer getting on with the job to seeking self-glory.

As a rule of thumb, the excessive pursuit of publicity, of communication with the outside audience, is a bad omen. The internal audience is another matter; but the proliferation of formal means of communication, from company newspapers to joint committees, is often another bad sign. It's the *informal* methods of communication that are crucial, none more so than the personal appearance and accessibility of those in charge.

Dr. Joachim Zahn, who had a spectacular fourteen years running Daimler-Benz, made a point of alternating the top management's meetings between the various sites, giving Zahn and his executives the chance to show their faces, and to see other people's, at each Mercedes plant in turn.

Not being seen, by the same token, also conveys a powerful message: that of disinterest or, worse still, of some impending disaster which management is hugging to its bosom. But though the internal world of the company is perennially full of potential anxieties and psychological needs, the external world, for the most part and for most of the time, cares very little about most organizations. The exceptions occur when:

1. Some event (the fatal crash of a DC-10 at Chicago, or the Three Mile Island nuclear leak, are only extreme examples) thrusts the company into the limelight.
2. The media approach the company out of non-specific interest in its affairs, or those of the industry.
3. There's a specific reason for the company itself to seek some public reaction.

The three can often be intermingled. For instance, oil companies in the last few years have been in perpetual limelight, even floodlight. They are constantly badgered by the media and have a multitude of most powerful reasons to want to sway public opinion. As the best of them have demonstrated, the basic rules are the same as those of communication in the workplace:

1. Be accessible—if people want answers to questions, give them, in person if necessary.
2. Be truthful—the liar (like the Bank of America) is doubly damaged, by the truth it sought to disguise and by its exposure when the truth escapes.
3. Keep cool—adverse publicity is seldom as damaging as the victims fear. Remember that there are only three possibilities.

Either (a) what's said or written is true and damaging—in which case you must urgently correct the fault, not the report; or (b) it's false and damaging, in which case you sue; or (c) whether false or true, it's not damaging—in which case, so what?

4. Be objective—use public communication as intelligently as public advertising should be employed, as a proven and effective means to a properly chosen end.

Some ends, like elevating the price of the shares into the stratosphere, are seldom proper. But one objective is paramount: to maintain in the eyes of the public and (above all) of those who work in the company an accurate portrait of what the organization really is. That projection should continually reinforce what the company is doing to meet all its other objectives—including such vital matters as hiring the best people and winning the best reputation in the market.

Mention a Kodak or an I.B.M., and a total image springs to mind. None of us can escape this image, because every aspect of these companies, for every year in which we've known about them, has projected the same invaluable identity. When the pervasive good image matches a pervasive truth, it's the ultimate excellence in communication, often silent, often not seen as communication at all. But what you are, what you look like, how you talk—these indivisible elements make the difference between a winning and a losing identity.

15

THE PARTICIPATIVE PANACEA

All over the developed world, the problems of handling workers have been increasing at the same time as their numbers have been falling. There's nothing new about the latter decline. It's been going on ever since man learned to substitute brain for muscle. Economic progress can come only by obtaining more output for less input, or the same input. Either way, it means that jobs provided cannot keep pace with the expansion of production.

Over most of the postwar period, this hardly mattered. Non-manufacturing employment took up any slack, and there was rarely enough manufacturing labor to go around. But ever since the oil-price rises of 1973 opened a great hole in the Western economies, managers have been forced to confront a new and powerful pressure—the pressure for work. The true nature of this pressure has been obscured by its alliance with something equally burdensome for many managers—the cry, especially in Europe, for more "industrial democracy," more "participation."

The logical connection is clear. A management decision to

close a plant will cost employees their jobs. Therefore, they have a democratic right to "participate" in the decision—meaning, to stop closure. If that were all, it would be difficult enough for managers to cope with. An incompetent plant can devour cash in a most horrible manner. But the "democratic" pressure has strong theoretical underpinnings provided by two schools of thought: the behavioral scientists, who challenge the old theories of work, and the political radicals, who see the corporation as the last bastion of reaction and denial of workers' rights.

While some managers find this deeply unpalatable, some are fully committed to the new cause, and most of them fit uneasily in between. The majority want to recognize the workers' right to a voice in matters that concern them; but managers also want to continue managing. Moreover, they won't be thanked by the work force for managing badly, even in the most participative manner imaginable. That is actually the way out of the maze—the manager's job is to build up the resources of the business, and to exploit them to the full. That remains his job under any political dispensation.

The approach of the Scandinavians to these issues attracted worldwide attention because the Norwegians, and even more the Swedes, seemed to have combined virtue with victory. High absenteeism and labor turnover were afflicting production and profits at Volvo's traditional plants. If the working methods favored by the social scientists could eliminate these negative factors, the company could afford the costs of abandoning the assembly line while also extending democracy and participation in its factories.

But were the various devices employed to these ends new techniques of management control? Or an extension of political suffrage into the workplace? Or the good, the new, the only way of working? The answers are still uncertain, because the evidence is as confusing as the motives are confused. But this much is clear. If participative methods do not improve the effectiveness of the firm, neither workers nor management can afford them. The proof of the pudding can only be in the profits—and the pay.

> **The good manager doesn't run a social laboratory, but a place where people work effectively and willingly.**

The methods which Pehr Gyllenhammar tried at Volvo's new Kalmar plant and elsewhere were potentially of the greatest importance to managers a long way from Sweden. This wasn't, like unjustly celebrated case histories of the past, some liberal-minded experiment with a few workers on a green-field site in the Midwest. Nor was it some bankrupt British engineering firm being kept alive by taxpayers' money in the guise of a worker cooperative. Volvo is an industrial company of European scale. What Volvo did today, the rest of the world might be forced to do tomorrow.

So the journalists and the professors and the unionists and the thinkers beat a trail to Volvo's door. What they saw seemed not only liberal and progressive, but common sense. The monotonous assembly line was replaced by work stations at which men, organized into groups, could carry out entire operations in their own time, instead of some boringly repetitive task timed to take a few seconds. The brand-new plant in which this apparently revolutionary principle was applied had, moreover, been designed after and with the most careful consultation between management and workers.

Surely this had to be a better way than the old system, in which managers imposed on the work force methods and working conditions over which the men and women never had a say. If Volvo at Kalmar (and the other Swedish experiments) worked, managers around the world might find themselves in a wholly new situation.

1. Traditional mass-production methods would have to be scrapped in favor of less economic, but more productive batch operations.
2. All operational plans and changes would have to be agreed by the work force.
3. Some kind of institutional framework would be needed to formalize the process of consultation and agreement.

This triple threat, as it must have seemed even to quite liberal-minded executives, has not materialized; and not only because Volvo has been through the worst financial period in its history. The basic reason why a Swedish revolution hasn't swept through world industry is that, not for the first time, and certainly not for the last, the management and social pundits have made the mistake of leaping from the particular to the general.

Whether Volvo was right or wrong to experiment as it did, Volvo is a particular company in a particular culture—and companies and cultures differ extremely, even within countries, let alone across the world. The clash of cultures became real when a group of Detroit car workers spent some time at Volvo's automotive rival, Saab, another site of experiments in group working. The Detroiters didn't like it at all. They said they preferred the monotonous, boring, repetitive life on the assembly line.

Such conservatism may be the despair of sociologists and social thinkers, but those who genuinely believe in giving the workers what they want can hardly complain if the latter want something of which social thinkers disapprove. The manager is under no obligation to turn his workplace into a social laboratory. He is obliged to make it a place where people work effectively and willingly. In some circumstances, that may well demand experiment; but experiments, in the factory as in the laboratory, are only sanctified by success.

It's true that Glacier Metal, the British firm of bearing makers, became world-famous, not for its bearings, but for its early ventures into consultation with the workers. It's equally true, however, that Glacier had a powerful motive. Faced with annihilating American competition, the top management had to find some revolutionary way of motivating its people and becoming competitive in a hurry. Volvo also had a problem, which, though less critical, was also serious. How could a small-volume car manufacturer, based in a small market with very high labor costs, compete successfully with firms in other countries which had much larger home markets, cheaper labor, and higher volumes?

One way, so any clever marketing man could see at once, was to enhance the image of the company by all available means. In the executive car market, where Volvo's Swedish factories mostly compete, image is decisive. Such cars don't vary a great deal in mechanical terms; but the choice between B.M.W., Mercedes, Rover and Volvo in image terms is extremely wide. The publicity which Pehr Gyllenhammar obtained for the Volvo experiments projected the company as progressive, bold and superior—an image which, rubbing off on the cars, could only do good.

But one of the oldest rules in advertising is that the performance must match the promise. Volvo's cars, in design and specification, were not progressive, bold and superior; they were stodgy, safe and reliable. Thus, while the new publicity for the company could reinforce the good feelings of existing Volvo customers, the non-Volvo buyers were unlikely to be attracted by an image that wasn't consistent with the product. Chapter 12 stressed the importance of asking the right question. Whatever Volvo's problems with its absentee workers (how do we keep them at work?), they were nothing like as serious as the lack of an attractive, up-to-date, broad range of cars (how do we compete with Mercedes-Benz?).

Moreover, while the latter problem was certainly within management's span of control, any change in the factories was not certain to improve Volvo's productivity figures. There's no telling whether the effort spent on revamping Volvo's labor organization and building new ideas into the new plants detracted from management's concentration on the product. But it's sure that the action Volvo took to broaden its range was a disaster—the purchase of Dutch Daf, whose slow, expensive small cars, made in another small home market, were hardly a perfect complement for Volvo's slow, expensive big cars.

The financial strains imposed by Daf intensified the pressures which must have explained Volvo's failure to modernize and develop its range in earlier years—a sheer lack of the resources needed to keep up with Mercedes on the open road. Small wonder that Gyllenhammar tried abortively first a merger with Saab, then the sale of a major stake to Norway, then a deal with Renault, finally merger with a local conglomerate, in the attempt to place Volvo on a more secure financial base. Small wonder, either, that people contemplating Volvo's plight concluded, with varying degrees of glee, that its labor experiments were at best irrelevant, at worst flops.

But that's to make the same mistake as the enthusiasts did in the first place; to jump headlong from the particular to the general. It doesn't follow that group working isn't a better method than the assembly line—*in some plants*. It doesn't follow that workers shouldn't be consulted about existing and planned facilities and methods—*to some extent*. It doesn't follow that managers shouldn't take note of Volvo-style social and political trends—*in some way*.

But these reactions are no substitute for getting the basic functions of management right. In fact, the Volvo experiments, although they won the most publicity, were neither the most interesting nor the most innovative in Sweden; and reports from other plants speak of substantial gains in cooperation, communication and so on as a result of the different methods adopted to escape from the tyranny of the line.

Perhaps, as some argue, Detroit would never have adopted the assembly line but for the fact that its work force, mostly fresh immigrants from Europe, couldn't understand English and had to be spoon-fed with work. But if group working and participative methods are "better," in the sense of "more effective," then managers who persist with older ways are not *social* reactionaries, but economic ones. They are emotionally and intellectually tied to what they know, and are afraid to venture into the unknown.

That's sloppy thinking and poor management; but it's also human nature. In revealing that the latter doesn't change, managers are no different from other workers. The evidence of unchanging human (or worker) nature is much more striking than the evidence of change—and that truth must be a governing factor in running and planning the factories of the future.

In any workplace, there's an implicit social contract between workers and management.

The idea that worker-management has become completely different because of basic shifts in the nature of the workers themselves would never have won so much support but for the extraordinary events at Lordstown, Ohio, in 1971–72. The unrest at this recently established General Motors plant escalated to something akin to revolution. Poor productivity degenerated into deliberate sabotage. Managers were pelted with rivets. The whole place became a byword for the alienation of the blue-collar worker, for which the sociologists had some convincing explanations.

The Lordstown labor force was younger and better educated than that of other G.M. plants. These assembly-line rebels were plainly the forerunners of a whole generation that would no longer accept the harsh disciplines and monotony of the traditional factory. Like the storming of the Bastille in the French Revolution, the rebellion at Lordstown was a demonstration by force that life and society would never be the same again.

Even seven years later, an article in the *Harvard Business Review* had a prologue referring to Lordstown in precisely such terms. The article itself reported on a series of employee surveys, starting in 1950 and continuing to the present day, which showed a steady rise in worker dissatisfaction. Or did they? The numbers of employees who expressed enthusiasm or liking for their jobs had, true, declined substantially. But did this mean that the remainder were positively discontented? Or did they, when asked, reply (like most people) that their jobs were "not bad"?

Any good market researcher (as noted earlier) knows that it's not the results, but how well you interpret them that counts. Exactly the same is true of case histories. But the writers and teachers who pounced on the Lordstown case didn't test their interpretation either against experience elsewhere—or (far more heinous) against later developments at this Ohio plant. At least one professor did his duty by the truth, though —John Child, whose report appeared in *Management Today*.

Child admits that he had been using the Lordstown case for his students in the standard way—just like that recent prologue in the *H.B.R.* But he then took the trouble to visit Lordstown and investigate (a) the events leading up to the 1971–72 riots and (b) the events since the 1970 work stoppage. This is what he found:

1. There were other assembly plants in G.M. with equally young and educated work forces where no similar problems had occurred.
2. The Lordstown plant was built to make the Vega compact car. The sales flop of this model played a major part in all subsequent troubles.
3. The trigger was the handover of Lordstown to a new management organization, which ordered a speed-up on the assembly line with no extra pay.
4. The angry reaction to this old-fashioned speed-up was compounded by the need for layoffs, and by inter-

union rivalry, caused by the consolidation of two operations, with previously independent unions, into one under the new management set-up.

Industrial-relations problems are never as clear-cut as they seem—and Lordstown was no exception. Moreover, money is somewhere at the bottom of most labor unrest, and again Lordstown was no exception. The failure of the Vega meant that the workers' expectations on jobs and earnings had been disappointed, and the speed-up was the final straw.

That diagnosis is strongly supported by what happened after the riots. Lordstown has had a long period of peace and today is no more worthy of social study than any other G.M. plant. Why? Here's what Child found:

1. The new management, against head-office advice, accepted, head-on, a total confrontation with the dissident workers—and won.
2. An important factor in the victory was the worsening economic climate in that part of Ohio, and the threat that the plant might close for keeps.
3. The management, having won, made a number of conciliatory moves; in particular, it reduced the speed on the assembly line.
4. While several liberal and important improvements in labor relations had been introduced, these were not central to the peace—nor were they any kind of response to any novel industrial climate in the plant.
5. The overwhelmingly important factor in the new atmosphere was that, with the Vega replaced by successful models, Lordstown was now giving its employees high and stable earnings.

In that context, it's significant that the *Harvard Business Review* article mentioned above found a sharp rise in the proportion of employees who are satisfied, not with their jobs, but with the much less nebulous matter of their pay. Considering that the seventies haven't been an especially rewarding time for American industrial workers, the result is fascinating. Could it be that, in times of economic anxiety, a good salary is simply valued more highly?

The moral goes deeper than that. The first duty of the manager to the work force is to provide the conditions that will secure them excellent pay. There are other duties; but they are all piled on top of this foundation. Sometimes this first duty to all the employees will involve hardship for some, when, for instance, numbers have to be cut or operations dropped. But it's not even a sentimental kind of folly to believe that the cooperative spirit, or anything else, can override the laws of economics. It's plain, crass idiocy.

It would still be a serious mistake to throw the Lordstown story on the rubbish dump as yet another piece of tough fact converted into soft theory. As John Child spotted, the real truth of Lordstown ran far deeper than the blue-collar revolt that wasn't. In any workplace, Child observed, there is an implicit social contract between workers and management: conventions of behavior on which both sides have come to rely. The new management installed at the factory broke the terms of that unwritten contract by introducing the speed-up. It restored the contract by magnanimous and sensible behavior after winning the strike.

The real problem of labor relations as the century draws to its end is thus not new, but old: sticking to the terms of a varying social contract, and ensuring that those terms don't conflict with the prime duty of guaranteeing the workers a satisfactory economic reward. To that end, a management may have to "hang tough"—to take a conflict, as the Lordstown management did, or to threaten the closure of a plant. The more you mean it, the less the chance that the unpleasant action will have to be taken. But if you don't really mean it, you will lose—and deserve to.

This may sound like a harsh, even obsolete doctrine. If matters deteriorate to that extent, in fact, management has failed—as the Lordstown people certainly had. The motivation and aspirations of today's labor force may differ (despite higher levels of education) from those of their fathers and mothers to a lesser extent than non-working-class observers have wanted to believe. But this helpful fact doesn't remove the responsibility of management for doing unto others—fellow workers, after all—as they would be done to themselves.

It's a sad fact that, even under the best-intentioned of managements, misunderstanding and mistakes will produce emotional and violent response among the workers—not as violent as at Lordstown, but nasty enough. The process is only a demonstration of the collective unreason which seizes reasonable individuals when they are banded into a group. The emotionalism on the shop floor imposes a great necessity on managers to keep cool—that is rule one. The second rule is to analyze the situation with the greatest care to discover what the real cause of the grievance is. The third stage is to propose a full and fair response to any genuine complaint. In other words, never react as the social pundits did to Lordstown, where they got overexcited, analyzed inaccurately, and used their incorrect deductions to propound inappropriate policies.

> *"People must feel they are part of an organization where their contribution is properly measured."*

The social contract in the firm is the foundation of its labor relations, good or bad. But the contract is not the foundation of the firm's success; that lies in the overall effectiveness with which all its resources are applied—in a word, in its productivity. The unwritten contract between the workplace and the executive suite has an important role in that outcome; and if participative methods are to earn their keep, they should presumably, somehow, contribute to higher productivity. If taking part in decisions, being consulted through new organizational set-ups, getting greater responsibility for one's work, and so on, have no effect on output—how do you prove that any benefit at all has arisen?

The purist might argue that these innovations are inherently good. But the practical manager can't devote too much time to inherent goodness, not when the procedure is so laborious and time-consuming as participation. It's so difficult, in fact, that you can't make it work unless you have extremely good managers. But (and here's the paradox) if you have extremely good managers, you don't need participation.

Three cases published in *Management Today* prove the point, although they might seem to prove a different one entirely. The first is that of Tannoy, a British company in public-address systems and hi-fi equipment, which was taken over by Harman, an American audio components group (itself now part of the Beatrice Foods conglomerate). Sidney Harman, the American entrepreneur concerned, took a degree in social psychology in his fifties and has become a leading light in the movement for work humanization. But don't jump to any conclusions. Harman has left Tannoy free to follow its own philosophy—with good reason, given the 40 percent rise in output per employee between 1974 and 1978.

The contributory factors included:

1. A clear statement by the management of its intentions on "security," "fairness," "individual fulfilment," and "involvement." "Individual fulfilment" means having enough flexibility so that people can move towards the job and the style of supervision which they prefer. "Involvement" meant letting individuals direct their own work so far as the job would allow.
2. The company was changed to a single status: the same hours for everybody, monthly salaries for all, everybody eating in the same place.

3. Productivity is closely monitored: "People must feel they are part of an organization where their contribution is properly measured."

In organizational terms, Tannoy has work groups, leading up to a work improvement committee that discusses every aspect of the operation. There's no inspection of work, though. Every operative stamps his or her work, so that quality controllers can trace back any errors. The moral is thus that of this book's Chapter 8: Tannoy combines its progressive ideas with rigorous, high-octane insistence on performance.

The performance in turn springs from factors which have nothing to do with the organization of work. The company had moved, lock, stock and barrel, to a new factory and new work force in an area of high unemployment. It dominates the quality end of a growth market. It is small enough for easy identification and communication. It is run by a committed, specially selected group of managers, whose leader, Jim Hughes, wisely said in 1978 that "No one should be over-enthusiastic for our solution—in my view, it suits only us, and even then I sometimes have my doubts."

At another of the cases studied, J.C.B., the quick and wrong conclusion might be the opposite. A sign in one office says, "Put products not people on a pedestal," and the corporate emphasis is on heavy investment—heavier per employee than that of Caterpillar and Clark Equipment, the firm's mighty American rivals in earth-moving equipment. Expenditure on good working conditions is likewise unusually high, but there's no sign of Tannoy's "humanization" or participation: except for one thing—to quote author Cheryll Barron—"At J.C.B., every capital sanction form is signed by the foreman, who may have been flown over to Germany in the company jet with an operative to help him choose machine tools."

The foreman's signature isn't the only one needed, of course. However, as at Tannoy, the crucial point is that the commitment to productivity is expected to run right through and down the firm. Since J.C.B. has been getting sales per employee of four times the United Kingdom industrial average, three times the European and twice the American, the commitment must be real enough.

In J.C.B.'s case, however, the traditions of a brilliant business built by one eccentric entrepreneur (Joe Bamford, who hated debt so much that he never acquired any) provided as strong an economic foundation as Tannoy's lock, stock and barrel move to Scotland. But the only common elements in these cases, and in the third, that of Davy-Loewy, which supplies plant to the world's suffering steel makers, were (1) correct orientation of the business towards its markets; (2) emphasis from top to bottom on competitive efficiency; (3) a high and good level of communication; (4) a high degree of commitment at all levels.

All four virtues should figure among the objectives of all managers in all companies at all times—and their achievement has no connection, in itself, with the social ideas of the presiding manager. The four common features also had little to do with participative machinery of any kind, least of all in making decisions. Frank Heller of the Tavistock Institute has reported on research which shows exactly why this should be so.

Decisions can be divided into (a) those that are particularly important for the employee, less so for the company; (b) ones equally important to both; (c) decisions very important to the company, less so to the employees; (d) ones which don't matter much to any party.

In practice, as opposed to theory, what you would expect to happen does. The employees have the highest degree of "sharing influence and power" in case (a), where they care most. In Heller's study it was 30 percent of the time—a figure which should obviously be higher. In case (b), where management also cares, the level of consultation is very high, the level of sharing is not. In case (c), where the employees don't care, consultation and sharing are both low, as in case (d), where neither side much cares.

This research, like most behavioral findings, contains no surprises. But it does convey a lesson. Participation is about sharing responsibility. Where people can't or won't surrender the responsibility, or don't want to accept it, participation is a dead letter. A manager who is paid to manage a company effectively can't fulfill his total responsibility if he's stopped by others who share it only in part—as witness that awful year of Volkswagen when labor's representatives on the board of directors stopped essential cutbacks.

Losses of jobs (as at V.W.) rank high on the list of worker concerns—if not at the very top. But there are limits to the extent to which the workers can *share* decisions on shedding labor—for the simple reason, as noted before, that they don't want those decisions to be taken at all.

Nor is there much evidence that the more neutral questions of product strategy or investment planning are ones in which workers want a share; but remember the J.C.B. foremen who must signify and sign approval of machine purchases. These men are *involved and informed*—and that is the participative thread of these three cases. The managements concerned have each found their own individual ways of telling people as much as possible about the business, and of involving them in the affairs about which they are informed—especially the matters of direct concern to them.

Bosses can contrive to win in secret; many multimillionaires have done so—and still do just that. But secrecy makes the job harder. If people are fully and honestly informed, they will quickly and responsibly let you know where they want their voice to be heard. That isn't democracy or even "participation"; but it is the essence of managing men—and women.

PART 5

CHALLANGES FOR THE MANAGER OF TODAY AND TOMORROW

16

SWINGS OF THE SEVENTIES

This book has contained far more about managing people than its predecessor of eight years ago, *The Naked Manager*. This is no accident. From halfway through the sorry seventies, "people problems," to use the jargon, have come to subsume many other management concerns. Not only can university pundits cite Maslow's hierarchy of human needs (as they do—at the drop of a fee), but many managers themselves are just as familiar with his needs theory, and just as ready to believe that nobody can manage effectively without such knowledge about human beings.

Nor is it only a matter of "people problems" within the firm. Top managers are now supposed to devote much of their time to questions of human relations in society as a whole. But watch out; we've all been here before—many times.

Looking back over the history of management thought, it's clear that its principal themes have appeared (and disappeared) because of real problems, often critical, that were on the anxious minds of managers at the time. Sometimes, like generals fighting the war before, inventors of management's current pet theories have been preoccupied with a real-life challenge that is already extinct. Thus, anxiety about the American competitive threat in Europe long survived its virtual disappearance. At other times, though, the problem being confronted was still alive—and kicking management: like the concern with declining productivity growth at the end of the seventies.

In the same way, managers only began to harp on marketing when the seller's market of the postwar world turned into a buyer's one. The race then began to go to the commercially swift, rather than to those who could produce anything at all. Not surprisingly, the commercially sluggish sought the magic ingredient which put so much power in their competitors' tanks. So "marketing" was born, developed and blown up into a cult which eventually tried to embrace the whole of management (except, perhaps, the legal department).

The rage for computerization was also a natural answer for managers who had suddenly fallen foul of the problems of scale. Recourse to the machine not only promised to alleviate a crushing clerical problem (it did), but to cope more effectively with the difficulties which, as growth worked its wonders, were raised by the great increase in corporate scale. The latter promise remains unfulfilled, and even unnecessary. The key to controlling the over-large corporation lies not in hardware, but in administration, in the organization of people.

At this point, obsession with people becomes understandable. All things seemingly conspire to make the manager into a practicing behavioral scientist, like it or not. To run his company, many times larger than the most megalomaniacal founder would have dreamed, he must find some means of motivating his managers without sacrificing the essential elements of control.

In the face of militant and articulate labor, too, the manager must find some means of remaining the boss, not only because of personal need, but also in the interests of operating efficiency. Yet he must simultaneously find some way of allowing labor to "participate" in what has previously been recognized as solely managerial work.

In fact, the signs in the late seventies were that people-preoccupation had lessened, like the marketing and computer ones before it, largely because, in a time of high unemployment, work had become more important than the nature of work. That new social importance of jobs *per se* in turn explains why the communal problems created by slow economic growth have spawned a whole series of books, articles and conferences on management's responsibility to society. No doubt, that fashion, too, will be modified or even obliterated as the nature of reality changes—or is seen to change in the mind of the manager. The would-be winner, however, is well advised, before falling for the current seductive set of supposed thoughts and theories, or the next lot, to remember what has happened to those of the past—the all too recent past: as follows.

Managers, under duress, have been quick to learn the lessons of their failure in the seventies.

The myths which *The Naked Manager* attacked, and which have surfaced from time to time in these pages, fall into three categories. Some are received views about the company as seen from the outside, or in its relations with the outside world. Others are received views about what actually does go on (because it has to) inside the organization. Finally, there's the whole quasi-academic, journalistic world, which only concerns itself with *ideas* about management—ideas which may or may not have anything to do with actual business events, but are quick to mirror changes in the *market* for ideas. Academics, too, must live, and journalists need stories.

To start with some external myths of 1970:

1. Big companies are best.
2. American multinationals are best of all.
3. The company is and must be run in the best interests of its owner, the shareholder.
4. Economies of scale are the key to economic success.
5. Government efficiency can be improved by the introduction of modern management techniques.

The extent of change over the seventies can be measured by the fact that today's received views are often exactly the opposite, namely:

1. Big companies are worse.
2. American multinationals are worst of all.
3. The shareholder is only one of the interests which the directors need to serve—and maybe not the most important.
4. Size is not only inefficient, it's immoral.
5. Government is bound to be inefficient, no matter what, so the less it does the better.

There's an element of caricature in the above ideas (and some of those who hold them certainly deserve caricature). But in every case the reality of events fully explains the swings of opinion. Take big companies as an example. For most of them, even the best, the seventies have been a period of humiliating failure to perform well, even by their own criteria.

General Motors has a claim to be among the very best of the giants, as well as the biggest—while outsold by Exxon, G.M. made much higher profits in 1978, at $3.5 billion. Total sales that year came to $63 billion—20 percent more than in 1973, measured in that earlier year's currency. But by the same exacting "real" yardstick, G.M. recorded no increase in profit at all between the two years.

Nor could inflation carry all the blame (although it was the crucial factor). In 1965, G.M. earned 10.3 percent on its sales. In 1978, the statistic, a vital one in any business, was only 5.5 percent. To put it one way (as chairman Thomas A. Murphy did to *Business Week*), "We've tried to focus more attention on the profit margin, because *we've seen it* [my italics] on a toboggan going down."

To put it another way, the great G.M.'s top management had watched (if the italicized words, "we've seen it," are taken at face value) while a deterioration of nearly half had afflicted the most basic measure in the business. Nor was the experience of this corporation in any way untypical. Looked at either in real, non-inflationary terms, or in the actual inflated numbers which they reported, big companies did badly all around the world, and American companies certainly did no better than the rest. In fact, in Europe, where American firms were expected to splatter the opposition all over the ring, some American entrants were the defeated contestants carried out on a stretcher, while the same Europeans who were supposed to offer easy meat were invading the American market in full and vigorous force.

One great help to the Europeans has been the collapse of Wall Street, which in the seventies crumbled into a state of permanent stagnation that left many prides of American business standing in the market at valuations far below the replacement cost of their assets. This, in turn, is the major element in the dreadful damage inflicted on shareholders during the period. Whether any board of directors believed the lip service they paid to the shareholder is beside the point. But the directors' bad stewardship was partly to blame for the inability of the American stock market, having first broken through 1000 on the Dow Jones Index in 1966, to struggle much out of the 800–850 range in mid-1979: 1000 was still the peak fifteen highly inflationary years later.

A clear error of big corporate strategy lies behind this sorry saga. In 1974, so *Business Week* worked out five years later, American companies paid an effective tax rate of 63 percent on their profits; and then gave 99 percent of what was left to their shareholders. This was truly a "shocking" performance, as the magazine described it; it was explained largely by a purblind refusal to account for rampant inflation.

Directors were behaving only relatively more sensibly in 1979. That year, an $84 billion tax bill on 1978 profits was $17 billion higher than it would have been if inflation had been taken properly into account, and shareholders were paid 65 percent of adjusted after-tax earnings. This might seem to be a favor to investors—until you reflect on two truths: (a) the excessive dividends still added up to a miserable return on the investors' funds; (b) the inadequacy of retained earnings has paved the way for miserable performance in later years.

In other words, while claiming to defend the interests of the investor, companies showed an unconvincing idea of what those interests were. This can be proved in the case of American companies by an elementary failure. They can, if they wish, switch from F.I.F.O. accounting for stocks to L.I.F.O.: meaning that they can choose to make the cost of the inventory consumed in making a product either that of the *first* item purchased (First In, First Out) or the *last* (Last In, First Out). In inflationary times, only an ass would choose F.I.F.O. when L.I.F.O. was available. On that basis, two-thirds of American companies were asses in 1979.

In Britain, the problem didn't arise, in that a benevolent government decided, under pressure, not to tax stock gains at all. But the same phenomena occurred: profits grossly overstated; shareholders severely mauled in both real and inflated money; big companies, with few exceptions, failing to perform as well as small; and those firms which, following the credo of the sixties, had become proudly and sizeably "multinational" finding that they were likely to be the most pilloried of all.

In consequence, the idea of big business being held up as model to government now seems just as ridiculous as it always was. Politicians and businessmen are in quite different trades; and the fact that neither group did well at its occupation during most of the seventies says nothing about their respective merits and demerits. The times simply became more testing, and people who had not excelled in less troubled periods naturally failed the new tests. But, under duress, the managers have at least been relatively quick to learn the lessons of their failure and to look for new and better ways of working. The politicians have hardly begun.

> *Compound annual growth plans are creeping back, and the crawly accountants will come back with them.*

The correction of past and terrible error by big corporations has started with the books. Even accountants now agree that what they have called "profit" for all these years may be nothing of the sort. The English profession, by taking a lead in the matter of finding new, inflation-proof definitions, looked as if it was in eventual danger of shutting the stable door after its horse had bolted. But, as in America, the government obliged by engendering a fresh bout of double-digit inflation; so the new bookkeeping (which many companies are now using for an extra page or two in their annual accounts, if nothing more) is on its way.

Inflation accounting, of course, is just as fictitious as the old bookkeeping, if not more so. Nobody has yet produced a theory that can truly rationalize the complex of changing values that is a company. There is no definitive answer to a question like this: "If your stock of a raw material has doubled in value, have you already made a profit?" Or, if the price of the end-product has risen in step, is *that* when you cash in—when (in effect) you sell the raw material, via the product, at its doubled price? Or, have you really made *no* profit, anyway, since you now have to replace the stuff at its new, higher cost?

Common sense can't help, except to say that the search for accounting truth doesn't much matter, save for tax purposes. Taking an unrealized profit on inventory maximizes the tax and pays it at the earliest possible point. Waiting until the stuff is used still yields a heavy tax charge, but later. The third course, which eliminates the profit altogether, is the most tax-efficient by far, and is the approach any manager with his wits intact would employ—if the tax authorities will let him.

Accounting for profits, in other words, is about paying tax (or, rather, not paying it), while also giving shareholders a fair idea of what can reasonably be paid out in dividends. You could be tempted, as I once was, to sum up the matter in a simple rule: when in doubt, always adopt the most conservative accounting principle—L.I.F.O., not F.I.F.O., for instance. It remains a sound *general* principle. But in accounting, as in life, there are always exceptions.

I was much impressed once by a building contractor, then richly successful, who, in contrast to all his fellows, refused to take any profit on work in progress over the long life of a contract. Even though, of course, he received payments as the work went along, he only regarded a profit as made when the "claims" (the extras above the contract price) had been agreed, and the final check was handed over.

Only later did I learn that this apparently virtuous course was inherently dangerous. It meant that the man's annual figures said nothing whatsoever about what had actually happened that year. The profit all related to jobs that might have been finished years before. Actually, he was realistic in one sense—all his profits lay in the extras, the "claims," so he truly hadn't made any money in the contract stage. But the upshot was that, in a poor year, when losses were being made on contracts, he could (and did) show superb profits—and promptly went bankrupt.

His form of accounting, although apparently deeply conservative, was as "creative" as its opposite: the man who takes in profits on sales that haven't yet been made, or buys another company to add its profits to the pile just before the end of an otherwise uninspiring year. All such fiddling is downright unpopular (and in America, an outcome which is worse than unpopularity, has led to alarming lawsuits against accountants and directors). But its unpopularity reflects less the spiritual or ethical conversion of the business community than the disappearance, as a corporate aim, of the compound annual growth plans that creative accounting can help along.

They are creeping back, though, and the crawly accountants will come back with them. An excellent company whose strategy meeting I attended in 1979 was committing itself to a growth number I remember well from the swinging sixties: 15 percent, the same target the gee-whiz boys used to pick to excite the stock market's adrenalin. I thought then, as I think now, that 15 was chosen because 10 (which means you take seven years to double) looked too low: and 20, which doubles you in three and a half years, looked too high: so ("hey presto") you split the difference.

But 15 percent, an annual compound growth rate that yields a double-sized company in precisely the standard corporate planning period of five years, is a foolish figure, too. In the first place, if one of those years (and this happens to the best of companies) is as flat as the Gobi Desert, the plan is immediately in deep trouble. Year two's index, say, instead of rising to 132.3, sticks at 115. To get back on plan by the end of year five, the firm must now grow at a galloping 74 percent in only three years. It will almost certainly never make it, and probably the company wouldn't even try—that is, (a) if the word "growth" had lost its emotive power, and (b) if it wasn't still so easy to buy other companies.

Growth worth having is the result of offering the right products or services to the right markets at the right time and in the right way (which means especially the right price). That truism is so blatantly obvious that it's astonishing how many clever managers miss the point. But the personal urges which drive men to seek larger and larger empires, and to call that enlargement "growth," remain strong.

The expression of those urges still creates flattering magazine and newspaper stories; and it's possible to argue convincingly that, with assets on Wall Street and elsewhere selling at a discount, it's better for shareholders if their directors buy existing undervalued assets rather than invest in new fully valued ones. Or else, like the oil and tobacco companies, you can make a plausible-sounding case for diversifying into other, less contentious activities. It takes a brave, or (in terms of career advancement) foolish, manager to fly in the face of evidence that most acquisitions don't work out, and are still dragging at the companies involved, like rusty anchors, years after the deals.

In one study, for example, the imposing academic combine of Ansoff, Brandenburg, Portner and Radesovich found this from the period 1946–65:

1. "Slow-growth firms embarked on acquisition as a result of an accumulated history of deteriorating performance and/or as a result of inferior current performance."
2. Among low-growth firms, "The acquirers did much poorer than non-acquirers, both on the pre- to post-acquisition comparison and the total history."
3. High-growth acquirers bought other companies because of a restless management drive to continue improving the firm's performance, and they too "showed indifferent performance on pre versus post comparisons."
4. "On the basis of the twenty-year history of the sample as a whole, one would conclude that acquisitions do not pay, and . . . are an inferior method of growth."

The approach to mergers in the late seventies may be more sober, but is no safer than the gung-ho enthusiasm and hubris that created the conglomerates in the sixties. The latter mostly linger on, some making massive profits; but they resemble a corporate mothball fleet, monuments to the dead idea that this kind of whole can be more than its parts, and that a central management, while not managing, can generate superior performance out of a business it doesn't understand.

The conglomerate myth was counterpart to the decentralization deceit: the notion that you could delegate responsibility without delegating power and authority. We know better today. But too many managers are still too easily tempted by the illusion that businesses are like the herrings in the Jewish story, just for buying and selling. They are for *managing*—and, unless you can manage them, they are never worth buying.

> **The iron laws of economics, not the discoveries of technology, are the ultimate deciding force.**

The sudden rush of mergers—especially in the United States—at the end of the seventies was a sharp reminder that the swings of the decade towards common sense were more a response to economic pressures than a permanent gift of wisdom. Some of the once-dominant modes and *mores* that are now out of fashion—like one-man-band bosses who try to run the whole company and everyone in it—have never really vanished from the scene. Other follies, like the habit of playing musical chairs with the executive suite in trying to manage phony decentralization, didn't receive the short shrift they deserved. But in areas like planning and marketing, probably some real and lasting advance has been made.

Corporations seeking a dynamic, planned, "market-oriented" future no longer ask themselves, "What business are we in?" and then use contrived answers to justify merger-laden plans for future aggrandizement based on businesses they aren't in at all. In fact, the younger executive generation often doesn't even recognize the above question, or even know of the famous Ted Levitt article, "Marketing myopia," which first asked managers to face the issue.

If I've been hard on that most stimulating of *Harvard Business Review* pieces, however, it's less because of the foolish empire building by others which it stimulated (that would probably have happened, anyway), than because of its own inability to grasp the central truth of the seventies, which is that the iron laws of economics, not the discoveries of technology, are the ultimate decisive forces. Levitt's "myopia," the failure of managers to perceive the technological change that will alter their business, is a permanent, incurable condition of man.

Indeed, Levitt's later admission that his own efforts at forecasting technology (solar-powered cars by 1980, and so on) had been woefully awry is more valuable than the original article—as mistakes often are. The electric utilities ran into big trouble, just as Levitt predicted, but not because, as he expected, of the industry's failure to stimulate customer demand. It was the economic difficulty of financing the mounting scale of investment needed to meet demand that first drove the utilities into their bankers' arms.

The winners in the marketplace—products and producers alike—are those which at market prices obtain the highest return on capital. The test of a new technology is not whether it works (Concorde plainly *works*), but whether it works economically. This trite but true fact explains why it takes so long for new technologies (even the micro-electronic marvels of our age) to journey from the lab and the military customer into the mass market. The same fact also explains why the great majority of the world's money-spinning products are relatively ancient.

The "product life-cycle" is another academic concept of the sixties that can be safely buried. Companies are fond of noting that half their products weren't on the manifest only ten years ago. By the same token, half their offerings are at least ten years old (and, what's more, usually provide well over half the profit); the exploitation of these base markets is what separates the winners from the losers, the sheep from the goats. Time and again, when diversifying firms run into difficulties with their diversified treasures, the shock wave that drives the whole company back on course is the discovery that the base business has also been sinking out of sight while everybody in command has been watching the new fleet founder.

On both sides of the Atlantic, titles like that of a magazine story in April 1979, "National Can: Getting back to the business it knows best," have become commonplace. In that case, a company which had sought to raise its United States sales outside cans to half the total is now back to 98 percent packaging. In terms of profitability, National is at least $10 million better off as a result—that being the sum lost by its diversifications in 1977–78.

All you can say in favor of such disasters is that they give such quick and easy scope for recovery. New managers in disaster areas can apply the tried and tested old rules with impunity, knowing that, in this dire situation, dire measures will not only be approved, but applauded. They win out of somebody else's defeat. But the art of winning management is something else: to act with the sharp surgical instincts of a company doctor when the business is in excellent health.

There are a few cases of successful discontinuity, like the conversion of W. R. Grace from a mere shipping line. (Its success owed much to the hiring of veteran, superannuated chemical executives from competitors like Du Pont—and more to a single plunge into energy.) But if the base business is sound, there's no doubt that the prime duty of a manager is to exploit that business continuously, leaving nothing to chance.

Consultants, who have often thrived on introducing discontinuous strategies, and academics, who love dramatic case histories, have not been conspicuous in articulating this simple truth. *The Naked Manager* was hard on both groups, especially the consultants; but it's no fault of mine that both have been through recessions since then. So has the computer industry, and there was a common element to all three setbacks: overselling.

This is clearly recognized, and perhaps inevitable, in the computer industry, where the salesman's commission on sales and the manufacturer's own interests combine to push the customer towards the most expensive configuration he can buy. To justify the expense, he must be promised marvels, which probably won't be forthcoming. Nearly a decade ago, a canny man observed that he would buy a computerized M.I.S. (management information system) on the day that a computer manufacturer installed one for its own use. So far as I know, that man is still waiting. But computers do work, and they are an essential, developing tool, without which firms of all shapes and sizes would find it increasingly hard to function.

Similar claims can't, alas, be made for sellers of consulting or of management education. In many cases, either the advice of the consultant or its implementation by the client has led to disaster. In consequence, the top-level trade of boardroom advice on corporate strategy has suffered long-term damage in Europe—not because the consultants themselves are bad (on the contrary, many are brilliant); but because management is only partly a matter of deciding what to do; doing it is what counts. A bunch of executives who need an outsider to give them a sense of direction can never be the likeliest people to stay on the road, even the right one.

The same type of objection can be leveled at the educators, and often is. They have inevitably sponsored the notion that management is a subject like Latin or chemistry, which can be taught in classrooms. It's true that all education has value, and that would-be managers at school can learn plenty that will be useful at work. But in the seventies opinion has swung heavily towards the view (which I've always held) that you can't so much teach managers as *train* them; that sophisticated mathematical techniques have mostly won their place in the schools because they are so useful as classroom fodder; and that case histories (as the president of their shrine, the Harvard Business School itself, has lately suspected out loud) are of very little value in developing managers.

The alternative approach, of training on the job, using the classroom only to give the guidance and educational back-up which prove necessary, has been taken to its extreme by Professor Reg Revans, whose "action learning" switches managers between companies to grapple with other people's real-life problems. The Revans approach seems to work, and it embodies many of the principles of what this book has identified as winning management; and unless management education does help in that cause, it is no help at all.

17

PLUS ÇA CHANGE

In a way, "scientific management" should have been perfectly possible. The science of war, after all, has been intensively developed, and it's not just marketing that gives managing its resemblance to military work. The manager, too, has to administer and lead large forces, to muster (and master) formidable technical equipment, to plan campaigns in which an opponent must be outwitted, or out-maneuvered, or overpowered.

The winning manager, like the general staff, can and does apply "science" (that is, knowledge and technique) to help in all these matters. But that can never be how he wins. The same, of course, is true of war. The actions, reactions and interactions of human beings determine the battle, to the extent that material and manpower leave the outcome to chance. But even at El Alamein, where Montgomery assembled an immensely superior weight of arms, his impact on the morale and training of the troops was undoubtedly an essential factor in the victory.

Management is about such human factors, the intangibles and the changing tides of individual men and women and of mankind in the mass. Uncertainty is the name of the game. Thus, reason's main task in management is to limit the zones of uncertainty as far as possible, to reduce risk to tolerable dimensions, to allow scope for changes when the unpredicted (not, note, the unpredictable) happens—as it always will.

It's because of this dominant human factor that management is so full of paradox. One that troubles many writers, including Peter Drucker, is the paramount role of the paramount man. Not only is it wrong in theory for an organization to depend on some Caesar, but in practice the dependence often proves dangerous. The excesses which the emperor commits can be bad enough. Worse still, he customarily bequeaths a legacy of inferior successors. So the correct response seems to be: no great men. Except that the ban would mean: no (or few) great businesses.

The paradox can only be resolved by accepting that human nature includes, among its quirks, the desire to respond to the personal qualities of someone we recognize as our superior. That's why one man gets better work from the same people who under-perform for another boss. Moreover, the advantages of having a single source of authority and dynamism are considerable. The disadvantages arise from the human nature of the boss himself—from his subconscious (which secretly tries to protect him by appointing acolytes and successors who are inferior to the "great man")—and from his conscious wish to impose himself on everything and everybody.

Self-awareness is the only defense, and it can work. Some great founder-proprietors do leave well-worked-out and protected successions, taking as much pride in their people as their products. But this difficult achievement is, by definition, a rare one. Most managers are not founder-proprietors, nor great men, nor anything like it. They may try to behave that way; that is one of the eternal faults of human nature which prevent the run-of-the-mill professional manager from delivering the exceptional performance which is within his reach.

> *Use of managers should conform to the value analysis ideal of Least Input for Most Output.*

The barriers to human perfection are many and varied. But any list of eternal management impediments would have to include:

1. The abuse of time.
2. The managerial lie.
3. The misrepresentation of risk.
4. The overpayment of managers by managers.
5. The misunderstanding of motivation.
6. The false assumption that somebody else's business can ever be like one's own.

The passage of the years has made little difference to the items on this catalogue, and maybe it never will. Managers waste time, which is in limited supply and not replaceable, because it's so hard to concentrate all their time on what is truly essential. They fib (or worse) about the facts, because the latter are less palatable than the manager's fictions. They portray themselves as "risk-takers" because it sounds romantic and glorifies their actually often humdrum role. They go on and on about motivation without facing up to the truth that corporate hierarchies are demotivating in essence, and that any venturesome young man would rather run a business that is truly his own than some operation where an older (but not necessarily wiser) man can call the shots.

If a manager, or a set of managers, can only break out of these traps, that alone will propel them much of the distance towards success. Take time. How many executives pause to think whether some project they have just launched is worth the expenditure of executive time required? Because every company above a certain size can always afford somebody to do something, the firm easily silts up with permanent and temporary assignments that are not worth the trouble—and specifically not worth the time. The time-logs which determined managers use to regulate their own days are also important to the company. Its use of its managers should conform to the value analysis ideal of L.I.M.O.—Least Input for Most Output.

But the same process which silts up the executive's personal day tends to clog up the corporation. Committees meet for no purpose with members who couldn't contribute to the objective even if there was one. External commitments, often of a quasi-social nature, also eat into time. I greatly approved the tongue-in-cheek idea of an author who suggested in *Management Today* that companies should use executives near retirement for these ceremonial purposes: men who know enough to alert the active management if anything important does, by accident, come up, but who otherwise earn *their* bread by allowing other managers to earn bread for the company.

The idea is unlikely to catch on, though, so long as managers hanker and hunger for the prestige which goes with outside bodies and internal committee membership. It's a sound rule that no fully paid manager should have any daytime commitments outside the company which pays him. His job should be strenuous and exciting enough to absorb him completely. If it isn't, something is amiss. Top men with a plethora of outside entanglements will claim that these jobs help the company. Almost invariably, those men lie. It won't be their only lie, of course—in fact, it sometimes seems impossible to get a manager to tell the truth, the whole truth, or anything like the truth about his corporate affairs.

More often than not, to be fair, this is because they don't know the truth themselves. Men will, for example, boast about profits or market share to others who, because of their own business knowledge, can spot the lie at once. But the liar has probably deceived himself. He doesn't want to face the fact that the business makes a pitiful profit or has a pathetic market share. It follows that he will be defeated—if he hasn't been already.

Far better to be like Philip Caldwell, during his climb to the succession to Henry Ford II. Confronted with the task of competing against the all-conquering trucks of Chevrolet, Caldwell sat down with his colleagues to list every attribute that might influence the decision of a truck buyer and rigorously compared the Ford and Chevrolet offerings on each criterion. (As I recall, the Ford came out ahead on only two items, and one of those was the windshield wipers.)

Now, Caldwell's unforgiving search for truth was made far easier by the fact that he was an outsider, thrust into the truck division to save a losing day. It's a pitiful aspect of human nature that it so often takes new brooms, not to sweep clean, but to raise any dust at all. Anything that any turnaround artist has ever achieved could in theory have been accomplished by the men *in situ*. But they would have needed the very quality, objectivity, whose absence helped to make them failures.

The best cure for this deficiency is an experience of real sharp-end contact and real adversity. I've never met a manager with factory-floor experience who didn't value that grounding above all; and I've never met one who has stared disaster in the face whose survival hasn't shaped his attitudes for the rest of a successful business life.

One such hardened-in-adversity manager likes to say that management is about taking the risk out of business—and his trade, women's fashion, is as "risky" as they come. But it's most important to be clear-minded about that word. The degree of risk is a measure of the possibility of being wrong. In some trades—like high fashion—it's much easier to be wrong than in others. But there's nothing particularly virile about sticking out one's neck. Older managers who encourage their juniors, if only by lip-service, to take risks are wrong; they really mean that their juniors should be "enterprising"—and that is a very different matter.

The whole concept of risk developed from mercantile trade. You sent a ship forth from Boston or Portsmouth to pick up a cargo of spices, knowing that, if it didn't sink *en route*, your investment would be repaid many times over. There was no risk in the venture, the project, only in its execution. The vast majority of commercial failures are plans which would have flopped no matter how well they had been carried out.

When failures occur, too, the more senior the manager, the less risk he runs of dismissal or demotion, even of any serious impact on his personal fortunes. Look at the highest salaries in any country, especially the United States, and it's hard to make any correlation between reward and achievement. Mostly, men rise to the top through age, and continue to fix matters so that, arrived at the summit, they get the biggest share of the boodle—paid, moreover, in as painless a way as possible.

How much the chairman or even the chief executive of a major company is worth to the shareholders is a question nobody asks—though there are cases where the boardroom remuneration is a fair, or unfair, proportion of the after-tax profits. But plainly a system of hierarchical rewards tends to encourage time-serving and to weaken the positive motivation, the venturesome drive, which the senior men claim to want. So they turn to devices which promise to inject motivation, like fixes of heroin, and are regularly disappointed.

The solution can only lie in the motivation of the whole company, in the way in which it is structured, and in the amount of true responsibility and early reward given to people who do their jobs successfully. What they run can never be a business like their own—because it isn't their money, a fact they should never be allowed to forget; and won't, if they are really good. But an individual manager's operation should be, quite clearly, *his* business, to run in *his* style; provided only that he runs it well.

> *No matter what relation the price paid by the immediate user bears to the full cost of the product, somebody, somewhere, somehow, is bearing that full cost.*

The seventies were a good testing and training ground for the new breed of managers, not least because the idea of discrete business units with full operational responsibility had started to percolate through the corporate establishments. But the relative harshness of the economic environment also helped to provide a more rigorous training ground; although, in truth, the world economy suffered nothing like so severe a setback as would have been supposed from reading the media.

But you can't avoid severe shock when the younger citizens of an affluent West, never having experienced world recession, actually have to endure a year of real decline in output, followed by distinctly slower growth than before. For some citizens—such as the managers of West Germany—the initial shock was so traumatic that they surrendered to daytime nightmares about everlasting zero growth. They were totally mistaken, of course. What happened was no cataclysm, like the seismic disaster of the thirties, but the impact of unprecedented inflation on a world economy which was, in any case, due for certain serious adjustments.

Oil falls under both definitions. Inflation in the West (a classic monetary inflation produced by over-expansion of the money supply in several countries at once, and in the extranational Euro-currency market) reduced the real price of oil. The producers reacted in the usual manner at a time when political developments—the Yom Kippur war—unfortunately emphasized both the power of the Middle East producers and the excessive vulnerability of the West to any interruption of Arab supplies. Had world growth continued at its previous clip, the oil crisis would still have arrived, and sooner rather than later. Coming as it did in the middle of galloping world inflation, the switch from cheap glut to expensive scarcity (one of the adjustments that were bound to come) very likely did have the equivalent effect, as *Fortune* magazine once calculated, of taking two machines in every hundred in the West out of production.

If managers can take any comfort from this uncomfortable experience, it lies in the supreme value of knowing that in economics there are forces that cannot be withstood. Governments might and did suppose that they could sustain growth by printing money. But as the value of that money inevitably declined, so the impact of inflation on savings, on interest rates, on earnings and on prices created the very recessionary effects that governments had tried to avoid. Managers, too, were forced to react as inflation and weak markets threatened to undermine some of the mighty corporations which make up the world's great economic powers.

That so few actually did crumble is some compliment to their managers, as well as to the better public, or governmental, defenses of private firms. But the time of test by recession —which may not be over yet, given the West's continuing propensity for double-digit inflation—did not paralyze consumer and industrial markets. Many went on growing—and growing abundantly. Nor is there any reason to suppose that growth and the exciting development of new markets will ever stop.

Those markets, however, will always be governed by "the rule of full cost." This means that, no matter what relation the price paid by the immediate user bears to the full cost of the product, somebody, somewhere, somehow, is bearing that cost. If the full cost exceeds the true market price (that is, the price which people are ready to pay out of their own pockets), then ultimately the product or service is doomed. Even if it survives, it will deteriorate. Rail systems in countries where the roads and the air are fully developed are a striking case: the full cost per passenger mile, with public subsidies thrown in, is enormous, and fully explains the contraction and worsening of the West's train systems.

Among managers, the fact that everything has a cost should have been swallowed with their mother's milk. But the stress on "profit centers" (an attempt to apply the "business-like-one's-own" theory at large) tended to move emphasis away from *cost*—cost being another word for "use of resources." In a context of scarce resources, it's more important than ever for managers to minimize their costs while maximizing their revenues; or, if they have no revenues (like an internal service department), to prove, first, that any cost at all is justified and, second, that the actual level of costs is the right one.

The value of "zero-based budgeting" (whose popularity may ultimately be President Carter's sole fairly beneficial contribution to the economies of the West) is to systematize this process of challenge: the attack on overheads, which dates back to the beginnings of business. But the attack on production costs is even more vital, since (on the full-cost theory) the lower the true cost of production, the greater the chance of finding successful markets.

A glance at the phenomenon of micro-electronics rubs in the point. As production costs have tumbled, the industry has developed from making specialist components for the few, to mass output of silicon chips for the millions. If pocket calculators still cost as much as $395, as they did in 1971, sales would have been a fraction of their volume later, when the price was $10.95—and the machine was actually better. It's a law of economics rather than the advance of technology which explains the development: the rule that, with every cumulative doubling of output, the price drops by 30 percent.

By no coincidence, the high-technology firms, including the chip-makers, have been immune to the fall in returns on capital that has plagued most industries in the seventies. The average American electronics firm had a profit margin of 5.8 percent towards the end of the decade, compared with 3.7 percent ten years before—not in spite of, but because of the barely credible deflation of their prices in an inflationary age. Investment in lower production costs and higher performance is a sure way to win; just as failure to match the investment of others is a guarantee of defeat.

Of course, everybody fails, no matter how fine their investment policies, if the whole market goes away. When demand collapses for ineluctable economic reasons (as in shipbuilding in the seventies), then nothing—not even the offer of ships at well under full cost—will resurrect the corpse, unless another economic cycle is allowed to work. In this cycle, over-supply leads to price cuts and withdrawal of capacity, and turns into under-supply as demand recovers; prices then rise sharply; investment in new capacity then returns and, in the fullness of time, creates over-supply all over again.

As with all attempts to resist the laws of markets and economics, efforts to stockpile in the hope of avoiding these swings and roundabouts are doomed. The known existence of the stockpile restrains output, prices and recovery long—and painfully—after the natural moment of upturn. Since such hard economic laws determine events, it's no surprise that humanistic theories which impinge on those laws are always subject to alteration at short notice.

One Swedish shipyard, for instance, seemed to have achieved both productivity and profit by applying enlightened theories of man management. The yard concerned, Kockums, was quite right to treat its people intelligently and well; but when the economic storm blew down on the shipbuilders of Europe, the fabric of Kockums' prosperity was blown away, and so, equally inevitably, was the company's reputation as a worker of management miracles.

But, as the management theories come and go, each adds something of lasting value. A few of the theories go on forever, not because of the preternatural brilliance of their originators, but because they are rooted in both sides of the equation: the malleable material of human nature and the iron laws of economics.

> *"Make quality products, constantly strive to improve, take care of regular customers and maintain good relations with suppliers."*

Konosuke Matsushita is a man of profound simplicity, and the overlord of one of Japan's greatest electrical firms. No doubt, the simplicity is exaggerated—but this passage is an excellent illustration of Matsushita's personality:

> Considering that I am rather sickly by nature, I am extremely surprised at the fact that I have been able to continue my business for such a long time. I started with only two persons and, over sixty years, the number of my employees has gradually increased. Today my company has more than 100,000 employees. . . . People say that I have become a great success in business. . . . With the help of my wife and brother-in-law, I started a small electrical supply company simply in order to eat. Of course, there were times when I considered how I might become successful in business. I tried to work hard, used common sense, and adhered to general maxims of practical business management in those days: "Make quality products, constantly strive to improve, take care of regular customers, and maintain good relations with suppliers." My business gradually prospered and expanded in both size and the number of employees.

You might suppose that this great Japanese businessman would continue by claiming that all his subsequent success had been founded on this simple formula. Wrong. He goes on to argue for "a management philosophy" as the foundation of success. By this, Matsushita means an ethical system, a set of morally based principles and precepts that binds together all the members of a company in the interests of the organization which they serve.

The idea comes more easily to a Japanese mind than a Western one. But Matsushita is right—a company does need a unifying ethos, and the more deeply this reflects man's non-material needs, the greater the contribution the ethos will make to the company and to society. The heroes of the last pages of my *The Naked Manager* were the Quaker businessmen: men excellent not only at their primary business task, but also at building for the future and at pioneering the better treatment of people at work. Among the solid and great manufacturing firms of America's Midwest, the same pattern is often repeated: commercial success founded on and imbued by an ethical view of life and the value of work.

A book like my present one, concerned mainly with ends, means and results, by implication ignores these broader, perhaps greater issues. It's wrong for managers to do so. They should, just as Matsushita says, have a philosophy; but that is essentially something which they (as Matsushita did) must work out for themselves. There is, however, one element which has an essential place in any management philosophy—it's the element which the Japanese electrical giant now tends gently to deprecate in that early common-sense credo:

> Make quality products, constantly strive to improve, take care of regular customers, and maintain good relations with suppliers.

Those few words have no great intellectual weight, and would never be written on tablets of stone. But maybe they should be. Their childish simplicity doesn't prevent them from being lastingly right. Many of the most important management truths share this same humdrum quality, but I don't hold that against them—although no less an authority than Robert Townsend, author of *Up the Organization*, apparently does.

Writing a review of my first book, he described its Ten Truths of Management, which were printed on the back cover, as "ho-hum." Well, so (and here) they are:

1. Think before you act: it's not your money.
2. All good management is the expression of one great idea.
3. No executive devotes effort to proving himself wrong.
4. Cash in must exceed cash out.
5. Management capability is always less than the organization actually needs.
6. Either an executive can do his job or he cannot.
7. If sophisticated calculations are needed to justify an action, don't do it.
8. If you are doing something wrong, you will do it badly.
9. If you are attempting the impossible, you will fail.
10. The easiest way of making money is to stop losing it.

Nothing that happened in the seventies has invalidated those ten ho-hum truths, any more than Matsushita's eighteen-word policy statement is less valid now than when he started in business sixty-one years ago. What's happened in the interim, above all, is to emphasize by example (much of it awful) the importance of mastering and sticking to what football coaches call "the basics." Once the corporate reflex has become to "get the basics right" in a continuing process, the company's future and the success of its more complex plans should be assured.

But the key to mastering complexity, too, can be summed up in a favorite acronym: K.I.S.S. Standing for "Keep it simple, stupid," it embodies (in the best K.I.S.S. style) several much more profound observations: like that insistence of Moltke's on an army system which mediocre officers can manage successfully, or the behavioral work showing how the chances of error are magnified with each additional level in the hierarchical structure.

It's another ho-hum truth, which the manager forgets at his peril, that even a hyper-intelligent man will master a simple system more readily than a complex system. Reducing the complicated to the simple is a key to success. *The simpler the task is made, the more easily it will be done.*

It follows that, the fewer the tasks, the easier it is to simplify them. That's why concentration, on a few markets or a few products, or structuring a company so that its constituents can so concentrate, both simplifies and strengthens the firm. The marketing consultant Andrew Tessler has shown beyond question that British exporters, in contrast to their far more successful German and French competitors, disperse and thus waste their effort by serving far more geographical markets. The same observation can be repeated anywhere in management: more means less—that is, M.I.L.O.

The translation is: Most Input for the Least Output. Every manager who has ever pruned a product line, removed a production unit, regrouped machines to eliminate unneeded ones, etc., can produce anecdotes to confirm this truth. L.I.M.O.—Least Input for the Most Output—is the only sound policy and, as noted before, it's one that must include the time of managers, like all other inputs. Not only does this principle bar the sixteen-hour day, the eternal working weekend and other abuses (all of which are evidence of structural and operational defects); it also means not placing people in positions where their ability isn't used to the full.

To express the point positively, ability is more important than seniority, and talent is more important than age. That has immediate relevance to a subject unmentioned so far: women. I was once taken to task by a lady lecturer in management for giving "a very chauvinist speech." My sin was to use the pronoun "he" for the manager—as in these pages. Adding "or she" expresses my feelings accurately, but the extra verbiage doesn't add to the sense. Manager is a female as well as a male word, and any firm where a woman has no chance of reaching any line or staff position is suffering from a self-inflicted wound. Apart from anything else, it's ignoring *half* the available pool of talent—and making itself a less pleasant company for which to work.

Pleasant may be a strange adjective in the context of management, but it has a vital role. If a company isn't pleasant to work for, it probably isn't worth working for. One of the notable developments of our times, a process which has gathered force over the seventies, is that companies have become more enjoyable places: in relatively trivial ways, like the introduction of flexible working hours; in broad social changes, like the spread of informality in manners and relationships; and in crucial managerial ways, like the devolution of real power to points closer to the real work of the business.

Under economic stress and strain, the company has continued to develop into a less stressful and strained form of organization. This social evolution has given managers a much better chance of performing well at their prime function—which is and must be economic, in both senses of the word: using resources economically in order to contribute to the economic well-being of society. The organization that wins and the manager who wins succeed by virtue of their economic contribution. And that is essentially a virtuous achievement, under any economic system known to man.

18

FIVE WHO WON BIG

Managers never dare forget that there's far more to business success than one set of superb results, even than a whole string of splendid statistics. Every business magazine inevitably has its Hero-of-the-Month Club. But heroes, remember, last much better in sports, even in politics, than they do in business. For idols of the business hour, nemesis always lurks in waiting—the chance that one day, like the burnt-out conglomerate kings, they will be shown to have great, clodhopping feet of clay.

Of course, the feet were clay all along. But there's a shattering difference between the knowledge of mortal frailty and its proof. It's the awful proof, like the famous collapse of Litton Industries' conglomerate profits, that brings heroes down from pedestals they should never have ascended in the first place. For business is not fundamentally a heroic activity. It's about basics, and the ultimate winners, more often than not, are those who, soberly and sensibly, lay foundations, on which not only they, but other men, can build.

Hero managers, too, often owe their rise in part to keen application of basic principles. But it's characteristic of the breed to neglect a basic or two, if not three—or more. The time must come when that neglect proves calamitous, if not to them, to those who follow, and who must try, sometimes forlornly, to clear up the mighty man's mess. By an injustice of history, however, those who manage such Herculean clean-ups rarely get the historical accolades of the titan who created the company—and the chaos. A special corner in the Management Hall of Fame should be reserved for men like Ernest R. Breech, who stepped into a postwar Ford Motor Company that was losing a million dollars a day. Breech built up a corporate world leader, not only in automotive design and production, but in the organized, creative and effective use of basic business disciplines.

Yet Breech's basic brilliance couldn't cure two equally fundamental defects at Ford: first, its market share in the United States was only half that of General Motors; second, the Ford family controlled the company. The first explains much of Ford's floundering struggles in 1980; the second explains why, one day, Breech had to pack his bags and depart, saying sadly that "Henry doesn't need me any more." As for Henry—Henry Ford II—he never matched either the managerial reputation of Breech or the genuinely heroic industrial stature of his grandfather.

All the same, Henry II, too, deserves a special place in that mythical managerial Hall of Fame. Under him, the Ford Motor Company succeeded where no other traditional manufacturing company had, and where General Motors hadn't even tried: operating a unified manufacturing and marketing operation across the disparate countries of Europe. This was done so effectively that the European empire could even give a financial transfusion to its bleeding American parent in those traumatic days of 1980, when Ford's record third-quarter losses, at over $6½ million daily, easily outdid the drain so efficiently arrested by Ernest R. Breech.

The contrasting merits of Breech and Ford II illustrate a bedrock truth about managers and entrepreneurs. Nobody is equally good at all things. Even the most capable executive builds his success on the few basic elements where he excels. If he's wise, he surrounds himself with colleagues whose basic expertise lies in the missing areas. But just as business success usually rests on the exploitation of one wonderful idea, so that exploitation, in turn, often owes its effectiveness to the pursuit of one basic excellence—even of one basic excellent objective.

The five case histories which follow prove this basic point, drawing on the careers and words of five very different men. Their similarities, however, are more striking than those differences. A half-dozen attributes appear to be common to all five: tenacity; loyalty to long-standing colleagues; tightness with money coupled with tight controls; ability to admit and learn from mistakes; the money-making drive; and, underlying all, an urge to simplify and build on simple foundations. None of them exemplifies this last attribute more than the first case.

"If that simple system had not been there from the beginning, I would have stayed in two shops."

"I said to Eric Hartwell that if we could take £400 a week, make 60 percent gross, keep wages below 20 percent and other expenses at 8 percent, on the rent we paid, we must make so much a week." The speaker refers to a milk-bar in Leicester Square, opened in 1938, and to an associate, Hartwell, who was still at his right hand 43 years later. By then, the milk-bar had metamorphosed into the 800 hotels, 3,000 catering outfits, and £772 million turnover of the global enterprise called Trusthouse Forte.

Its founder, Sir Charles Forte, went on to explain how "From that beginning, we have always known what we were doing, and have always compared one place with another by the use of percentages or ratios. They are the basics of the business. The system has been refined into more statistics, into graphs and so on. . . . But if that simple system had not been there from the beginning, I would have stayed in two shops, turning up morning, noon and night, and asking, 'how are you doing, have you taken any money today, can I pay the rent tomorrow?' "

The quotes give some idea of the personal style which enabled an energetic, short, and politely spoken Anglo-Italian, without benefit of formal training in management, or any initial capital worth mentioning, to create and hold together a vast, rich business. What's more, its major growth came in the later middle age of both Forte and his close colleagues. Hartwell was one of four associates who joined Forte in the earliest days, and who, according to Forte, provided an essential element of collaboration. Thus, a crucial moment of lift-off came in the early fifties, when Forte had the chance to buy the marvelous Criterion site in Piccadilly Circus for £800,000 which he didn't happen to have. Referring to that deal, he said, "I am not sure that I would have had the courage if I had been on my own. But with four or five other people you can get together and say 'Look, why do you think we can use this? Where are we going to find a chap to run it?' Then somebody says, 'maybe so-and-so can do it.' Gradually you can find that the operation is quite simple."

"Simple" sounds much too simple. In fact, Forte pioneered rather subtle schemes like the lease-back, in which you sell an acquired property to an institution that promptly and obligingly rents it back. Clever financing of sound property purchases set the pattern by which Forte pursued a clearly expressed basic objective: "I have always been ambitious to undertake projects which will earn money, because that is my principal job—to earn more money and in greater safety." To that end, Forte employed: "(a) a certain cash flow, (b) a bank that has always been very good to us, and (c) financing the business through property purchases." It's a marvelous winning recipe.

True, Forte's nutritious ingredients, especially (a) and (c), are more easily applied to hotels and restaurants than to many businesses. Cash customers provide the cash flow, and the property values are not only obvious, but intrinsic to the trade. The security is double—the site of the Pierre in New York City, or Grosvenor House in London, or George V in Paris, is worth a mint merely as land, while the premium position simultaneously generates the premium prices and prime profits.

But any manager in any business should heed Forte, and avoid overly trusting reliance on income streams unbacked by assets. They can prove to be a desperately dangerous support —on this point Forte speaks from hard experience. He bought a soft ice-cream firm in the sixties, for its earning power, and had to sell off the error at a costly loss. But the lesson was well and truly learned. "For the first time in my career," Forte has admitted, "I made a very bad mistake, and I was principally wrong because I was overanxious. If you allow any deal to hallucinate you, it's liable to go wrong."

There's nothing hallucinatory about the lush product of Forte's latter-day deals—even though his crucial 1970 merger with Trust Houses, which added some prime hotel properties and thousands of rooms, appeared to backfire disastrously. Forced to fight for his business life, in possibly the best-publicized boardroom brawl of postwar Britain, Forte provided a textbook demonstration of entrepreneurial tenacity. Pumping his personal fortune into buying shares and producing a final, overwhelming power-play, he remained in undisputed command (and in undisputed direct and indirect ownership of stock now worth £30 million).

Whether or not this trauma revived, or reinforced, the flow of his business adrenalin, Forte's further deals truly transformed the group—coups like picking up control of the Travelodge motel chain for £9.5 million in 1973, or relieving the suffering J. Lyons group of assorted prime hotels such as the Cumberland at Marble Arch in 1978. As recently as 1969, the group was only an eighth of its present size. At that date a dispassionate observer would surely have ruled out any skyscraping rise simply because of the founder's fairly advanced age: he was already 62.

Nor did visions of 40,000 beds in the United States, or world sales outstripping an American giant like the Marriott Corporation by 1979, seem to dance in Forte's head. His ambition before the Trust Houses deal wasn't "planned in specific terms of doubling the company or trebling it or making it 10 times bigger. What is clear is that we will take the opportunities that come along, and that these opportunities are getting bigger."

Taking opportunities is one thing: exploiting them another. Forte's managers have been expected to achieve—one of his management tenets being that, "It is amazing if one sets a target, how easily one hits that target." Noses are kept close to grindstones; and the business is controlled by equally close concentration on those early basics. As Forte summed it up, after a team of management science experts imported into the business was disbanded some years ago, "we have since gone back to basic common sense, allied to very good accounting." It's the combination punch of successful entrepreneurship.

Common sense, very good accounting, hitting targets and ratios are catnip to another Briton, the General Electric Company's Lord Weinstock. Like Forte, he is making the breakout from a United Kingdom-based business to a global concern—although even the £52 million A. B. Dick copier buy, G.E.C.'s largest in the United States to date, represents a mere splash in that business ocean. Weinstock's basic principles appear to translate into American practice with little difficulty. They begin with the proposition that, if you maintain efficiency at satisfactory levels and improve it continuously, the financial results should flow through in deeply satisfying quantities. Under this regime, you wouldn't, as one director remarked long ago, with feeling, "get a word of thanks if the profit was up but the overhead was higher than budgeted."

It's hard not to read into this philosophy the tough lessons from Weinstock's early career, when he faced fierce pressures as a supplier of radio and TV sets, mostly to rental groups. The eventual hard-won success was founded on skill at squeezing factory costs to the lowest possible level. Overheads were kept to irreducible minimums—such as only 145 non-productive employees out of 2,400, with no private secretaries. In the process he developed a famously abrasive management style. This brilliant performance took Weinstock's original business into G.E.C. at a price which gave his family and friends a critically large chunk of the equity—critical both for the influence and incentive it provided, and for their own fortunes. Weinstock's personal stake alone, considerably smaller than his non-beneficial family holdings, is now worth £16 million. But still greater managerial bravura was required to transform a deeply ailing group from near-bankruptcy to today's $7.2 billion in sales and (a far better indicator of effectiveness) 32 percent pre-tax return on capital employed.

Weinstock, a definitely clever man who has been heard to deny his cleverness, is a passionate exponent of thinking simply and directly about means and ends. "I'm not a pattern weaver," he says; "you can draw charts and define tasks and relationships, but if you think that's all management is you're deceiving yourself." Uncovering self-deception is a facet of the uncomfortable assessments which his managers must undergo. As one described the process of budget approval, "Weinstock is paging, and everyone else is paging with him. With every page turned, your heart rises." Yet for all that abrasive reputation, for all his own undisputed dominance of the management style at G.E.C., Weinstock was a very early pioneer of the flat structures, with the smallest possible central organization (and central overheads), that, with luck, will be the prevailing fashion of the eighties.

Each of the more than 130 domestic businesses, into which G.E.C. is currently divided, has its individual boss and is supposed to have enough autonomy to follow its own destiny. Sir

Kenneth Bond, who has worked with Weinstock since the radio and TV days, says, in words that would be heresy in most large firms, that, "Our managing directors approve their own capital expenditure. The justification for it is not really a head office business." But if these sub-bosses don't ask questions ceaselessly about their performance, markets and objectives, it's a fairly safe bet that Weinstock will.

Inevitably, failings and shortcomings are thrown up by the process, and Weinstock has shown more tolerance towards error than towards attempts to conceal it. His business philosophy sometimes seems to suggest that management must fight a continual war against management's own backsliding into waste and slackness—which, of course, is absolutely true. When G.E.C. was the wonder of whiz-kid managements in 1966, the 42-year-old Weinstock told *Management Today* that his group was "not half-way in terms of the efficiency of some operating units"; and he meant it.

G.E.C., though, was rapidly becoming quite efficient enough to absorb the two giant competitors—Associated Electrical Industries and English Electric—which once held equal ranking with Weinstock's company. Neither of the absorbed colossuses was renowned for its razor-sharp efficiency; with A.E.I., the reputation was the reverse. Thus, nobody can rival Weinstock's knowledge of how big companies can generate expensive incompetence, and of how simple, direct, tough controls can turn that folly into a fortune. Even G.E.C.'s very own management college received the treatment, and the tale provides an instructive, non-academic illustration of the basic method.

For control purposes, the college was split into three parts; each had to make a profit, or else. The academy was to make money by selling courses, at what the traffic would bear, to all comers, including G.E.C. companies—if the latter wanted to buy. The residential operation had to sell its rooms and food at a profit to those attending the courses. Even the grounds had to earn their keep, by developing and selling market garden produce (the vegetables eventually fetched such high prices that the college couldn't afford to buy them itself, and rich citizens of Rugby reaped, or, rather, ate, the harvest).

This directly effective style has its detractors, and so, amazingly, do the results: although it's surely impossible to argue with a decade's expansion in net capital employed of 170 percent, against a 225 percent surge in sales, a 559 percent rise in pre-tax profits and 590 percent leap in the net. Weinstock has said that "the object is to be efficient, not to be big. Growth is something that comes through efficiency." True enough; yet size counts in today's world, the electronic world especially. G.E.C.'s phenomenal performance still leaves it well behind the sales of world competitors (G.E., Philips, Siemens, not to mention the Japanese). The critics argue, with conviction, that G.E.C. is also weaker than any of the mammoths in consumer durables, from cookers to stereos, or, at the opposite end, in advanced electronics—at the frontiers of new technology.

In much the same way, critics can point out that Charles Forte's combination of solid business basics and skilled opportunism hasn't answered the question of whether a lasting corporate management exists to take his business forward after the founder's magic touch, inevitably, has gone. Although both Forte and Weinstock have shown an essential virtue in keeping close associates with them for years, that virtue too has its vice; equally inevitably, one day must see a relatively wholesale changing of the guard.

The unknown future is the final test of a manager's known past and present. In both these British cases, basic excellence has carried two entrepreneurial businesses far further, in far shorter time, and to a scale of success far greater than anybody could have expected at the outset. How they did it is relatively clear: less obvious is what happens next.

> "*I am working here for myself, not because I am the company president, and I hope you're working for yourselves, too, and not for me.*"

If ability to ensure continued growth and prosperity into an unknown future, when he himself isn't around, is the supreme test of a winning manager, then the Japanese start (as in so many matters) with an unfair advantage. The renowned social system of the Japanese gives an inherent stability to the firm, and to the relationship of people within it, which the individualism of the West can only match with difficulty. So, admiration for the achievements of a man like Konosuke Matsushita has to be tempered with the knowledge that an English, an American, or even a German Matsushita would have had to build his business in a very different way.

Probably he wouldn't have been able to build so high and so fast, either. At $11.1 billion in sales, Matsushita's empire towers over Weinstock's G.E.C. and is substantially larger than Westinghouse ($8.5 billion), the also-ran to General Electric in the United States. But it's not enough to say that Japan is different—profoundly true though that statement is. There are Japanese entrepreneurs whose mastery of the basics is so brilliant that their success has to be explained by far more than a national urge for self-sacrificing creation and development of other people's businesses.

Of those masters, my favorite is Soichiro Honda, not least because, to quote an apparently bemused journalist from the sixties, "Mr. Honda is a management executive who always wears red shirts and tells naughty stories when drinking. We have to admit that a new type of executive has appeared who could not have been imagined in the conventional sense." This unconventional behavior by Honda has one enormous argument in its favor—it is *human*. Many of the business basics prove far more effective if only they are applied to the company with the human touch; that's what convinces people that the boss is in truth behaving towards others as he would wish them to behave towards himself.

The son of a blacksmith, Honda stayed close to his earthy roots in a way somewhat reminiscent of the first Henry Ford. Like Ford, he is an engineer first and foremost, who at one point raced cars. It's unlikely, however, that old Henry ever passed through anything like Honda's postwar fallow period. Then, according to a Japanese business magazine, the future tycoon "purchased a fifty-gallon drum full of alcohol and did nothing but drink alcohol and water with his friends for about half a year." Having survived that major health hazard, Honda bought 500 small war surplus engines, and was off and running, or, rather, riding, on his first two-stroke. He had to adapt the engines to run on a mixture of pine-root extract and black-market gasoline (the white-market stuff being in short supply).

Romantic tales of business beginnings such as these make lovely reading, but they do little to explain dynamic success. Part of Honda's corporate dynamism has obviously always been Honda himself. What made the sheer personal energy so effective, however, was its marriage to engineering both brilliant and sound, and its application to design and production. As long ago as the mid-sixties, Honda had abolished stocks (and their financing costs) in his factory. The guiding principle—materials and parts are to be consumed by the assembly lines as soon as they are delivered—is even now too rarely followed in Western plants. Honda has presumably never forgotten the cash shortages of his early years, when, again like Henry Ford before him, he saved the day financially (Honda had, typically enough, ordered its first American machinery without the means to meet the bills) by making his dealers pay for Honda cycles in advance.

The Ford imitation was devised by Takeo Fujisawa, one of

two key colleagues who have been with Soichiro Honda since the postwar start. The other, Kijoshi Kawashima, was actually Honda's very first postwar employee. This long-standing association with close partners (which, as noted, Weinstock and Forte also exemplify in the wildly different conditions of Britain) hasn't led to a closed mind, either technically or managerially. In fact, Soichiro Honda appears to have gotten around to thinking seriously about management only as late as 1958, after a rare labor dispute had ended up in the Japanese courts.

Far from crowing about the company's initial victory over the unions, Honda felt much happier when a court reversal held both sides equally to blame. Since then, his management policies have been developed as carefully as his engineering, hinged around the following philosophy: "I am working here for myself, not because I am the company president, and I hope you're working for yourselves, too, and not for me."

Of course, words (the above were delivered to union representatives) are not the same as deeds. But Honda's symbolic acts reinforce the message: no private offices (conference tables, however, are round, to facilitate communication); no company cars; one huge cafeteria for everybody; white coats for all. The use of "quality circles," with no inspectors, but full participation of the work group, under an elected foreman, in obtaining the desired high standards, is basic to shop-floor organization. That in turn is geared, not to frantic efficiency, but to consistent, orderly, high-speed performance.

Still, it's nonsense to correlate all this desirable democratic procedure, and that alone, with the results that took Honda from nowhere to a 1978–79 turnover of $5 billion. Those results are truly founded on aggressive marketing. For instance, Honda early on sold into the bike shops, far more numerous than Japanese motorcycle outlets, while Kawashima did a legendary job in breaking into the West Coast with 1,500 dealers. As one director explained, "In the United States, we didn't want to put a small cage on our business even at the first stage.

Five Who Won Big 275

From the beginning we have always wanted to be large. We wouldn't have gone in for Grand Prix racing otherwise. Our policy of selling is not primarily to confirmed motorcyclists but to members of the general public who have never before even given a motorcycle a second thought. When many companies look at market potential, they examine only the market at the time. Not us."

Superb technical development has also been fundamental. Long ago, Honda set up a separate research company, and gave it 3 percent of Honda's total annual sales income. That was back in 1961—a year when Honda already accounted for half of Japanese two-wheel production. For years afterwards, the firm didn't see that its future on four wheels, as opposed to two, would be especially big or bright. But (like its car competitors) Honda management itself underestimated the penetrative power of its own marketing, design and manufacturing. This latter power is epitomized by a British rival's quote when Honda racers ran away with the first five places in both Tourist Trophy classes on the Isle of Man: "When we stripped a Honda, frankly it was so good it frightened us. It was made like a watch and it wasn't a copy of anything, and very good thinking."

Now, great engineering is only to be expected from a great and compulsive engineer like Honda. But nothing in the whole of his remarkable performance at the top became the great man more than his leaving at the summit. At the age of 66, he retired. His conventional reasons were as follows: "I know what I can't do. I don't understand data processing and electronics. Today, automobiles require automation. I am too old to study computers; I have no willingness to learn new technology any more...."

However, it wouldn't be Soichiro Honda to leave matters as simply as that. He also observed that "I lost my sex power. I don't say I have lost all my sex, but, I must admit, frequency of doing and recovery have not been the same as when I was young. Great leaders love sex, and I am not a great leader any more." Moreover, "I can't drink any more. Two cups of sake is enough. For entertaining customers and employees, presidents should be able to drink more. . . . Without sex power, drinking habits, and work desire, I should quit the life of an entrepreneur. . . . I want my employees to be happy. If I had any more to say, I would not retire from the company."

A basic business principle of supreme importance runs through both this endearing eccentricity, and the Japanese belief in the identity of sexual and other forms of prowess. Honda is recognizing that, unless the organization has indeed become more important than the man, the latter has failed—and so, one day, will the organization. If even so dominant a personality can't safely step aside at a normal retiring age, far from managing the company sensibly, he has been offending against basic organizational principles. Because he had followed these principles to the letter, Honda could, on retiring, say with evident and merited satisfaction, "The deputy president and I have not signed any papers nor attended any executive committee meetings for the past ten years." How about that?

> "I'd noticed that a few companies like Du Pont and G.M. made 20 percent on equity, so I said, 'Why not shoot for that?'"

The basic preaching of Soichiro Honda, carried out in practice with such self-control and admirable results, is a creed which all big bosses, and many little ones, should follow:

1. Spend your time correctly judging future trends.
2. Leave details of daily operations to the responsible personnel.
3. Insist that the latter make consensus decisions.

4. Always approve what they ask to be done for short-term tasks.

This is a code, a text, a potted sermon, for the man who wants his business to make the transition from an entrepreneurial creation to a long-lasting, creative, evolving corporation. It's a vital change, and one which has to be made much earlier now in the eighties than was once the case. Even a relatively small company has a more complex management task than large concerns did in the fifties. It needs far more information, far better systems, far more effective controls—and those needs demand the kind of personal delegation and combined operations summarized above by Honda.

But the task also demands a basic directness and simplicity that convert perfectly from Japanese into American and back again. Take this for an example: "I'm sure that as the founder of the business, I would have been a real pain in the neck to [the] management if I had stayed on the board." The writer is Royal D. Little, an engaging character who shares with Honda a great deal more than perception of the necessity for founding fathers to get out of the way.

One of those shared characteristics is amiable eccentricity. Many American tycoons have lost $100 million, no doubt, but only Little has written a book about it (*How to Lose $100,000,000 and Other Valuable Advice*). That only exemplifies Little's extreme willingness to own up to his mistakes and to learn from them—with spectacular results. From 1964 to 1979, Textron, with an earnings per share increase of 16 percent a year compound, was the sixth fastest-growing of all the companies listed in *Fortune*'s 500 in both 1955 and 1980. Though Little himself bowed out in 1962, he had chosen his own successors (Rupert C. Thompson and William Miller, later boss of the Federal Reserve System and Secretary of the Treasury), and nobody questions that the setting-up and development of Textron owed everything to Little's basic genius.

He had started off by founding a New England textile

company in 1928 with $10,000 of bank money. "I guess I had a natural flair for business. During the first five years . . . we almost broke even," he recalled. Though the textile company somehow survived the early fifties, the real turning point came when Little first began to think as simply and directly as possible about what he was doing and why. After some thought, Little concluded, "I didn't see how the textile business could ever be good in my lifetime. But I'd noticed that a few companies like Du Pont and G.M. made 20 percent on equity, so I said, 'Why not shoot for that?' "

The target of a high return on equity became translated into the guiding principle of the Textron conglomerate as it burgeoned. After a brisk, small-beer start (upholstery cushioning, radar antennae and an electronics firm), Little ran into a big problem: little or no cash. So he bought deadbeat textile companies for their saleable assets and tax losses, borrowed heavily and launched his "acquisition of the month" plan. In eight years, Little bought 40 firms; by 1967, sales in all manner of diverse enterprises, many of them highly technological, almost hit $1½ billion (turnover has doubled since). Yet the organization stayed as tight as a drum—with a measly $10,000 limit on what a division head could spend without approval.

The sailing wasn't always plain. One of the many self-deprecating stories Little loves to tell concerns the cruise ship *Leilani*, a minor venture on which Textron lost $8 million. Like Forte with his soft ice-cream failure, Little typically learned his lesson: "If an investment goes sour, the first loss is the best loss. If Textron had thrown in the sponge at the time the operating companies could no longer pay the rent, the losses would have been limited to the initial cost of $1.8 million."

But the error did produce an invaluable management tool. "Whenever I was considering a new acquisition," Little remembers, "Rupe Thompson and Bill Miller . . . would escort me to the picture [of the *Leilani*, hung in the main office in Providence] and say, 'Roy, do you still want to go ahead with this new deal?' " The "bold, imaginative, impulsive and unpredictable" Little (to quote a memo written by one disaffected director) sometimes needed reminding to assess each business and business opportunity with all the objective facts and logic he could muster. As Forte noted, it's easy and deadly to get "hallucinated" by a deal.

In his post-Textron days, Little (he says that unemployed retired bosses "wither on the vine real fast and die early") became a practicing expert at "deconglomerating the conglomerates" by the so-called "leveraged buy-out." Helping managers to buy pieces from their conglomerate employers with a mixture of debt and equity is a neat way, to take one example, of turning $500,000 into $4.7 million in under four years. Little, who was also earning whopping $800,000 fees for fixing merger and acquisition deals in his eighties, no doubt benefited from his past Textron errors: one such error being to set a price ceiling if you're buying a business on a formula linked to future profits; if you do, the man will play safe and make less money for both of you.

In all of the "deconglomerating" that he has helped to finance, Little can think of "only one business that appears to have any serious problems at the moment, and that is one we bought in 1973. It is currently in trouble because it is in a no-growth, over-capacity industry. The amazing thing is that I personally arranged this purchase, believe it or not, from Textron, and therefore can blame no one but myself for this mistake. I also selected the management to run it. The less said the better in this case."

With that major exception, Little has shown that the basics of entrepreneurial success can be applied to backing others —and backing others can make money very handsomely indeed. In fact, Textron itself bought, long after Little's departure, a venture capital company, founded by General Georges Doriot, which made a famously spectacular investment in another man's success: Digital Equipment. At Digital, Doriot's original $60,000 had turned into $350 million at one wonderful point.

This investment, as New England in its essence as is Textron, was prudently nurtured by Digital's founding entrepreneur, Kenneth H. Olsen, on business principles as basic as apple pie. Simplicity has been cherished, even though the company's short and stunning career, as the I.B.M. of small computers, has been lived at the complex heart of the greatest postwar technology boom. No one has boomed more than Olsen's company. Digital Equipment has grown at an almost ludicrous pace: 37.6 percent annually in sales since 1973, 28.3 percent in earnings per share since 1969. Yet, incongruously enough, Olsen could say in all sincerity that "we've been quite conservative. It always looks to many in the company that we're growing too slowly. We've lost a lot of people because they felt we weren't growing fast enough."

That conservatism amid explosive expansion is symbolized by the fact that Olsen has stuck for years to headquarters in an uninspiring former woolen mill. Olsen even went without a carpet on the floor, and shunned any such extravagance as a corporate dining room. "Our customers come here to work. They'd rather eat sandwiches at lunch. They come here to see the equipment, work out the details and then go home," Olsen reasons. His own attention is concentrated predominantly on the engineering in which, like Honda, he was trained. The way he talked about it back in 1962 has a Honda-like ring, too: "I still keep my hand in at engineering; for fear that I might one day be out of a job. I do it some Saturday mornings; though I don't tell anybody."

Apart from one near-fatal mistake with an aberration called the PDP-6 (Olsen broke his own rules by allowing the product to be shipped before the engineering was complete), the company has added to the D.E. small computer family with one market winner after another. Olsen concentrated simply and effectively on supplying machines whose "price-performance ratio" was the best on the market. Similarly, the chief management idea is effectiveness: an informal, hard-working, product-oriented and Puritan ethic. "We can't afford to have our people interested in status," Olsen has said, preferring a company with a "withdrawn personality," that doesn't "build up stars" (especially himself), but that does rely heavily on the questioning basic.

As one executive told John Thackray, quoted in *Management Today*, "Ken Olsen has insisted that we in management . . . have open communications. Nobody does things in secret, off in a corner. There are no protected pieces of the company —everything is exposed and subject to being examined and questioned." The correct answers to the incessant questions have enabled Olsen, like Honda, to develop a company and a management simultaneously.

What ultimately ties all the management basics together is a binding ethos which creates more than a success story, more than a personal fortune, which builds a company that can become an institution, but can avoid being institutionalized, and can build the basics into its continuing systems. Such an ethos, then, isn't Eastern in essence. The Littles and the Olsens —and the United States and Europe have many of them— have shown that lasting corporate cultures can be created, and can create lasting success, in the West.

This ultimate objective of winning, naturally, doesn't benefit only the successors. The better-based the business, the better for the founder's own fortunes—even if, like Royal Little, he quits the scene early with his stock. At the end of 1980, just one percent of Textron would have been worth over $90 million: and that is a mere smidgen compared to the enormous wealth of a founder's stake like Olsen's. But all five cases prove another basic fact: the truly winning manager not only has his cake, but others eat it, too.

19

THE WINNING COMBINATION

This book began with the true fairy story of a Sleeping Ugly, which was kissed into vigorous life and growth by the efforts of its own management. But only in fairy stories do people live happily ever after, and companies are no different. Just as yesterday's failures, as in the case of the Sleeping Ugly, can become today's successes, so today's heroes can, with equal ease, become tomorrow's bums.

The corporate world is one of constant shifts: not some unchanging landscape, dominated by mighty, invulnerable peaks. The high and the mighty can fall as far as the humble, and change can topple even the tallest. I.B.M.'s billions upon billions of cash holdings were once the envy of many nation-states; yet in 1979 it was forced by cash shortage to borrow money in unprecedented billions. This fact is no criticism of I.B.M.; it merely affirms that nothing stands still, and that everything changes—or nearly everything.

The situations with which managers must cope, the opportunities for profit which they must grasp, the threats of losses which they must avoid: these are what change, and change all the time, along with (and just like) the societies which throw up both challenges and chances. The methods and styles which best meet situations, opportunities and threats have changed much less over time, because the laws of human nature and economics, in which management method is rooted, while they also change or become modified with time, change at a relative snail's pace.

Prophets, however, are prone to exaggerate both the speed and extent of social change—and to get the direction badly wrong. Today's popular seers talk of a post-industrial society, in which growth will become an archaic concept, technology an irrelevance and microcircuits (a technological product, of course, but let it pass) will replace human labor—for good or ill, according to taste. The post-industrialists (or anti-industrialists) could conceivably be right this time, despite the poor track record of preceding seers. The odds of history, however, are against them.

Yet it hardly matters, in management terms, whether the world economy grows at all, or only slightly, or at a pace much nearer to the wonderful expansion of the fifties and sixties. Companies and all other organizational life-forms will still need to be managed, and, within any overall economic scenario, some companies and some managers will still outperform the others. Thus the rules in the Introduction's acronym, **BACK TO BASICS**, will apply just as strongly in any foreseeable circumstances.

BACK TO BASICS

1. Behave toward others as you would wish them to behave toward you.
2. Assess each business and business opportunity with all the objective facts and logic you can muster.
3. Concentrate on what you do well.
4. Keep the company flat—so that authority is spread over many people instead of being piled up at the apex of some unnecessary pyramid.

5. Think as simply and directly as possible about what you're doing and why.
6. Own up to your failings and shortcomings—because only then will you be able to improve on them.
7. Budget your time and tighten up the organization whenever you can—because success tends to breed slackness.
8. Ask questions ceaselessly about your performance, your markets, your objectives.
9. Save costs—not just because economizing is an easy way to make money, but because doing the most with the least is the name of the game.
10. Improve basic efficiency—all the time.
11. Cash in—because unless you do make money, you can't do anything else.
12. Share the benefits of success widely among all those who helped to achieve it.

Reading over these principles, and over the key sentences which head each section in this book, emphasizes one fundamental point: that the manager's job is essentially simple, while its successful execution is extremely difficult. There are ball games like that: the fundamentals can be written down on one piece of paper, but when you're actually playing, it's hard enough to concentrate on one rule at a time, let alone to obey all these simple principles at once in the heat and fury of the contest.

The champion player has instincts and talents which, enhanced by intensive coaching and practice, give him almost automatic performance—especially against weaker rivals who can't put him under pressure. The same is true of the best winning managers. Practice has perfected their attributes, and they can make success seem easy. But game analogies—including this book's very use of the word "winning"—shouldn't be taken too far: because managers aren't playing a game. Their business is the stuff of everybody's lives, starting with those who work for the firm.

The starting point, however, is never the finish. The basic economic fact of our times is that managers of all kinds and at all levels have become responsible for the dominant proportion of the activities which shape society. The responsibility of managers, expressed in these terms, is awesome. But the genius of our times, or their inevitable historical development, or both, has been to break down this responsibility into parcels which are of more manageable size and shape.

The entrepreneur starting a new business in a garage is no less a maker of his times than the man succeeding to the top spot in some vast multinational corporation. Both, however, now have a great deal of freedom—perhaps more than ever in the past—to do what they want in the way that they want, provided only that it works, and works within a context of well-defined social and human responsibility. That is surely a saving grace of the times—the fact that it is harder than it was to perpetuate failure or perpetrate anti-social offenses. This is a benefit not only for the customers of management, but for managers themselves. Serving time, going through the motions and cheating or damaging other people are not fit occupations for grown men and women.

All this means that the dedication to *The Naked Manager* of 1972 seems to me, in today's context, to be unduly cynical:

> This book is dedicated to all those managers who did the right thing for the wrong reason, and were acclaimed as geniuses and heroes; and to all those who did the wrong thing for the right, the wrong or no reason at all and still hold their overpaid jobs.

Today I would be more inclined to acknowledge the work of those managers who did and do the right thing for the right reason, and who don't care whether they are acclaimed at all: who share the intolerance of all right-thinking people for incompetence: but who seek the organizational and personal solutions which make it easier for other managers to perform to the best of their ability, and which match that ability to the job.

In some respects, this is an attitude which the Quaker businessmen, and the other deeply religious non-conformist money-makers of long ago, would have understood and adopted instinctively. Time has moved on, but the ethical and practical necessities of the past have on the whole only been emphasized by the passage of the years. Today's winning manager obeys old-fashioned principles and precepts by using contemporary tools and techniques. He deserves his successes.

APPENDIX

BIG NAMES IN BUSINESS

ROY ASH
With Tex Thornton (q.v.) as chairman, Roy Ash won business fame as president of Litton Industries, now a $4 billion West Coast conglomerate, which was the most fashionable company of the sixties—and one of the fastest-growing ever seen. Its marriage of high technology with high appetite for mergers seemed irresistible; until, in 1970, profits actually fell, and the Litton bubble burst. Later, Ash became Richard Nixon's budget director and federal management expert before returning to civilian life, where, alas, he ran into growth troubles and eventual ouster as boss of Addressograph-Multigraph.

JOE BAMFORD
Joe Bamford was one of the rare breed of determined, individualistic Britons who made fortunes in the fifties and sixties by dedicated manufacturing and marketing—in his case, of excavators. While small compared to an American earth-moving giant like Caterpillar, Bamford's J.C.B. grew fast and fat enough to avoid borrowing (as a matter of principle), to stay privately owned and to afford a fabulously high standard

of corporate amenity. In 1980, Joe's son, Anthony, with his father retired from the scene, staked everything on the success of a much-needed new range of machines.

LORD BEAVERBROOK

What Hearst was to America, Northcliffe and Beaverbrook were to Britain: rampant press tycoons who changed the nature of the media. Born Max Aitken, Beaverbrook was a Canadian—like Lord Thomson (q.v.). A wealthy financier before he entered newspapers, Beaverbrook achieved enormous success with the *Daily Express, Sunday Express* and *Evening Standard*. He was more interested in power than money, and his extravagant management methods are widely blamed for the decline that hit Fleet Street after Beaverbrook's death in 1964—and hit Beaverbrook's own empire hardest of all.

FRED BORCH

Chairman of General Electric at the start of the seventies, Borch, as president in 1968, set up a five-man President's Office imitated by many other corporate giants. This was only one of his many organizational innovations. "The first thing we had to recognize," he said then, "is that the company has grown at a rate of almost a billion dollars a year." In recognition of that, Borch took hold of the huge group and shook it up from stem to stern. His emphasis on strategic planning and his redivision of General Electric into "strategic business units" have provided the model for modern management decentralization. It also paid off in a sharp improvement in General Electric's profit trend, carried on under Borch's successor (now also retired), Reginald Jones.

AUGUST BUSCH III

Other U.S. brewers (notably Miller and Coors) stole the limelight while the Busch family business (headed by August III since 1974) concentrated powerfully on maintaining its position as Number One. Anheuser-Busch owes its strength not just to the company's traditional emphasis on quality, but to August Busch III's readiness to bring able non-family executives into a business which, with $2.78 billion of sales, is actually almost four times the size of Coors.

PHILIP CALDWELL
Caldwell was the first of several heirs-apparent to Henry Ford II (q.v.) to get his hands on the golden chalice. Eventually it proved to be poisoned: Ford's losses in the awful year of 1980 set new records. Caldwell and his co-managers have had to carry the can for the company's inability to match the massive investment of General Motors under Thomas Murphy (q.v.) in down-scaled cars.

SIR JOHN DAVIS
Much of the fabulous success of Xerox has been achieved outside the United States, and much of that xerography harvest was reaped by Britain's Rank Organisation, thanks to the brilliant deals worked by Davis. An accountant with a tremendous appetite for work (and a tremendous hire-and-fire reputation), Davis turned an unpromising British cinema empire into a growth superstar by exploiting the Xerox machines. But his management methods didn't work in other diversifications. His reign ended on an unhappy note in 1977.

PETER DRUCKER
Not a businessman, Peter Drucker is probably still more influential in shaping business thought than any tycoon. Drucker came to America after a background in European banking and economic journalism. He owed his take-off as a management authority and consultant to an extraordinary assignment: a no-holds-barred study of the General Motors built by Alfred P. Sloan. The resulting book, *Concept of the Corporation*, is a classic text. Drucker's many works on the arts and crafts of managing remain unique.

Appendix: Big Names in Business

SIR MICHAEL EDWARDES

Sir Michael became probably the best-known British businessman at the start of the eighties, because of his constant struggles, mostly with labor unions, to save what was left of the national automobile industry. A Rhodesian, Edwardes came to attention through a masterly turnaround job at the Chloride battery business. His initial results at the British Leyland car firm—in terms of market share and huge losses—have been awful. But nobody can deny his tenacity or toughness.

HENRY FORD I

A great engineer who, more than any other man, shaped modern industry, Ford not only developed the assembly line, but created the mass market in private transportation. In the process, he pioneered dealer networks, worldwide branding and other now familiar features of big-time industry. Not an intellectual and not a manager, Ford survived one potentially disastrous threat—the inter-war rise of Chevrolet—but left it to his grandson to survive another—the postwar collapse into colossal losses.

HENRY FORD II

An enigma among world-class businessmen, he employed some of the ablest managers in America and Europe, and applied their talents through a famously effective management system. Yet he was notorious for taking all decisions himself—and for cutting down heirs-apparent (such as Lee Iacocca, who became boss of Chrysler). History's final verdict could be adverse: far from breaking General Motors's massive hold on the American domestic car market, Ford saw that grip tighten dramatically in his last years.

PEHR GYLLENHAMMAR

Gyllenhammar became internationally famous in the seventies, not because his Volvo cars achieved any great feats, but because of much-publicized experiments in group working—

schemes for abandoning the monotony of the assembly line without too much economic sacrifice. Less was heard of the experiments as the decade ended in a period in which jobs seemed more important than their character. Gyllenhammar's Sweden no longer looks like a success story, and Gyllenhammar, after two abortive attempts at rescue by merger, has accepted the embrace of a huge Swedish trading conglomerate.

SIDNEY HARMAN

Harman was part founder of the audio components group Harman International, which was sold to the Beatrice Foods conglomerate in 1977. Harman, when in his fifties, went back to college to take a degree in social psychology. He was already a successful businessman, but he used his newly acquired knowledge to stage experiments in "work humanization"—the concern of many progressive businessmen as the seventies unfolded.

NEISON HARRIS

A legendary figure in consumer marketing, Neison Harris, a Chicago entrepreneur, made his first breakthrough with the first home perm. Harris created his legend and his fortune, not only by persistence and a renewed attack when his first attempt on the market failed, but also by saturation advertising. Two of his slogans have become classics: "Which twin has the Toni?" and "20 million American women can't be wrong." The 20 million women each made Harris a dollar when he sold out to Gillette.

WILLIAM HEWLETT

With David Packard (q.v.), Hewlett built one of the most consistently successful of the companies which have exploited postwar electronics advances. The technology is Hewlett's main concern. The partners kept as far away from I.B.M. as possible, making small calculators, mostly for scientific and professional use. But advancing technology made Hewlett-Packard's machines more and more powerful, until the company became a genuine and rich ($3.1 billion in sales, $269 million in profits) competitor at the small end of computing.

CHARLES F. KETTERING

One of the greatest inventors of all time. Kettering's most notable invention was the self-starter, which made the first of his fortunes. Others sprang from lighting and ignition systems, the electric cash register, accounting machines, small farm generators, etc. He was closely associated with Alfred P. Sloan during the latter's construction of General Motors, heading its research efforts. Kettering died in 1958 at the age of 82. By then, he was better known for his philanthropies (such as Sloan-Kettering Memorial Hospital) than for the vital technological and business breakthroughs that financed them.

SIR FREDDIE LAKER

An aggressive British entrepreneur, Laker cashed in on three economic facts: one, you can always buy airliners on credit; two, the cost of flying passengers in full wide-bodied jets is very low; and three, given a chance, the big airlines will always pitch their prices for passengers very high. By undercutting the giants over the Atlantic, Laker Airways (the airline is still privately owned) ushered in a new era of low-cost mass transport.

EDWIN LAND

Edwin Land was the greatest inventor/manager of his day. Polaroid, which sprung from Land's original research, developed into a superbly managed marketing and production organization under his leadership. His progressive development of instant photography, though, led the business into increasing complexity. Making his own film, and making the greatly improved SX-70 cameras for which the film was developed, gave Land his first serious faltering in 1974. He cured it, only to run into the great instant movie camera flop in 1979–1980. But $1.45 billion of worldwide sales are testimony enough to the prowess of the now retired chief executive, who is still running the all-important labs. A Land quote: "The bottom line is in heaven."

BILL LEAR

Of several fortunes made in American aerospace, that of the Lear family is among the largest, even if it was made from planes that are among the smallest. The Learjet is the best seller among executive jets. Lear, who started his company back in 1930 and climbed on the jet bandwagon in the sixties, was an old-fashioned engineer and entrepreneur whose best-publicized venture was a flop: a doomed 1967 effort to bring the deceased steam car back to life. But his products were still showing the old master's technical wizardry in his own market after his death.

JAMES H. MCDONNELL

The world's most successful builder of military aircraft, "Mr. Mac" (who died in 1980) had his last years clouded by tragic accidents involving his biggest civil project, the DC-10 airliner. Merger with the troubled Douglas Company took McDonnell into a much bigger league (1980 sales: $6.1 billion). But the California aircraft business couldn't be run as closely as the St. Louis military plant, where Mr. Mac made his world-leading Phantom fighters and where he demonstrated how a huge factory could be run in an intimate style.

DAVID J. MAHONEY

Mahoney won out in a power struggle to succeed Norton Simon at the head of the latter's ketchup-to-steel conglomerate. The winner did a phenomenal job of tidying up the group and turning it into an operation predominantly in packaged consumer goods. Later ventures, such as the purchase of Avis

Rent-a-Car, have done less well for the business and for Mahoney's image as a red-hot marketing boss. All the same, $3 billion of sales and a collection of top brand names can't be sneezed at.

LOUIS B. MARX

In a toy business which has seen more than its fair share of debacles, the firm founded by Louis Marx (born in 1896) has suffered peculiar indignities. It was bought, from its first purchaser, Quaker Oats, by an English company, Dunbee-Combex. Yet worse was to follow. Laid low by its American losses, Dunbee-Combex went spectacularly bust. But the name of founder Louis Marx deserves to be better remembered as that of a great pioneer in branded, nationally advertised and distributed toys.

KONOSUKE MATSUSHITA

The Matsushita name does not have the currency outside Japan of, say, Sony. But none of the founding fathers of modern Japanese industry looms larger in his field than Konosuke Matsushita, fourth biggest in the world electrical league. Matsushita expresses his social and ethical philosophy through a little magazine, but he combines his ethics with a strong taste for profits. In 1978-79 Matsushita made $463 million on sales of $11.1 billion—or well over three times those of Sony.

REINHARD MOHN

Scion of a family which started in theological publishing in the last century, Reinhard Mohn has made the company into one of the biggest ($2 billion of 1978-79 sales) in books, book clubs, printing and magazines. Bertelsmann's *Stern* magazine boasts the largest circulation in the world. Mohn spent two years in the United States after release from a POW camp and gained an extremely healthy respect for American business methods. He returned the compliment by buying Bantam Books.

THOMAS A. MURPHY

A typically long-service General Motors veteran, Murphy, as chairman, presided over the world's largest manufacturing company during a crucial development in its strategy: a $50 billion investment program, launched in 1974, to re-engineer and down-scale its gas-guzzling product line. The first of G.M.'s new world cars helped take the company's United States market share up from a low of 38 percent to a wholly unprecedented 61 percent in 1980. A Murphy quote: "We're gaining market share by competing aggressively and respecting the law. Whatever share we obtain is properly ours."

HEINZ NORDHOFF

Without the Volkswagen Beetle, West Germany's economic miracle would have been much less miraculous: without Heinz Nordhoff, there would have been no Beetle. His resurrection of Hitler's People's Car and creation of a manufacturing and worldwide marketing empire (now the eighth largest outside the United States, with $16.8 billion of sales) was nearly faultless. It ran into trouble only towards the end of Nordhoff's career (he died in 1968), when V.W. was stranded, almost fatally, with an inadequate model line-up.

ROBERT N. NOYCE

The emperor of Silicon Valley is bidding fair to take over the scientist/entrepreneur palm from Edwin Land (q.v.). Noyce was the scientific brain behind the fantastic growth of Fairchild Camera in semi-conductors. Breaking away to California to start Intel, Noyce struck pure gold in the explosion of microcircuit technology, in which his leadership has taken Intel to $854 million in sales and $97 million in profits almost overnight. In 1979, investors in Intel achieved a total return of 104.55 percent as Noyce chalked up one of the highest returns on sales (11.7 percent) and on stockholders' equity (25.7 percent) of all the large manufacturing companies outside oil.

DAVID PACKARD

David Packard was doubly fortunate in having Bill Hewlett (q.v.) as his partner in Hewlett-Packard. Not only did Hewlett provide the technological strengths to which Packard could add his business prowess, but he was there to mind the store while Packard went off for a stint as Richard Nixon's secretary of defense. For every year that Packard was in the Pentagon and his shares were in trust, he made $77 million in capital gains.

H. ROSS PEROT

A former I.B.M. salesman, Perot gave the most spectacular demonstration that a new kind of company had been born: one that may manufacture little or nothing, but sells its expertise expensively. Perot's specialty is computer services. The huge value Wall Street investors placed on stocks like his Electronic Data Services made him the fastest billion dollars ever recorded—on paper. The collapse of the stock also gave Perot the biggest one-day paper loss known. But his company is still a leader in its field, and Perot's personal dividends top $4 million a year.

DAVID PLASTOW

David Plastow was the head of a team of managers long employed as executives of the luxury-car division of the Rolls-Royce aero-engine firm, who suddenly found themselves independent when the latter went bankrupt. By taking steps that had always been possible—like raising production and controlling costs—Plastow took the long loss-making company into sharply rising profits. In 1980, he took it into a merger with the armaments-based Vickers Group, giving Rolls a broader base for a decade when gas-guzzling limousines won't be the surest winners around.

FERDINAND (FERRY) PORSCHE

Son of the great Ferdinand Porsche, inventor of the Volkswagen Beetle with which Heinz Nordhoff (q.v.) conquered the world mass market, Ferry Porsche concentrated on applying the founding father's ideas to minority motors—fast and expensive sports cars. The 911, launched in 1965 by Ferry, together with other engineering and design work, brought unique success to the Porsche trademark and gave the family one of West Germany's largest miracle fortunes. It allowed them to retire from active management, and in 1980, chairman Ferry broke German tradition by appointing an American, Peter W. Schulz, as chief executive.

SAMUEL REGENSBRIEF

Regensbrief is one of those largely unsung heroes of American entrepreneurial capitalism who emerge when a magazine like *Fortune* lists the latest crop of hugely rich men. His little-known company, Design and Manufacturing, is remarkable not only for its 40 percent of the American dishwasher market, but because its founder and proprietor came from two backgrounds which are usually inimical to self-made business success. Regensbrief has been both a management consultant and a full-time executive of a large corporation, Philco, now part of the Ford Motor Company.

JIM SLATER

The most talked about success story of the sixties in Britain was the rise of Slater Walker: a small conglomerate that mushroomed via a series of acquisitions into a financial institution of more prominence than substance. History may record much the same verdict on its founding and presiding genius, Jim Slater, an investment whiz kid whose business talents were unable to withstand the collapse of the property and other markets in the early seventies. The Bank of England directed and financed a temporary rescue operation, but the rump of Slater Walker now left doesn't even bear its name.

MICHAEL SMURFIT

Michael Smurfit was one of four sons in a business which his father started in Ireland—by buying, for £500, a half-share in a corrugated-box factory from the priest who married him. Michael was brought back to run the company after a family row had exiled him to England. British interests in paper and packaging became one of the main elements in a ferociously fast multinational growth (sales up 200 times in 12 years) which made Jefferson Smurfit the largest industrial firm in Ireland.

LORD THOMSON
Like Beaverbrook (q.v.), the late Roy Thomson was a Canadian who had already made his fortune before coming to Britain. Unlike Beaverbrook, Thomson made his money in the media—starting in middle age with a radio station in Timmins, Ontario, and ending with chains of newspapers and broadcasting stations in the United States and Canada. Beginning in Britain with *The Scotsman*, he won a self-styled "license to print money" in commercial television in Scotland, bought the Kemsley newspapers and magazines, and gave himself a license to lose money by buying *The Times*. Roy Thomson was made a peer in 1964 at the age of 70. A Thomson quote: "You make a dollar for me, and I'll make a dollar for you."

CHARLES B. THORNTON
Charles Thornton built up a famous group of statistical analysts for the United States Air Force in the war. After the war, he sold the team *en bloc* (including himself and former Defense Secretary Robert McNamara) to Ford Motor. Later, at Hughes Aircraft, "Chuck" Thornton increased sales 130 times in five years and met Roy Ash (q.v.). Together they built the huge Litton conglomerate on the back of inertial guidance navigation systems for the Defense Department. Thornton has subsequently had to steer Litton through its disasters (like shipbuilding) of the seventies.

ROBERT TOWNSEND
Robert Townsend has become widely known, less for his work at restoring the fortunes of Avis Rent-a-Car at the behest of

Wall Street investment bankers, than for the brilliant management book he based on his Avis experiences, *Up the Organization*. After its purchase for Norton Simon by Dave Mahoney (q.v.), Avis stayed well behind Hertz, despite the superb Doyle, Dane, Bernbach advertising, sponsored by Townsend, with its resounding slogan, "We try harder."

SIR SIEGMUND WARBURG
Warburg is the most respected of all the new names to rise in the City of London since the war. The S. G. Warburg bank was opened in 1946 (its founder had started his banking career in prewar Hamburg), and carved out its powerful position in British finance by dint of greater skills and harder work. At one point, the City establishment ganged up on Warburg to stop his client, an American firm, from buying a British aluminium company. He won—permanently.

THOMAS WATSON
The founder of the $26.2 billion I.B.M. learned most of his business while working as an executive for John M. Patterson, the megalomaniacal boss of N.C.R. (now a mere seventh of I.B.M.'s size). Watson, in his own company, was just as dominant and hard-selling, but without the mania. Before the war, he built up a company whose stranglehold on the market for punched-card machines foreshadowed its later dominance in computers, and which became the model for the modern American corporation.

THOMAS WATSON, JR.
Lacking his father's all-powerful personality, the younger Watson nevertheless played a crucial role in the postwar transformation of I.B.M., catching up on its four-year late start in computers and building up the product and marketing strengths which have made I.B.M. the hardest nut to crack in world business. Another brother, Arthur, masterminded the interna-

tional expansion which created a non-American entity of enormous wealth in its own right.

KEMMONS WILSON

A successful Memphis house builder in 1951, when he was 39, Wilson went on a family holiday which was to change the face of the hotel industry worldwide. Wilson didn't like the middle-class hotels and motels he found. So, with another Memphis builder, Wallace Johnson, as partner, Wilson began Holiday Inns. Three ideas made their huge fortune: universally high standards, concentration on building costs as the economic key, and franchising—letting other businessmen put up the capital, a device which played a vital part in the growth to $1.113 billion in worldwide sales for 1979.

JOACHIM ZAHN

Joachim Zahn's stewardship of Daimler-Benz (1971–79), the twelfth-largest industrial company outside the United States, was one of the most successful runs in the history of the motor industry—even though Zahn was not a car man by training. A lawyer, with experience in pulp and paper, he was tapped by the company's bankers and proved to be exactly the right man to foster the continued progress of the technical excellence and single-minded product development which have made the Mercedes niche unique. Zahn took Daimler-Benz sales to $14.9 billion without ever having recourse to the mass market. A Zahn quote: "The man who has a clear view is the man who sees from afar."

INDEX

ABC television network, 21
A. B. Dick copier company, 268
Added value (A.V.), 35–37
Addressograph-Multigraph, 287
"Advise and consent," 85–87
Aerobics, 140
Airline problems, 159–62
 charter companies, 161
Allen, Michael G., 95, 96, 169, 175–76
Ambition, 52–53
 personal, 55
American Management Association poll of managers on attitudes toward their work, 83
American Motors, 158
Anheuser-Busch breweries, 101, 109, 110, 130–31, 133, 288–89
Ash, Roy, 119, 287, 298
Associated Electrical Industries (A.E.I.), 34, 270
Authority
 of expertise, 88–91
 and seniority, 88–89
 traditional and new, 80–81, 84, 85
A.V. See Added value
Avco, 16
Avis Rent-a-Car, 119, 293–94

BACK TO BASICS
 mnemonic acronym for key concepts of winning management style, 4–5, 116, 283–84
Bamford, Anthony, 288
Bamford, Joe, 229, 287–88
Bank of America, 207, 208, 214
Bank of England, 297
Bantam Books, 294
Barron, Cheryll, 228
Basics of winning management, 3–5. See also BACK TO BASICS
Beatles, the, 170–71
Beatrice Foods, 227, 291

Beaverbrook, Lord (Max Aitken), 55, 288, 298
Beecham Group, 172, 174
Beeson, Richard, 119
Bell, Daniel, 13
Bertelsmann publishers, 134
 acquired Bantam Books, 294
Big business
 myths concerning, 236–39
B.M.W., 220
B.O.C. International, 124
Body-scanner, 174
Boeing, 45–46
 747 airliner, 160
Bond, Sir Kenneth, 270
Borch, Fred, 96, 288
Boston Consulting Group, 156
 and PROBE procedure, 167–68
Brain Book, The (Russell), 145
Brain-scanner, 171–79 *passim*
Braniff, 160
Breech, Ernest R., 264
British Leyland, 84, 290
Brown, Mark, 148–49, 204
Buick cars, 157
Burmah Oil, 12–13
Busch III, August, 131, 132, 133, 288–89
Business Week, 60, 114, 178, 185, 188, 237

Caldwell, Philip, 252, 289
Canada Dry, 119
Canadian Pacific, 153
Carter, Jimmy
 and zero-based budgeting, 155, 256
Cash-flow management, 26
Caterpillar earth-moving equipment, 228, 287
CBS television network, 21
Charter air travel, 161

302 Index

Chevrolet cars and trucks, 157, 252, 290
Child, John, 223-24, 225
Chrysler Corporation, 17, 79, 110, 290
  problems, 156-58, 159
Citroën, 110
Clark Equipment, 228
Clausewitz, General Carl von
  his maxims of war applicable to marketing, 98-103
Color film market, 18, 20, 152, 153-54, 156
Communication, 201-15
  clarity of language, 206-7
  distortion, 203-4
  failures, 203-4, 207
  misunderstanding, 203-4
  non-verbal (N.V.C.), 205
  telling the truth, 207-15 passim
  understanding the message, 203-7
Competitive management
  need for "insight/outsight" perceptions, 11-13, 14-15, 16
Compound annual growth plans, 239-43 passim
Computerization
  rage for, 234, 246
Concentration on strong points, 39-42, 101, 245, 265
Concept of the Corporation (Drucker), 289
Concorde, 244
Conformity, 82
Consent, 82-91 passim. See also "Advise and consent"
Consultants, 245-46
Consultation with employees, 189-92, 218-22
Control, 80
  techniques of controlling people, 183-85, 190-91
Cooper, Dr. Kenneth H.
  aerobics program, 140
Coordination by leaders, 124, 125
Coors breweries, 288, 289
"Corporate Strategists, The" (Ohmae), 154
Corporation Man (Jay), 93
Crosby, Philip, 111-14
Crown Agents, the, 202

Daf cars, 221
Daily Express, 288
Daimler-Benz, 214, 300. See also Mercedes-Benz
Davis, Sir John, 70-71, 289
Davy-Loewy, 229
DC-9 airliner, 45
DC-10 airliner, 45, 162, 214, 293
De Bono, Edward, 157
Decision-making, 164-79
  decisions guilty until proved innocent, 175-79
  new and unpredictable decisions, 170-75 passim
  planning ahead, 166-70

PROBE procedure, 166-69
  and trade unions, 164-65
Delegation, 147-49
Design and Manufacturing Company, 16, 297
Digital Equipment (D.E.), 279-81
Discipline, 80, 81, 115-16
  self-discipline, 82
Dishwasher market, 16
Disinvestment, 63
Dissatisfaction
  executive, 83
Diversification, 48, 58-59, 245
Doriot, General Georges, 279
Doyle, Dane, Bernbach advertising, 299
Drift process, 111, 113
Drucker, Peter, 35, 147-48, 249, 289
Dunbee-Combex, 294
Dunlop, 62
  and Pirelli, 175-77
Du Pont, 17, 47-48, 245, 278
  Corfam synthetic leather, 178

Earnings per share (e.p.s.), 22-23, 26-31, 34
Eastman Kodak, 102, 109, 154, 188, 215
Economy of effort, 49-50
Edwardes, Sir Michael, 84, 290
Einstein, Albert, 143
Electronic Data Services, 296
E.M.I.
  and the Beatles, 170-71
  and the brain-scanner, 171-72
  medical electronics, 171-75
Emotional drive, 56
Employee relations, 183-200 passim
  communication, 201-5
  consultation, 189-92, 218-22
  insecurity of managers, 195, 199
  manipulation devices, 189-92
  O.D. (organization development), 195-97
  participation, 189-90, 216-30 passim
  techniques of controlling people, 183-85, 190-91
  at Texas Instruments, 185-89
English Electric, 34, 270
E.p.s. See Earnings per share
Evening Standard, 288
Executive Stress (Norfolk), 141
Exercise
  value to managers, 139-42
Expertise
  authority of, 88-91
Exxon, 236

Fairchild Camera
  and semi-conductors, 295
Family businesses, 130-34, 264
Fathers and Sons (Turgenev), 69
F.I.F.O. accounting, 238, 240
Financial Times, 84, 103

Fitness, physical and mental
 of managers, 137–42
Five-star companies, 38–50
 concentration on strong points, 39–42
 desire to be best, 43–45
 economy of effort, 49–50
 evolution into plurality, 46–49
 self-criticism, 42–50
Ford I, Henry, 126, 273, 290
Ford II, Henry, 252, 264, 289, 290
Ford Motor Company, 17, 57, 157, 252, 264, 289, 290, 297, 298
 import of cars from Europe to U.K., 163
 problems in Britain, 163
 Thunderbird and Mustang, 157
Forte, Sir Charles, 274, 278, 279
 business objectives and principles, 265, 266, 267, 268
 and Trusthouse Forte, 265–68, 271
Fortune magazine, 15–16, 17, 30, 131, 133, 255, 277
Friden, 59
Fuji
 and color film market, 18–20, 152
Fujisawa, Takeo
 and Soichiro Honda, 273–74

Gamesman, The (Maccoby), 195–96
Gellerman, Saul, 164, 197–98
Gellerman Memos, The, 197–99
General Electric (G.E.), 16, 17, 44–45, 74, 97, 100, 271, 272, 288
 PROBE procedure, 166–70, 175–76
 strategic business units (S.B.U.'s), 74, 95–96, 288
General Electric Company in Britain (G.E.C.), 34–35, 90, 268–71, 272
 efficiency, growth and profit, 34–35, 271
 management college, 270–71
General Motors (G.M.), 17, 76, 156, 157, 264, 278, 289, 290, 292, 295
 financial results, 236–37
 the Lordstown events, 222–26
 Vega compact car, 223–24
Germany
 industrial achievement, 91
 industrial engineering, 94–95, 97
Gillette, 291
 and competition, 97–99
Glacier Metal, 219–20
Grace (W. R.)
 conversion from shipping to chemicals, 245
Greening of America, The (Reich), 83
Group management, 120–34 *passim*
 group analysis, 125–26
Grunfeld, Henry, 55
Gulf Oil, 168
 decisions, 178–79

Gyllenhammar, Pehr, 218, 220, 221, 290–91
Haldeman, Robert, 67–68, 70
Haloid Corporation, 173
Handyside, John D., 51–52
Harman, Sidney, 227, 291
 and Harman International audio components group, 227
Harris, Neison, 98, 291
Hart, Moss, 85
Hartwell, Eric, 265, 266
Harvard Business Review (H.B.R.), 27–29, 30–31, 223, 224, 244
Harvard Business School, 22, 131, 247
Hawthorne Effect, the, 105–6
Head office
 reduction in size, 116–17
Heath, Edward, 202
Heller, Frank, 229–30
Hertz Rent-a-Car, 299
Hewlett, William, 128, 129, 291, 296
Hewlett-Packard, 128, 129, 291–92, 296
Holiday Inns, 128, 155, 300
Honda, Soichiro, 272–77, 280, 281
 master of business basics, 272, 276–77
 policies on work and workers, 274, 276
Honda
 motorcycles, 19, 273–75
 and world car market, 58, 275
Honeywell computers, 62
Horizontal organization, 72–75, 77, 79
Hounsfield, Geoffrey, 171–72
How to Lose $100,000,000 and Other Valuable Advice (Little), 277
Hughes, Jim, 228
Hughes Aircraft, 298

Iacocca, Lee, 290
I.B.M., 17, 77, 109, 127, 128, 151, 152, 156, 188–89, 280, 282, 291, 299–300
 and competition, 99, 100, 104
 concentration on data processing, 39
 model of modern American corporation, 215, 282, 299
I-DOCTOR devices, 190–91, 193
Immigrants
 their fresh perspective, 14–17
Impediments to management, 250–53
Imperial Chemical Industries (I.C.I.), 47–49
 competition from German and American firms, 47–48
 diversification, 48
Inflation, 26, 236, 254–57
 accounting, 239
Innovation, 41–42, 78–79

Index

Insecurity in managers, 194–96, 199–200
Insight. See Competitive management
Instamatic camera, 102
Intel, 127, 295
I.Q. tests, 143
Issigonis, Sir Alec
  and the Mini, 158–59
I.T.T., 17
  and zero defects, 114

Japan
  color film market, 18, 20, 152, 153–54, 156
  competition of, 19–20, 80, 81, 91, 114, 115, 153–54, 185
  decision process, 87, 88–89, 90
  outsider techniques, 18–21, 153–54
  and plurality, 46–47, 87
  and quality, 114, 115
  social system sustains business organizations, 81, 272
Jay, Antony, 93, 183
J.C.B., 287
  and productivity, 228–30
Jefferson Smurfit, 74–76, 298
J. Lyons hotel group, 267
Job enrichment, 82–83
Johnson, Dr. Samuel, 89
Johnson, Wallace, 128, 300
Johnson and Johnson, 173–74
Jones, Reginald, 288

Kaiser Aluminum, 117
Kawashima, Kijoshi
  and Soichiro Honda, 274
Kellogg's cornflakes, 109
Kemsley publications, 298
Kettering, Charles F., 41, 292
Keynes, John Maynard, 23
K.I.S.S. ("Keep it simple, stupid"), 260–61
Kockums shipyard, 257
Kodak. See Eastman Kodak

Laemmle, Carl
  Universal Pictures tsar, 130
Laker, Sir Freddie
  and Laker Airways, 292
  and Skytrain service, 161–62
Land, Edwin, 90, 127, 292–93, 295
Lateral contacts, 72–75
Leaders and leadership, 120–24
  and coordination, 124, 125
  different roles, 122–25
Lear, Bill, 42, 293
Learjet, 293
Learning curve, 113
Leitz cameras, 19
Levitt, Ted, 38, 40–41, 244
L.I.F.O. accounting, 238, 240
L.I.M.O. (Least Input for Most Output), 251, 261
Line and staff, 84
Lip watches, 189
Little, Royal D., 281

"acquisition of the month" plan, 278
  and Textron, 277–79
Litton Industries, 29–30, 118–19, 263, 287, 298
Lockheed, 44
  TriStar, 45, 172
Long-term needs, 23–24
Lordstown case, the, 222–26
Louisiana-Pacific, 117
L.T.V., 17

MacArthur, General Douglas, 121–22
Maccoby, Michael, 195–96, 197
McDonnell, James H., 45, 46, 293
McDonnell-Douglas, 45, 46, 293
  DC-9 airliner, 45
  DC-10 airliner, 45, 162, 214, 293
  Phantom fighters, 293
McGregor, Douglas, 67, 69
Machiavelli, Niccolò
  and modern management practice, 157, 189, 190, 193
McKinsey consultants, 31, 154, 167
McKinsey Quarterly, 95
McNamara, Robert, 298
Mahoney, David J., 119, 293–94, 299
Majaro, Simon, 152
Management by objectives (M.B.O.), 85–87
Management education
  criticism of, 246–47
Management information systems (M.I.S.), 246
Management Today, 42–43, 83, 98, 102, 124, 128, 167, 190, 223, 227, 251, 270, 281
Marginal costing, 161
Marketing, 92–104, 235
  market orientation, 93–95
  plan of battle, 97–101
  "small is beautiful," 92–93
  strategic business units (S.B.U.'s), 95–97
  understanding the enemy, 101–4
Market share
  growth in, 25–26
Marks and Spencer, 43–44, 128
Marriott Corporation, 268
Mars, Forrest, 60
Mars confectionery and foods, 49
  and quality, 60, 109
Marshall, Colin, 119
Marx, Karl
  and surplus value, 36
Marx, Louis B., 294
Matsushita, Konosuke
  and his electrical firm, 258–60, 272, 294
M.B.O. See Management by objectives
Measurement of results, 22–27
  creative measures, 24–25
Medical electronics, 171–75
Medium-term needs, 23–24

Index 305

Meetings
  attendance at, 149
Memory and memory training, 143–44
  associative method, 143–44
Mental fitness, 139, 142–50
Mercedes-Benz, 214, 220, 221, 300
Merchant banks, 54–55
Mercury Securities, 54
Mergers
  approach to, 242–43
Micro-electronics, 244, 256, 295
Miller, William
  and Royal D. Little, 277, 278
Miller breweries, 101, 102, 103, 130–31, 288
M.I.L.O. (Most Input for Least Output), 261
M.I.S. See Management information systems
Mohn, Reinhard, 134, 294
Moltke, General von
  and modern business structure, 73–74, 80, 97
Murphy, Thomas A., 237, 289, 295

Naked Investor, The (Heller), 153
Naked Manager, The (Heller), 9, 50, 172, 233, 235, 245–46, 259, 285
National Can, 245
National Cash Register. See N.C.R.
NBC television network, 21
N.C.R. (National Cash Register), 78, 151, 299
Nepotism, 130
Nixon, Richard M., 67–68, 287, 296
Non-verbal communication (N.V.C.), 205–6
Nordhoff, Heinz, 90–91, 295, 296
Norfolk, Donald, 141
Norton motorcycles, 19
Norton Simon International, 119, 299
Norway, 217, 221
Noyce, Robert N., 127, 295
N.V.C. See Non-verbal communication

Obedience, 81–84, 88–91
O.D. See Organization development
Ohmae, Konichi, 154–55
Oil crisis, 254–55
Oldsmobile cars, 157
Olsen, Kenneth H.
  and Digital Equipment, 280–81
Organization development (O.D.), 196–97
O.S.T. system (objectives, strategies and tactics), 188
Outsider techniques, 14, 16–21, 154
Outsight. See Competitive management

Packard, David, 128, 129, 291, 296
P. & A. E. (people and asset effectiveness), 188
Pareto's law (factor), 59–63, 149

Participation, 192–93, 216–30
  the Lordstown case, 222–26
  and productivity, 226–29
  Scandinavian experiences, 217–22
  and a social contract, 225–27
Partnership, 121, 126–30
Paternalism, 82–83
Patterson, John M., 299
P.C.C.'s (product-customer centers), 188
Pearl Harbor, 46–47, 87
People-preoccupation, 234–35
Perot, H. Ross, 77, 296
Personnel departments, experts and policies, 196–200 *passim*
Petitpas, George, 86
Peugeot, 156, 157
  and quality, 109–11 *passim*
Philco, 16, 297
Philip Morris, 101–2
  takeover of Miller breweries, 101, 102, 103, 130–31
Philips electronics, 271
Physical fitness, 139–42
Pickford, Mary, 104
Pirelli
  and Dunlop, 175, 176
Plastow, David, 89, 296
Plato, 86, 127
Plurality (plural management), 46–49
Point of no return, 56–59
Polaroid, 39, 90, 127, 128, 292–93
Pontiac cars, 157
Pope, Douglas, 153, 154
Porsche, Dr. Ferdinand, 131, 296
Porsche II, Ferdinand (Ferry), 131, 296–97
Porsche cars, 109, 131–34
  Porsche family, 131
  family surrender of managerial control, 132, 134
Potential
  of individuals within organization, 68–72
  management, 137–50
Powell, Dr. John, 173
Pratt and Whitney, 44, 96
Pravda, 87
Prestige, 52–53, 55–56
PROBE procedure, 166–70
Problems, 151, 156–63
  and questions, 151–52, 159–63
Procter and Gamble, 40
Productivity, 226, 227–29
Psychologists and management, 51–52

Quaker Oats, 294
Quality, 60–61, 109–15, 228, 258–60
  learning curve and drift process, 113
  and quality control, 61
  zero defects (Z.D.), 111–15, 124
Quality is Free (Crosby), 111–13

Index

Questions and questioning, 151–56
  as competitive tool, 153–56
  and problems, 151–52, 159–63
Rank Organization
  and Rank-Xerox, 70–71, 173, 289
R.C.A., 21, 100, 132
Reading and reading speed
  and a manager's work, 144–46
Reddin, Bill, 86–87
Regensbrief, Samuel
  and dishwashers, 15–16, 17, 297
Reich, Charles, 83
Relaxation techniques
  for stress protection, 141–42
Return on investment (R.O.I.), 28, 29, 31–33, 34, 48, 107–8
  methods for improving, 31–33
Revans, Reg, 247
Right Guard deodorant, 98–99
Risk-taking
  and concept of risk, 250, 252–53
R.O.I. *See* Return on investment
Rolls-Royce, 30, 44–45, 49–50, 89, 95, 296
  RB-211 jet engine, 44
Rootes Group, 157
Rover cars, 172, 174, 220
Russell, Peter, 145

Saab, 219, 221
Sakura
  and twenty-four-frame film, 18–20, 152
Sales growth, 25
Sarnoff, General David, 132
Sarnoff, Robert W., 132
Saunders, John, 190–91. *See also* I-DOCTOR
S.B.U.'s. *See* Strategic business units
Schult, Peter W., 297
Schumacher, Ernst, 92
Scotsman, The, 298
Searby, Fred, 27, 30–33
Sears, Roebuck, 16
Sedgwick, Alastair, 97, 98, 102
Self-criticism, 42–46
Self-management, 137–38, 183–84
Self-neglect by managers, 139
Shell, 175–77
  and PROBE procedure, 167–69
Short-term needs, 23–24
Siemens electronics, 271
Simca, 157
Simon, Norton, 293. *See also* Norton Simon International
Singer Manufacturing
  and diversification, 58–59
Size
  and growth, 20–21
  myth of size, 236–39
  and remoteness, 76
Skytrain service, 161–62
Slater, Jim
  and rise and fall of Slater Walker, 53–54, 297
Sloan, Alfred P., 289, 292

Sloan-Kettering Memorial Hospital, 292
Small companies, 76–79
  and innovation, 78–79
  marketing, 92–93
Smurfit, Michael, 75, 77, 297–98
Social contract between workers and management, 225–27
Sony, 114, 294
Sorensen, Charles, 126
Stein, Gertrude, 156
Stern magazine, 294
Stockpiling, 257
Stock-turn, 36
Strategic business units (S.B.U.'s), 74, 95–97, 288
Stress
  experienced by managers, 140–41
Sunday Express, 288
Sweden, 72, 217, 218, 219, 221, 257, 291
  and trade unions, 191–92
  Volvo experiments in participation, 218–22

Tactical action programs. *See* T.A.P.'s
Tannoy, 227–29
  and productivity, 228–29
T.A.P.'s (tactical action programs), 188
Tavistock Institute, 229
Tenneco, 17
Tessler, Andrew, 261
Texas Instruments (T.I.), 173, 184–86
  concern for people, 186
  corporate culture, 187
  employee relations, 185–89
  O.S.T. system, 188
  productivity targets, 188
Textron, 277, 278–79, 280, 281
Thackray, John, 83, 167, 281
Theory X and theory Y, 67–71, 79, 81–82
Thinking, 151–56
  positive, 152
Thompson, Rupert C.
  and Royal D. Little, 277, 278
Thomson, Roy, 87, 288, 298
  and *The Times*, 103, 298
Thornton, Charles B., 119, 287, 298
Time
  delegation, 147–49
  meetings, 149
  organization of manager's, 147–50
  schedule, 149–50
Time magazine, 208
Times, The, 103, 298
Toklas, Alice B., 156
Toni home perm, 98, 291
Tora! Tora! Tora! (film)
  depiction of Japanese plural management, 46–47
Townsend, Robert, 67, 108, 260, 298–99
Trade unions, 188–89

and management decision-making, 164–65
and Swedish law, 191–92
Training on the job, 247
Travelodge motel chain, 267
Trusthouse Forte, 265, 267–68
Turgenev, Ivan, 69

Union Carbide
 and new polyethylene process, 178
Univac computers, 99
Up the Organization (Townsend), 67, 108, 260, 299
U.S. Steel, 17

Value analysis, 251
Vertical organization, 72–79 *passim*
Vespa motorcycles, 19
Vickers Group, 89, 296
Vision magazine, 119
Volkswagen (V.W.), 90–91, 175, 176, 230, 295
 Beetle, 91, 165, 295, 296
 and trade unions, 164–65
Volvo, 217
 experiments in participation, 218–22, 290–91

Warburg, Sir Siegmund
 and S. G. Warburg bank, 54–55, 299
Waterford Glass, 106, 109, 128–29, 131
 and partnership concept, 128–29

Watson, Arthur, 299–300
Watson, Thomas, 127, 151, 299
Watson, Thomas, Jr., 77, 299–300
Weinstock, Arnold
 and G.E.C., 34–35, 50, 90, 268–71, 272, 274
Western Electric, 17
Westinghouse, 17, 272
Whirlpool Corporation, 96
Wilkinson Sword, 99
Wilson, Kemmons, 128, 155, 300
Women in management, 261–62
Words
 use of in management, 144–47, 205–7
Writing
 and a manager's work, 144, 146–47, 205–7

Xerox, 12, 39, 40, 70–71, 100, 109, 128, 173, 176–77, 289

Yamamoto, Admiral, 46
Yom Kippur war, 13, 254

Zahn, Dr. Joachim, 214, 300
Z.B.B. *See* Zero-based budgeting
Z.D. *See* Zero defects
Zeiss cameras, 19
Zero-based budgeting (Z.B.B.), 155, 256
Zero defects (Z.D.), 111–15, 124